S. J. Perelman

S. J. Perelman. *Photo by Jill Krementz.*

S. J. PERELMAN

A Critical Study

STEVEN H. GALE

CONTRIBUTIONS TO THE STUDY OF POPULAR CULTURE,
NUMBER 15

GREENWOOD PRESS
NEW YORK · WESTPORT, CONNECTICUT · LONDON

Library of Congress Cataloging-in-Publication Data

Gale, Steven H.
  S. J. Perelman : a critical study.
  (Contributions to the study of popular culture,
ISSN 0198-9871 ; no. 15)
    Bibliography: p.
    Includes index.
    1. Perelman, S. J. (Sidney Joseph), 1904–   —
Criticism and interpretation.   I. Title.   II. Series.
PS3531.E6544Z66   1987   818′.5209   86-12106
ISBN 0-313-25003-0 (lib. bdg. : alk. paper)

Library of Congress Catalog Card Number: 86-12106
ISBN: 0-313-25003-0
ISSN: 0198-9871

First published in 1987

Greenwood Press, Inc.
88 Post Road West, Westport, Connecticut 06881

Printed in the United States of America

The paper used in this book complies with the
Permanent Paper Standard issued by the National
Information Standards Organization (Z39.48-1984).

10 9 8 7 6 5 4 3 2 1

Copyright Acknowledgments

The following publishers and sources have generously granted permission to use material:

Portions of this study originally appeared in ''S.J. Perelman,'' which originally appeared in *Dictionary of Literary Biography,* volume 11, edited by Stanley Trachtenberg. Copyright © 1982 by Gale Research Company. Reprinted by permission of the publisher.

From *The Marx Bros. Scrapbook* by Groucho Marx and Richard J. Anobile. Copyright © 1973 by Darien House, Inc. Reprinted by permission of Richard J. Anobile.

From *Nathanael West: The Art of His Life* by Jay Martin. Copyright © 1970 by Jay Martin. Reprinted by permission of Farrar, Straus, & Giroux, Inc.

From ''Perelman's Rasping Wit Becomes an Anglo-File'' by Myra MacPherson. *The Washington Post,* October 18, 1970. Copyright © *The Washington Post.* Reprinted by permission.

From ''That Perelman of Great Price is Sixty-Five,'' by William K. Zinsser. *The New York Times Magazine,* January 26, 1969. Copyright © 1969 by William K. Zinsser. Reprinted by permission of the author.

From the interview with S. J. Perelman by William Cole and George Plimpton in *Writers at Work: The Paris Review Interviews,* Second Series, edited by George Plimpton. Copyright © 1963 by *The Paris Review, Inc.* Reprinted by permission of Viking Penguin, Inc., and Martin Secker & Warburg, Ltd.

To Kathy, Shannon, Ashley, and Kristin,
and to my mother and father,
with all my love and thanks

Contents

Preface

I first became acquainted with S. J. Perelman's work when I was in high school and my father shared with me his brand new copy of *The Most of S. J. Perelman*. I immediately became a Perelman fan, and when I was required to compile an original bibliography for a graduate course in bibliography at the University of California at Los Angeles, I chose Perelman as my subject. The result, "Sidney Joseph Perelman: Twenty Years of American Humor," appeared in the *Bulletin of Bibliography* about eight years later, my first scholarly publication.

Over the years I have read pieces by Perelman as they came to my attention, and I even included one of my favorites, "The Idol's Eye," in the supplementary reading section of a composition text that I edited several years ago so that others could be exposed to the pleasure that I experienced on discovering his work. Over the years, too, I have been aware of some scholarly interest in Perelman, as occasionally someone would write to me to ask for information about him. Since my bibliography was the first, and for a while the only, scholarly work devoted solely to the author, I suppose that I received more inquiries than might normally be expected from one small publication. In a roundabout way, that bibliography was also responsible for my writing this study. Late in December 1980, I received a telephone call from Professor Stanley Trachtenberg of Texas Christian University. Trachtenberg was in the process of editing a volume of the *Dictionary of Literary Biography* titled *American Humorists, 1800-1950*. He had hoped to write the major author entry on Perelman himself but found that his editorial duties were too time consuming. Very little scholarship has been done on Perelman, and when Trachtenberg was looking for someone to take on the article, he remembered my bibliography and invited me to contribute the entry.

This present study of Perelman's work is an expansion of my *Dictionary of Literary Biography* essay. I have added a chapter on his filmscripts, updated and increased my comments on several of his volumes of prose and on his plays, enlarged the sections relating his biography to his writing, and included a bibliographic essay and an index. Not counting the bibliographic essay and the index (two elements that I consider vital in serious scholarship), this study represents more than a quadrupling of the material in the *Dictionary of Literary Biography* article.

I was surprised when Trachtenberg reminded me of how little writing had been done on Perelman, and when I worked on the *Dictionary of Literary Biography* piece I realized how much there was to be done and that Perelman's work warranted the attention that I have paid to it in this study. (Anyone who can compose the line, ''A girl on the couch is worth two on the mind''—*One Touch of Venus*, Act I, scene vi—bears watching.)

Given the length of the humorist's career and the large amount of writing that he did (in three different genres), I decided to examine his works by genre rather than follow the chronological format that I had used in the *Dictionary of Literary Biography* entry. It seems to me that, while there are definitely connections between his prose, movie scripts, and dramas, it is easier to trace his development in each of these areas if they are examined separately. I have maintained a chronological structure within each area, and I have crossreferenced from area to area where I feel that this helps in the understanding of either or both pieces of writing being treated. I have also included comprehensive stylistic analyses of many individual works as I look at their thematic content, again for the sake of clarity. Rather than treating all of the stylistic elements in a separate chapter, I believe that it makes more sense to examine them within the context in which they appear; a better sense of stylistic evolution develops out of this approach. Much in the way of plot summary that I have included was done not because I doubt that the reader will be familiar with Perelman's massive canon but because this serves to demonstrate typical and thematic patterns. (I have tried to keep the summarizing to a minimum.)

When the reader has finished with this volume, I hope that Perelman's themes will have been made clear and that there will be an appreciation of the writer as one of the major prose stylists of American literature in the twentieth century. There may be, however, some question about how I chose the selections to be examined. Given the tremendous number of prose pieces that Perelman wrote, I decided not to try to comment on every one. There is no need to, actually, since some are not particularly either enlightening or entertaining, and since a sampling of representative pieces is sufficient to illustrate the author's themes and techniques. I chose, then, those essays and short stories that I consider his best and most representative works. Taste in humor is a very individual thing; I hope that I did not slight anyone's favorite piece.

Acknowledgments

I was given a great deal of help in writing this study, which I am sure helped improve it and which I know saved me an enormous amount of time. I would like to thank my father for introducing me to Perelman's work, and my mother and father for the lifetime of help, encouragement, and love that they have given me so freely. Charles and Marcia Johnson have been good friends to me. Lawrence Hetrick gave me a copy of *Look Who's Talking* because he knew of my appreciation of Perelman's work. Stanley Trachtenberg gave me the opportunity to put my interest into concrete form, and he and the editorial staff of the *Dictionary of Literary Biography* made friendly suggestions regarding both the style and contents of my entry. Librarians have been proven invaluable in helping me gain access to Perelman's works and to reviews and criticism. These include Joan Banks and Fran Lundy, and others at the Joplin Public Library, and especially Carolyn Trout, Mary Lou Dove, David Reiman, Gay Pate, Arlene Moore, Barbara Beard Wales, Cindy Papp, and Cindy West at the George A. Spiva Library at Missouri Southern State College. My colleagues offered encouragement, and Dean Ray Malzahn arranged for my taking a summer off from my administrative duties to be a fulltime scholar. Ron Foster and his staff always worked hard to get material to me as quickly as possible. Sharon Campbell, in particular, was helpful in gathering bibliographical information. Teresa Plew did a find job of typing the manuscript, and she never complained, even when she had trouble deciphering some of my handwriting—I hope that working on this project made her job more enjoyable—and Jill Womack also helped with the typing. Greenwood Press Production Editor Lisa Reichbach and copy editor Dolores Abbott helped make sure that the manuscript was accurate, and Maureen Melino kept track of permissions. As always Pat Martin's help in transferring the manuscript to a computer disk was invaluable, as was the help of proofreading and indexing supplied by my wife, Kathy, and daughters, Shannon, Ashley, and Kristin.

Finally, of course, there is no way that a study of this kind and length could ever be completed (or have any reason for being initiated, for that matter), if it were not for my family. Kathy and my daughters, Shannon, Ashley, and Kristin, all deserve more thanks than I can ever express for their patience and understanding.

Chronology of Major Events

1904   Perelman born in Brooklyn, New York, February 1.

1917   Wins first prize for "Grit" in a contest sponsored by *American Boy*.

1917–   Attends Classical High School in Providence, Rhode Island.
1921   Chairman of debating team and editor of the literary magazine the *Accolade*.

1921–   Attends Brown University; leaves without earning a degree.
1925   First publication, in the *Brown Jug*. Goes to work for *Judge*.

1929   July 4, marries Laura West, Nathanael West's sister. First collection of prose, *Dawn Ginsbergh's Revenge*, is published. Becomes a prose contributor to *College Humor*.

1930   "Open Letter to Moira Ransom" is first contribution to *The New Yorker*, December 13. *Parlor, Bedlam and Bath*, co-authored with Quentin Reynolds, is published.

1931   Sketches in *The Third Little Show*, produced in New York City. *Monkey Business* (film) is released.

1932   With Bert Kalmer and Harry Ruby creates *Horse Feathers* for the Marx Brothers. Contributes sketches to the Broadway revue *Walk a Little Faster*. Buys farm in Bucks County, Pennsylvania.

1933   *All Good Americans*, written with Laura, runs for forty performances. *Sitting Pretty* is staged on Broadway and sold to Metro-Goldwyn-Mayer as the basis for the 1934 film *Paris Interlude*.

1934   *Paris Interlude* is released.

1936   *Florida Special* is released.

1937   *Strictly from Hunger* is published.

1938   *Sweethearts* is released.

1939   With Laura, co-scripts *Ambush* for Paramount. Hosts *Author! Author!*, a summer radio quiz show on whodunit theme. *Ambush* is released. *Boy Trouble* is released.

1940   *Look Who's Talking* is published. Sketches included in review *Two Weeks with Pay. The Golden Fleecing* is released.

1941   *The Night Before Christmas*, a play co-authored with Laura, is staged at New York's Morosco Theater.

1942   *Larceny, Inc.* is released.

1943   *The Dream Department* is published.

1944   *Crazy Like a Fox* is published. *One Touch of Venus*, co-authored with Ogden Nash and Kurt Weill, is staged in New York City. *Greenwich Village* is released.

1946   *Sweet Bye and Bye*, a musical with a futuristic theme, closes in Philadelphia during tryouts. *Keep It Crisp* is published.

1947   *Acres and Pains* is published.

1948   *Westward Ha!* is published. *One Touch of Venus* is released.

1949   *Listen to the Mocking Bird* is published.

1950   *The Swiss Family Perelman* is published.

1951   *A Child's Garden of Curses* is published.

1952   *The Ill-Tempered Clavichord* is published.

1954   *Hold That Christmas Tiger!* is published.

1955   *Perelman's Home Companion* is published.

1956   *Around the World in 80 Days* is released. Perelman receives the New York Film Critics Award and the Academy of Motion Picture Arts and Sciences Award (''Oscar'') for best screenplay.

1957   *The Road to Miltown* is published.

1958   Writes script for Cole Porter television musical, *Aladdin. The Most of S. J. Perelman* is published. Perelman is elected to the National Academy of Letters.

1959   ''Malice in Wonderland,'' a satiric spoof of Hollywood, is telecast on NBC's *Omnibus. The Big Wheel* is televised.

1961   *The Beauty Part* is staged. *The Rising Gorge* is published.

1965   Honorary Litt.D. awarded by Brown University.

1966   *Chicken Inspector No. 23* is published.

1970   Laura West Perelman dies April 10. Perelman sells his Bucks County farm and moves to London in October. *Baby, It's Cold Inside* is published.

1974   Revival of *The Beauty Part* at the American Place Theater.

1975   *Vinegar Puss* is published.

1977   *Eastward Ha!* is published.

1978   Receives first Special Achievement Award of the National Book Awards Committee.

1979   "Portrait of the Artist as a Young Cat's-Paw," his last comic essay, is published in *The New Yorker*. Perelman dies of cardiac arrest in his apartment at the Gramercy Park Hotel in New York City, October 17. Awarded (posthumously) New York City's "Mayor's Award of Honor for Arts and Culture."

1981   *The Last Laugh* is published.

1984   *The Old Gang O' Mine* is published.

1987   *The Letters of S. J. Perelman* is published.

S. J. Perelman

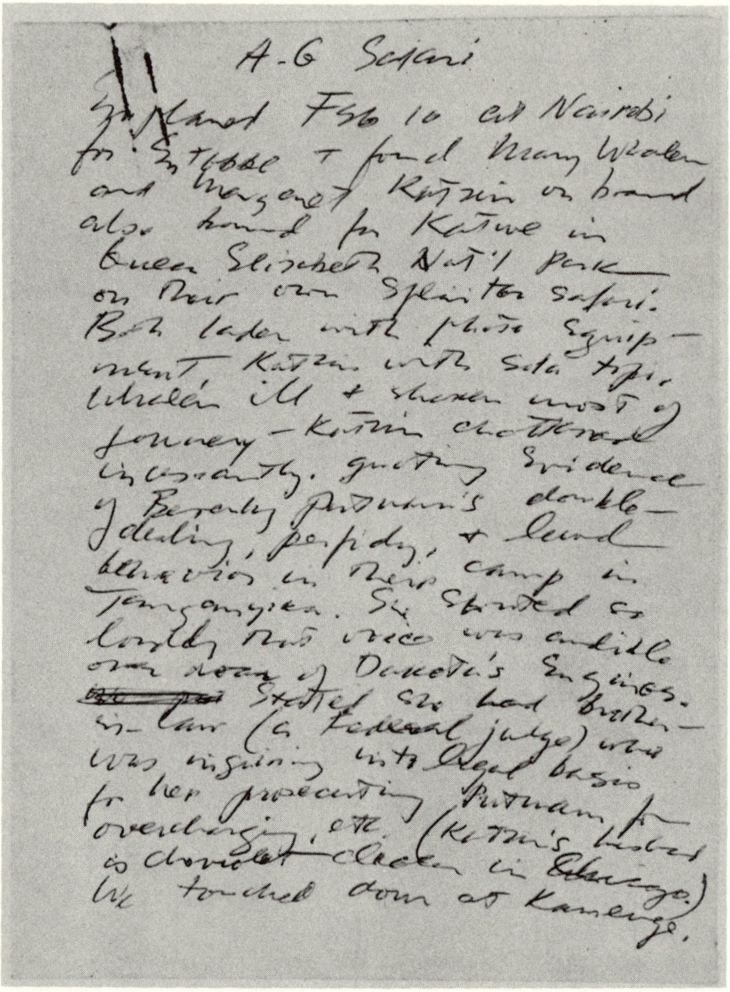
A-6 Safari

Got planed Feb 10 at Nairobi
for Entebbe + found Mary Whalen
and Margaret Katzin on board
also bound for Katwe in
Queen Elizabeth Nat'l Park
on their own splinter safari.
Both laden with photo equip-
ment, Katzin with sola topi.
Whalen ill + shaken most of
journey—Katzin chattered
incessantly, quoting evidence
of Beverly Putnam's double-
dealing, perfidy, + lewd
behavior in their camp in
Tanganyika. She started so
loudly that voice was audible
over drone of Dakota's engines.
Stated she had brother-
in-law (a Federal judge) who
was rigging up legal basis
for her prosecuting Putnam for
overcharging, etc. (Katzin's brother
is divorce clerk in Chicago.)
We touched down at Kamenge.

Manuscript copy of Perelman's material.

Introduction

It would not seem to be the kind of background that would produce one of America's greatest and most prolific humorists, a writer whose forte was a witty mastery of the English language combined with an ability to focus on peculiarly American clichés in order to reduce them to their innate ridiculousness. S. J. (Sidney Joseph) Perelman was born in Brooklyn, New York, on February 1, 1904, to Joseph and Sophia Charren Perelman, Russian Jews who had immigrated to the United States twelve years earlier. He grew up in Providence, Rhode Island, where, as he told *New York Times Magazine* interviewer William Zinsser in 1969, his father, who once backed an unsuccessful attempt to adapt Sir Walter Scott's *The Bride of Midlothian* as a Yiddish musical, was a machinist, ran a dry goods store, and tried unsuccessfully to raise poultry. "It was the American dream that if you had a few acres and a chicken farm there was no limit to your possible wealth. I grew up with and have since retained the keenest hatred of chickens," the humorist told Zinsser.[1]

Perelman was a voracious reader—a habit perhaps at least in part stimulated by his appreciation of the success stories of Horatio Alger and others—and this pastime exposed him to other worlds. He was soon reading the wide variety of books that captured the attention of youngsters at that time: the Toby Tyler books, *Graustark*, *Girl of the Limberlost*, *Trail of the Lonesome Pine*, *The Woman Thou Gavest*, *The Mystery of Fu Manchu*, *The Winning of Barbara Worth*, *Three Weeks*, *Scaramouche*, *Polyanna*, and the novels of Charles Dickens.

In many ways the style and subject matter of these books embody the essence of turn-of-the-century America—an innocent, enthusiastic, slightly romantic, and good natured humor that perceives life as an enjoyable experience, yet an experience that people sometimes take too seriously, almost a mixture of the lighter side of Mark Twain with Booth Tarkington's *Penrod*. This attitude seems to form the foundation on which much of Perelman's humor rests.

As a young man, however, Perelman showed interest in writing. At Classical High School in Providence he was interested in the use of language and served as chairman of the debating society, but there is no record of his being involved in creative writing. Furthermore, he told Zinsser that his "chief interest always was to be a cartoonist," and he spoke of drawing, at an early age, "cartoons in my father's store on the long cardboard strips around which the bolts of Amoskeag cotton and ginghams were stored."[2] In fact, while at Brown University as a pre-medical student and then English major from 1921 to 1925 he joined the staff of the *Brown Jug*, the campus humor magazine, as a cartoonist.[3] John Held, Jr., the recorder of the flapper era, was the prime influence on his drawing and, even though Perelman later became the magazine's editor and began to write for publication, his humor always contained the somewhat stylized feeling of Thurber-like cartoon images at its base. It is as though he saw situations in his mind as pen and ink line drawings. These he translated into a prose that captures the essence of a sketch whose meaning goes far deeper than would be expected from the deceptive simplicity of its outline. It seems especially fitting that most of Perelman's writing first appeared in *The New Yorker*, a magazine that for many readers is built around droll cartoons.

Perelman's editorials in the *Brown Jug* (advocating, among other things, "the dismissal of the dean and all the other pompous old fools on the faculty") reflects the first literary influence that he recalls: "H. L. Mencken was the Catherine wheel, the ultimate firework. . . . He loosened up journalism. With his use of the colloquial and the dynamic, the foreign reference, and the bizarre word like *Sitzfleisch* he brought adrenalin into the gray and pulpy style of the day."[4] However, when he left Brown without graduating and moved to Greenwich Village, it was as a cartoonist that Perelman first sought a job.[5] He was thrilled, therefore, when Norman Anthony, the editor of *Judge*, a popular weekly humor magazine, offered him a contract "to provide two cartoons and one humor piece every week.'' The cartoons were not great—one example of Perelman's cartoon art that he included in the *Brown Jug* shows two Jewish men, one standing with a Hebrew-language newspaper under his arm, the other sitting at a table with a liquor bottle and a half-empty glass in front of him. The caption reads: " 'For vy you marry Abie's widdow? She's old enough to be your mother vunce.' 'I know, but Abie's clothes fit me like a glove.' " A pun, one of the humorist's favorite literary devices, is the basis of another cartoon which depicts a carpenter and an old sailor. "That new wooden leg will cost you $10," the carpenter says. The "Sailor Fellow" responds, "What, are you going to charge me $10 for just remembering me?" In another cartoon a pasha is seen saying to his grand vizier, "Who's been eating my Kurds and why?" In Perelman's most famous drawing a man is seen dragging a second man into a doctor's office and announcing, "I have Bright's disease and he has mine, sobbed the panting palook." It is likely that the mature Perelman would have ended the sentence at the comma.

Most of the drawings were pen and ink, styled to look like wood-cuts (although Perelman actually did use woodcuts too) in a kind of double parody of both the form and the content of earlier cartoonists' work. As often as not, in fact, there was no relationship between the illustration and the words underneath it. A depiction of two men in Victorian bathing attire and playing harps is designed like an ad. "Learn to play the Harp!! Easy! Profitable! Uncanny!" is the legend, but the caption and the picture are in no way connected: " 'What do you consider the first requisite in business?' inquired Smithers of his friend Serime, who deals in goose feathers. 'Pluck,' reported the latter, his eyes twinking merrily. The first speaker's jaw dropped in chagrin." The cartoons, as Richard Marschall has pointed out, are "filled with allusions and metaphors" that make them "illustrated clichés" that are obviously closely related to his prose.[6]

Although the artist's style changed over the next few years to become more abstract as he came to favor geometrical shapes drawn with rulers and templates, a sense of the zany was still an integral part of Perelman's drawings. Marschall describes a character in one cartoon, for instance, whose vest is "patterned with photographic detail of tenement windows,"[7] a detail that has no bearing on either the subject of the drawing or its unrelated caption, and the illustration of an apartment building that accompanies the short story, "For Rent—

Thirty-Room Apartment, No Baths,'' is a schematic diagram of the interior of a human torso with everything carefully labeled in the manner of a medical illustration, but all of the parts are pipes, gears, and other mechanical devices.

It was about this time that Perelman's avant-garde art style began to get the better of him. His close friend, caricaturist Al Hirschfeld recalls:

He was drawing and writing, but mostly he was interested in graphic drawing . . . he used to do these one-line jokes and then they became two lines and then they became six lines and finally the editors said to him: "Listen, Sid. Why are you bothering with the drawing? Why don't you just extend the caption?'' Which is what he did and that's how he started writing.[8]

Perelman spoke to British interviewer Philip French about this period in his career, which French labels a "crossroads":

I had progressed through a number of stages in my drawing and I was rapidly approaching a point when I felt I was getting into design. I had been doing collages and things of that sort. I was influenced by what was happening in Europe and I could see myself drifting into something that was getting away from sheer comic art. But I think the thing that really stopped my drawing altogether was the fact that I encountered the Marx Brothers and drifted into working in film so that I could keep on with my writing for the printed page. But drawing seemed to be a little remote from that, and it just naturally faded away.[9]

Nevertheless, Perelman remained with *Judge* from 1925 until 1929. Later he would work for former *Judge* co-editor Harold Ross when Ross was the editor of *The New Yorker*.

In 1930 Perelman moved to *College Humor*, and it was there that a prose style of his own began to emerge. "I was beginning to develop a sense of parody," he told Zinsser, "and of lapidary prose."[10] This style shows the influence of many writers, but as do all great artists, Perelman had the ability to make what he borrowed his own, and to go beyond his source, even though, as he admits in a 1963 *Paris Review* interview, he "stole from the very best sources."[11] The first author to influence him as a humorist was George Ade. "Ade had a social sense of history," Perelman told Zinsser, "his humor was rooted in a perception of people and places. He had a cutting edge and an acerbic wit that no earlier American humorist had.''[12] Other writers mentioned by Perelman as having influenced his writing were Stephen Leacock, Max Beerbohm, Ring Lardner (''at his best . . . the non-pareil''), Robert Benchley, Donald Ogden Stewart, Frank Sullivan, Flann O'Brien, W. Somerset Maugham, and T. S. Eliot. In addition, he told Myra MacPherson of the *Washington Post* in 1970 that he had ''developed a fondness for whatever Dickens'' he read, which may be related to his admission that ''My names and titles spring out of my lifetime devotion to puns.''[13] Raymond Chandler (who ''took the private eye legend . . . and refined it and added an element that was not very obvious, and that was humor''), E. M. Forster (''His story, 'Afternoon at Pretoria,' is one of the finest pieces of comic writing I know''), Henry David Thoreau, George Jean Nathan, and James Joyce (''I've come over the years to realize that *Ulysses* is the greatest work of the comic imagination that exists for me'') are among those more serious writers whom Perelman recognized as having had an influence on his own writing.[14] For his work he was named to the National Institute of Letters, and he received a New York Film Critics Award and an Academy of Motion Pictures Arts and Sciences ''Oscar'' (both for *Around the World in Eighty Days*, 1956), and a special National Book Award in recognition of his contribution to American letters (1978). Shortly after his death it was announced that Perelman posthumously had been awarded the Mayor's Award of Honor for Arts and Culture by New York City's Mayor Ed Koch.

While many of Perelman's stories revolve around incidents in his everyday life, real or imagined, only occasionally do actual details and facts from outside his writing become incorporated into his writing. Some of these will be dealt with later, as they relate to specific pieces. There were, however, certain things that had a great impact on Perelman's life. At Brown one of his best friends was Nathanael West, who was a year ahead of him and who would later write *Miss Lonelyhearts* and *The Day of the Locust*. The authors-to-be met in 1922 when they enrolled in the same class. In 1923 Perelman designed a bookplate for West that ''shows a figure with his arm affectionately thrown around the neck of an ass, above a motto from Goethe, 'Do I love what others love?' and the signature, 'N. Von Wallenstein Weinstein.' ''[15] The two men formed a lifelong allegiance, and Perelman, who served as the best man at West's wedding in 1940, is also credited with having served as West's literary advisor occasionally. J. A. Ward in his interesting study "The Hollywood Metaphor: The Marx Brothers, S. J. Perelman, Nathanael West"[16] and Jay Martin, West's biographer, have commented on this relationship. Martin goes so far as to state that Perelman was "West's shrewdest critic," and that West respected Perelman's judgement. In fact, according to Martin, West "always spoke with deep affection for only two men, his dead father and Perelman."[17] Moreover, he was "particularly" influenced by Perelman from the very beginning of his career: "West gave Lillian Hellman the impression that he regarded his college acquaintance with Perelman as crucial in his development."[18] Perelman's "Miss Klingspeil Takes Dictation" influenced West's "Business Deal," a satirical sketch about Hollywood (with a character named Eugene Klingspeil) which appeared in a 1933 issue of *Americana*, and Perelman reportedly advised him in his writing of *A Cool Million* and *Miss Lonelyhearts*.[19] At one point Perelman and his brother-in-law wrote a play together (see the discussion of *Even Stephen* in Chapter Two), and toward the end of the summer of 1934 they considered collaborating on a novel, but the Perelmans returned to Hollywood before the project could be begun, and it was never revived.[20] The extent of West's respect is indicated by his dedicating *A Cool Million* to Perelman and naming him his literary executor.

As a result of his friendship with West, Perelman met his college chum's sister, Lorraine, called Laura, whom, he recalled, he "found . . . very pleasing."[21]. Perelman and Laura West were married on July 4, 1929, and after a honeymoon in Paris they settled near Washington Square in Greenwich Village. They had two children, first a son, Adam, and then a daughter, Abby Laura. Laura and Perelman appear to have been a close couple. In fact, they collaborated on several plays and movie scripts. Although he had been planning the move for several years, it was only after his wife died in 1970 that he sold the farm that they had lived on in Bucks County, Pennsylvania, for nearly forty years and moved to London.

Amusingly, two of the things that occupied much of Perelman's time seem contradictory, the Bucks County farm and travel. He spent most of his life in Manhattan and at the farm outside Erwinna, Pennsylvania. There were infrequent sojourns in Hollywood (a place that he detested) and numerous trips abroad. Paul Theroux, in his introduction to *The Last Laugh*, notes that "at the age of 74 . . . [Perelman] tried to drive his vintage 1949 MG from Paris to Peking, commemoráting the trip of Count Something-or-other. . . . He had been around the world a dozen times.''[22] Both the farm and the travels figure prominently in Perelman's writing.

Besides his collaborations with Laura, Perelman wrote several pieces with others. He formed close friendships with Ogden Nash and Hirschfeld, and some of his writing clearly grows out of his relationships with the two. He was also acquainted with most of the literati of his time. James Gould Cozzens, Max Bodenheim, Michael Gold, Israel Kapstein, and Robert Hillyer were classmates at Brown, and Perelman's writing and work in the theater brought him into contact with Bennett Cerf, Robert Coates, John Houseman, Lillian Hellman, Robert Benchley, Dorothy Parker, George S. Kaufman, Alexander Woollcott, James Thurber, Peter Arno, John Sanford, Norman Krasna, A. Lincoln Gillespie, John O'Hara, Edmund Wilson, Marc Connelly—a partial list that begins to take on the semblance of one of Perelman's own catalogues. While the Perelmans lived at the Sutton Club Hotel in New York City during West's tenure as its manager, Dashiell Hammett also stayed there and took the name of Laura's dog, Asta, for Nick and Nora Charles's dog in his novel *The Thin Man*.

Since a full-length biography of Perelman has been published by Dorothy Herrmann, I will not attempt to recount his life in any greater detail. However, a collection of tidbits from the humorist's life will help round out the picture of his personality. When his father immigrated in 1892, it was '' 'with dreams of becoming an engineer,' '' Perelman told MacPherson, but instead his father became third engineer on a steamer—'' 'the first ship into Havana harbor after the sinking of the *Maine*.' His was an interesting and difficult life.''[23] The elder Perelman never had a chance to go to college. At eleven "Sid" was a golf caddy, and during his vacations in college he had to work at a Providence department store. In high school he "had four years of Latin and three of Greek. I was very fond of reading and gave myself tremendous airs. I was an early discoverer of Joyce, who I venerated." After his wife's death, he held an auction at the farm, attended by five hundred people, at which he sold Mr. X (a brown horse), as well as other items, including two filmscripts that went for $7. He was unwilling, though, to sell any of the eleven copies of Joyce's *Ulysses* that he owned. Finally, when he had begun writing, he used his initials as a signature because, "I hated my first name and simply retired it to anonymity."

Physically, Perelman was of medium height and slight build. He was splay-eyed and is usually seen in photographs wearing a pair of wire-rimmed glasses that he acquired on a trip to Paris in 1927. He frequently wore a hat, and he was always immaculately dressed, at least in public, often in the tweedy garb usually associated with English country gentlemen.

Before Laura's death Perelman commuted between their farm and a one-room office two flights up at 1626 Broadway in Greenwich Village. West had used a small separate cottage at the farm for his office, but apparently Perelman needed to be in the city to write (he also kept an apartment in the Village). The office was furnished plainly, with a desk, two rocking chairs, a cot, some books, and a miniature typewriter. On the wall behind his chair there was a bright Stuart Davis water color of Paris and a photograph of the author's friend and favorite *New Yorker* editor, Gus Lobrano. On the wall opposite the desk hung framed photographs of James Joyce and Somerset Maugham. There was also a photograph of silent screen actress Jetta Goudal ("the great crypto-Eurasian vampire of all time," Perelman asserted to Zinsser), and the hat worn by David Niven in *Around the World in Eighty Days*, which he kept mounted on a pedestal.

On October 17, 1979, Perelman died of natural causes in his sleep in his apartment at the Gramercy Park Hotel in New York City. "The day before, and the day before that, he had dined with friends and created for them the Perelman illusion that if all was not well with the world all was at least funny."[24]

"I don't regard myself as a happy, laughing kid. What I really am, you see, is a crank. I deplore the passing of the word 'crank' from our language. I'm highly irritable and my senses bruise easily and when they are bruised, I write," he told *Life's* Jane Howard.[25] But, Theroux has observed that in spite of his curmudgeonly demeanor and instinct for slashing satire, Perelman the man had another dimension that underlies his writing, and that those around him knew. Theroux's reflection serves as an accurate tribute:

Perelman's friends liked him very much. He was generous, he was funny, he was enormously social, he didn't boast. Travel has the effect of turning most people into monologuists; it made Perelman an accomplished watcher and an appreciative listener. When he talked in his croaky drawl he did so in the elaborate way he wrote, with unlikely locutions and slang and precise descrip-

tions diverted into strings of subordinate clauses. . . . In his pockets he carried clippings he tore from the newspapers. . . . He read the London *Times*
every day (he had an airmail subscription), more, I think, for the unusual
names than for anything else. In today's *Times*, Sir Ranulph Twisleton-
Wykeham-Fiennes has just reached the South Pole; Captain Sir Weldon
Dalrymple-Champneys has just died; and both Miss C. Inch and Miss E. L. F. I.
Lukenheimer have just got married. Perelman welcomed news of this kind.[26]

NOTES

1. William Zinsser, "That Perelman of Great Price Is Sixty-Five," *New
York Times Magazine* (January 26, 1969): 26.

2. Ibid.

3. In *The American Humorist: Conscience of the Twentieth Century* (Ames,
Iowa: Iowa State University Press, 1964) Norris W. Yates says that at Brown
Perelman had " 'a brief, precarious toehold as assistant art editor' of *Case-
ments*, a literary magazine" (p. 322).

4. Zinsser, p. 76.

5. Most scholars have assumed that Perelman received a degree, but he
did not. No one has been sure why he did not graduate after four years in
attendance. In a letter to me dated June 30, 1981, however, the current Re-
gistrar notes that Perelman simply did not fulfill all of the graduation require-
ments. In an interview with Israel Shenker that appeared in *Publisher's Weekly*
(May 19, 1975): 91, Perelman offered the following explanation: "I attended
[Brown University] for four years and was never graduated—I lacked three
points, because I could never finish a course in trigonometry which I took
three times." In 1965 Brown awarded Perelman an honorary Litt.D.

6. Richard Marschall, "Foreword" to Perelman's *That Old Gang O' Mine*
(New York: Morrow, 1984), p. 8.

7. Ibid., p. 10.

8. Quoted in Philip French's "Perelman's Revenge or the Gift of Providence, Rhode Island," *Listener* (November 15, 1979): 668.

9. Ibid.

10. Zinsser, p. 76.

11. William Cole and George Plimpton, "S. J. Perelman," *The Paris Review* 30 (Fall, 1963), reprinted in *Writers at Work: The Paris Review Interviews, Second Series* (New York: Viking, 1965), p. 247.

12. Zinsser, p. 76.

13. Myra MacPherson, "Perelman's Rasping Wit Becomes an AngloFile,"
Washington Post, October 18, 1970, sect. E, pp. 1ff.

14. See both the Zinsser and *Paris Review* interviews.

15. Jay Martin, *Nathanael West: The Art of His Life* (New York: Farrar,

Straus, and Giroux, 1970), p. 57. West was a *nom de plume* for Natahan Weinstein.

16. J. A Ward, "The Hollywood Metaphor: The Marx Brothers, S. J. Perelman, Nathanael West," *Southern Review* 12 (July, 1976): 659-72.

17. Martin, p. 22.

18. Ibid., pp. 101, 68.

19. Ibid., p. 250. In the "Introduction" to West's *The Day of the Locust* (New York: Bantam, 1958; p. xiii), Richard B. Gehman states that Perelman's "shadow can be detected in *A Cool Million* in particular."

20. Ibid., p. 251.

21. MacPherson, sect. e, p. 4.

22. Paul Theroux, in *The Last Laugh* (New York: Simon and Schuster, 1981), p. 11.

23. MacPherson, sect. E, p. 4.

24. "The Talk of the Town: Notes and Comment," *The New Yorker* (October 29, 1979): 29.

25. Jane Howard, "The Cranky Humorist," *Life* 52 (February 9, 1962): 85.

26. Theroux, p. 10.

1

Prose Writing

An early linking of Perelman's delight in cartooning with his interest in literature came in Professor Thomas Crosby's class at Brown when he drew caricatures of the modern dramatists that they were studying. Perhaps the drawing was done out of boredom, since Crosby's lectures did not include twentieth-century playwrights. Perelman also was involved in providing art work for the *Brown Jug*, as mentioned above, and in writing for *Casements*, the Brown University literary magazine. One of Perelman's earliest pieces, "The Exquisites: A Divagation," was published in *Casements* in 1924. It satirizes the posturing of poets who wrote in the style of Ernest Dowson and Lionel Johnson, asking "Where can we find the Paters and Beardsleys of this day and generation?" Jay Martin suggests that the essay at least partially is intended to mock the poem "Death" by West, which appears in the same issue.[1]

Another little magazine in which Perelman's early work appeared was *Contact*, a short-lived journal co-edited by West and William Carlos Williams. "Scenario" was published in the inaugural issue in February 1932, and Perelman contributed another piece to the third and final issue of the magazine in October of the same year. By and large, though, there is no need to talk about Perelman's contributions to journals, *per se*, since so much of his work that originally appeared in magazines has been reprinted in book form. While many of the pieces were published in two or more of his twenty-three volumes of prose (excluding *Parlor, Bedlam and Bath*, but including *The Best of S. J.*

Perelman and *The Most of S. J. Perelman*), still, his output is astounding. Over five hundred of his individual essays have appeared in his collected volumes (441 were collected in the twenty-one volumes published during his lifetime; since his death, two additional volumes, containing another seventy-five pieces, have been published), and this is by no means a comprehensive list of his canon, for nearly half again as many pieces were *not* reprinted. The essays were written primarily for *The New Yorker*. Amazingly, between December 13, 1930, and September 10, 1979, he contributed 278 "casuals" to that journal alone, publishing at least one piece in every year except 1932, 1934, 1947, and 1971, with a high of fifty in one year, 1953, for an average of 5.67 essays a year for forty-nine years. A large number of pieces also were published in *Holiday* and later in *Travel and Leisure* (the American Express club members' travel magazine), but Perelman's work appeared in the following journals as well: *Broun's Nutmeg, Brown Jug, College Humor, Contact, Diplomat, Escapade, Funny Bone, Judge, Life, McCalls', Redbook, Stage Magazine, The Country Book, The New Masses, The Saturday Evening Post, This Week Magazine, TV Guide, Venture,* and *What's New*.

THAT OLD GANG O' MINE

Although not published until 1984, *That Old Gang O' Mine* actually represents the earliest of Perelman's writing to be reprinted in book form, and thus it seems reasonable to examine it out of chronological order. Edited and with a foreword by Richard Marschall, the anthology was published by William Morrow. Subtitled *The Early and Essential S. J. Perelman*, the collection contains fifty-five prose pieces that originally appeared in *Judge* between September 18, 1926, and December 13, 1930, together with around 124 cartoons and other illustrations.

As mentioned above, to this point in his career, Perelman's literary endeavors had been published in *The Brown Jug*, the college humor magazine that he edited. There was already a well-established tradition of college humor magazines in the United States when Perelman matriculated at Brown. The *Yale Record* was founded in 1872, the *Harvard Lampoon* in 1876, *The Princeton Tiger* in 1882, and *The Dartmouth Jack-o'-Lantern* in 1909. *The Brown Jug*, which had been preceded by the *Brunonian*, was first published in 1920. *College Hu-*

mor (1922), in which some of the author's writing appeared, attracted a national audience with its reprints drawn mainly from these publications. It was a natural move, then, for the humorist to submit material to *Judge* (established in 1881), which also reprinted material from the college magazines and was second in renown only to *College Humor*.

Most of the essays in *That Old Gang O' Mine* have two things in common: they are short, and the humor is obviously juvenile, considerably less sophisticated than that that the author will develop. Even in these early writings, many of the elements are present that will become his trademarks—the unconventional titles, Dickensian character names, puns, careful attention to language, subject matter, and comic devices such as reductionism.

Among the typically Perlemanesque titles, for instance, are "Not-So-Indian Love Call," "Spare the Rod and Spoil the Relative," "Do Your Christmas Necking Now," and "The Wolf in the Servidor." Orliansky Roof in "Dance Madness in Coney Island," Henry Tregaskis and Dollie LaRue in "A Tip to the Radio Boys" (one of the humorist's first pieces to involve a scenario format), Dudley Crud in "How Love Came to Dudley Crud," Titheradge, Todhunter, Apthorpe, Aspinwall, and Rapfogel in "How to Board a Street-Car," and George Twombly Beaver, Stanslaus Prouty, Dahlia Lark-Horowitz, Fred Whitebait, and Hazel Bummer Wheatcraft in the epistolory "Very Truly Yours" are randomly chosen samples representative of the names that appear in almost every selection.

Even more ubiquitous in Perelman's humor are the puns and wordplay. Undoubtedly it would be easier to list the few stories that do not include puns than it would be to discuss all of the puns in almost any of the pieces found in *That Old Gang O' Mine*, or any of the volumes that preceded it. In "The Love Racketeer," for instance, the narrator speaks of a young woman "sporting a mop of golden hair with which she dusted her dormitory room."[2] When the hero of "Master Sleuth Unmasked at Last!" is accused of having memory lapses, he replies, "No, I'm too fat to have any lapses."[3]

The earliest published example of Perelman's wit to be reprinted is the "Puss in Boots" segment of a three-part series entitled "Judge's Fairy Tales for Tired Clubmen" that first appeared on September 18, 1926. The 835-word article is merely a "modern" retelling of the old Charles Perrault French fairy tale. Perelman's young hero is named

Irving, his cat is called Morris, the ogre, who looked "like all the parts Lon Chaney ever played rolled together"[4] is named Bernstein. Subways, new model Fords, and lawyers who are the only winners when a will is contested are the details that the writer uses to "modernize" the old folktale.

Even shorter are the anecdotes collected under the banner "Judge's Own Kiddie Korner," subtitled "Brave Deeds of Bright Boys." The story "Tommy and his Fish" is only 163 words long. It tells how four-year-old Tommy, who keeps a collection of dead fish under his bed, managed to sneak out of a night club to avoid paying his bill.

"Daisy's Revolver" is a tale with a twist. A young girl who has been given a candy-filled glass revolver surprises a burglar and attempts to capture him with the fake pistol—but the burglar sees through her charade and, after advising her that she must "read the wrong books,"[5] throws her down three flights of stairs.

It may well be that the pieces collected in *That Old Gang O' Mine* are more spontaneous in tone than Perelman's later work, as editor Marschall claims in his foreword, but by and large they are not particularly funny. Obviously the seeds of the humorist's later masterpieces are present, and some of the pieces included in this volume could have been written at almost any time during Perelman's career, yet it is equally clear that the author's style improved dramatically over the next couple of years as he focused on subjects that are well-suited to his satiric attack, and he polished his techniques for expressing himself.

"How to Board a Street-Car" is one of the humorous essays in the collection. In it the writer describes this new contraption metaphorically as an animal that must be appeased with the proper foods, and then he suddenly moves into a series of *non sequiturs* about toothbrushes, then foot care, and finally tin-foil and the "dread Hun menace." As with the cartoons that Perelman was drawing at this period, a portion of the amusement is derived from the absolute lack of connection between the piece's title and any and all of the sections of the essay itself.

With the exception of a few other pieces in which passages plunge wildly off in all directions, though, there are not many examples of the explosive, madcap verbal fireworks that highlight the humorist's best later writings, and Perelman seldom deals with the personal frustrations that contemporary society imposes upon the Little Man and with which his audience can identify. While Perelman's imagination rambles over many topics in may ways (adopting female personae on occasions, supposedly reporting straight facts, narrating histories, and so forth), he has not yet identified those subjects—character types, fakery, pomposity, foolish institutions, elements of contemporary life such as advertising and malfunctioning gadgets—that he will delight in savaging over the next forty years. The selections that comprise *That Old Gang O' Mine* remain essentially what they are, examples of college humor. They are pretty much typical of the genre, with little true wit or sophistication. But, they do contain the elements that will later coalesce to become the distinctive art of one of America's major humorists. His ability as a parodist is evident in this anthology; his talent as a satirist is still to be developed.

DAWN GINSBERGH'S REVENGE

In 1929 Horace Liveright published Perelman's first book, though through an amusing oversight the author's name was not printed on the title page. As Perelman recounts in the *Paris Review* interview, "it was really an oversight of my own. I was so exalted at being collected for the first time that, in correcting the galleys, I completely overlooked the fact that there was no author's name on the title page. Unless one happened to look at the spine of the book, there would be every implication that it was written by its publisher."[6] The first hint of the author's approach to his material appears in a dust jacket blurb noting that this is the first volume of a trilogy called "Sean's Way Down Yonder in de Cornfield."[7] The collection, entitled *Dawn Ginsbergh's Revenge*, bore the legend "this book does not stop in Yonkers," and this bewildering *caveat* epitomizes the forty-nine selections contained in the volume, for it is a *non sequitur* based on a common experience. A similar notice on a bus or subway train car would not give us pause, but when applied in this new context, it carries with it a sense of absurdity.

Most of the selections in this first volume originally appeared in *Judge*, and, as was the case in the pieces contained in *That Old Gang O' Mine*, some of the characteristic elements of Perelman's comic style are already established and evident. The titles of his pieces have always been intriguing and amusing in their own right, and it is clear that many readers first were drawn to reading Perelman by the titles themselves. A sampling from this collection suggests the type of title that the author used throughout his fifty-year long career. *Dawn Gins-bergh's Revenge*'s "Puppets of Passion," "Lindbergh Hop Impossible, Says Expert!" "Do Spark-Plugs Think?" "Billiards and Their Prevention," and "Why I Should Like to be a White Slave" sound as though they could easily be substituted for "Hail, Hail, the Ganglia's All Here," "Who Stole My Golden Undies?" or "No Starch, No Tunic, No Chicken Fat," from *Vinegar Puss* (1975) or "Paris on Five Dolors a Day," "The Nearer the East, The Shorter the Shrift," or "Back Home in Tinseltown" from *Eastward Ha!* (1977) and *vice versa*.

Presumably at the time that this collection was compiled it was felt that these selections were funnier than those that Marschall would choose to publish fifty-five years later. Still, these relatively short early pieces (they are about one-third the length of those later written for *The New Yorker* and *Holiday*) are definitely not the work of a mature writer, though certainly there are moments of Perelman at his best in the collection. Moreover, the innocence and exuberance that mark many of the selections are, naturally enough, more strongly present here than in Perelman's late period. "Puppets of Passion," for example, is a satirical look at a young woman, Dawn Ginsbergh, who is courted by three suitors, "any one of them an ideal catch": "Nicky Nussbaum, tall, dashing, soldierly . . . DuBois Moskovicz of the Foreign Legation, and Hastings Berman, the great portrait painter."[8] A parody of women's magazine romances of the first quarter of the twentieth century, the tale (subtitled "A Throbbing Story of Youth's Hot Revolt Against the Conventions") shows Perelman's predilection for having fun with the names of his characters, for punning, for incongruity, and for reversal. Dawn's room is described as large enough to hold a regiment—"To tell the truth, the Sixty-ninth Regiment *was* in the room, in undress uniform." From the beginning of a Perelman story the tone is always such that there is seldom any question that the author's approach is humorous:

Dawn Ginsbergh lay in her enormous sixteenth-century four-poster bed and played tag with her blood pressure.

Oh, it was so good to be alive on this glorious May morning instead of being dead or something. Dawn, you must know was very fond of being alive. In fact, as she used to remark . . . "I would rather be alive than be Alderman." (p. 11)

While Perelman's use of language, a major trademark, would improve, he joyfully made fun of others' purple prose, as when he draws Dawn's portrait, the "impetuous dashing Dawn of the flame-taunted hair and scarlet lips bee-stung like violet pools and so on at ten cents a word for a page and a half."[9] The puns flow one after another: "A knock on the door aroused Dawn from her lethargy. She hastily slipped it off and donned an abstraction. This was Dawn, flitting lightly from lethargy to abstraction and back to precipice again. Or from Beethoven to Bach and Bach to Bach again."[10]

When Perelman introduces Dawn's mother, she is described as a "slim nervous woman, nervous like a manatee or a Firpo."[11] This image combines the writer's appreciation for incongruity with his constant references to people, places, and things (often of a literary nature, as will be discussed later) with which his audience should be familiar. The manatee is a huge, docile mammal, in no way nervous; Firpo was Luis Firpo, a professional boxer from Argentina who fought for the heavyweight championship in 1923. "Puppets of Passion" concludes with Dawn proposing marriage to the iceman, whom she has never seen before, and romantically proclaiming that she will work on his route with him—though Moe Feinbloom, whom she immediately rechristens Marvin Furbish, wonders who will hold the horses (a gag line that figures in a later piece in the collection).

The rest of the selections in *Dawn Ginsbergh's Revenge* incorporate similar comic devices and stylistic elements. " 'Bell's Folly,' or the First Telephone" begins, "The other day, whilst I was glancing through my encyclopedia for a corkscrew which had gone astray . . . "[12] "Sea-Serpent Menace again Rears Ugly Head" contains a picture of an old-fashioned bathtub titled "The sea-serpent following the steamer" and takes place on the tramp steamer "Max Beerbohm," crewed by "one Jim Hawkins, a powder monkey" who "had got thirsty for an apple and had crawled in a barrel," Israel Hands, and Long John Silverman (names taken in part from Robert Lewis Stevenson's *Treasure Island*).[13] "Why I Should Like to be a White Slave" has nothing to do with white slavery, though there is a character named Bjack Bjohnson, which is amusing, since Jack Johnson, a black man who was heavyweight champion from 1908 to 1915, got into legal trouble for traveling with a white woman. The reduction of logic to the point of absurdity is illustrated by the quick jumps that occur. From Bjohnson, Perelman moves to a horse who substitutes as a college dean (and subsequently is court-martialed and shot) to Germany's declaration of war on Latvia for the third time to the narrator's wife's renewing a dog's license to his conclusion: "The next afternoon we motored out . . . and were divorced by Vincent Lopez [the leader of a popular big band]. I now have a good job in the Water Department and no longer need fear the hydrant-headed monster of Jealousy. And to think that a fuzzy little wire-haired wombat first drew us together!"[14]

One format that Perelman experimented with at this time was a series called "The Complete Speech-maker." This involved speeches made at times when one would like to make speeches—on being fired, on being thrown out of college for gambling, on being spurned by a girl friend. Unfortunately, while the sentiments expressed were accurate, they sounded like sour grapes and were not funny. He subsequently abandoned the form. Finally, Perelman's amusement with foreign languages is evident as when he translates *la jardin de ma soeur* as "the power of speech" in "Do Spark-Plugs Think?" The remaining selections are not particularly distinctive.

At the same time, for a first published collection, *Dawn Ginsbergh's Revenge* showed good promise. The fact that Liveright published the volume indicated the publishing company's assessment of its new author's potential, and Liveright had a distinguished record in this sort of prognostication, having published works by Sherwood Anderson, Hart Crane, William Faulkner, Ben Hecht, Theodore Dreiser, Eugene O'Neill, and Ezra Pound, as well as E. E. Cumming's *The Enormous Room*, T. S. Eliot's *The Waste Land*, and Ernest Hemingway's *In Our Time*.

PARLOR, BEDLAM AND BATH

Perelman's only attempt at the novel format, *Parlor, Bedlam and Bath*, was written in collaboration with Q. [Quentin] L. Reynolds and published by Liveright in 1930. Reynolds, a star college football player and heavyweight boxing champion whom Perelman had met at Brown, later became famous as a newspaper reporter and war correspondent.[15] Dedicated to "L. W." (Laura West?), the book was originally titled *Through the Fallopian Tubes on a Bicycle* (a phrase retained in the summary that precedes Chapter Two).

Although a collaborative effort, this novel is Perelman's longest single work, and it merits close attention not because it is his best but because it is useful in displaying his utilization of certain techniques in a work of substantial length. It is characterized by the light comedy-of-errors tone found in many of the B movies of the 1930's. The shallow characters, the convoluted plot, the ignoring of contemporary economic and political events, the proto-absurd, bustling, helter-skel-ter activity and dialogue convey the same escapist entertainment ap-proach of the Mervyn LeRoy, Frank Tuttle, Busby Berkeley, and Ernst Lubitsch films of the time (*Gold Diggers of 1933; The Big Broadcast; Whoopie; Roman Scandals; 42nd Street; Paramount on Parade; Monte Carlo; The Smiling Lieutenant*). In a handwritten dedication, signed "Quent Reynolds," Perelman's co-author wrote: "Dear Bob; What this country needs is a good five cent novel—Here it is!"[16] This prob-ably pretty well summarizes the authors' attitude toward their crea-tions; they did not mean for their work to be taken seriously, and the play on Thomas Riley Marshall's maxim ("What this country needs is a good five cent cigar!") indicates their willingness to borrow freely from any source and to turn their borrowing to humor. The value that Reynolds places on the volume further emphasizes this, in a self-mocking way, since the novel originally sold for $2 a copy.

Borrowing, and the incongruous application of the borrowed mate-rial, is immediately evident in *Parlor, Bedlam and Bath*. The novel's twelve chapters draw on music and literature for their titles: "Alle-gretto," "Cadenza," "Pizzicato," "Dante and Andante," "Il Pen-seroso," "Con Amore," "Dolce Far Niente," "Mazurka," "Acce-lerando," "Kentucky Mountain Fugue," "The Hermit Speaks," and "Retribution." The running together of tempo designations with lit-erary allusions to Dante and Milton as though they are musical terms is humorous to the reader who recognizes the pattern while it simul-taneously devalues the classical context, making it seem stilted and snobbish. By contrast, the book, then, can be expected to be less pre-tentious and more informal than the serious art that it is poking fun at. There is an obvious awareness of the world of classical art and a con-comitant compact not to be drawn into it. Because the terminology is Latinate, it also permits the authors to insert other foreign phrases for comic effect. "Con Amore" and "Dolce Far Niente" sound as though they could be musical expressions, but the former is Italian meaning "with love" and the latter phrase translates literally as "sweet to do nothing" (i.e., idiomatically "delicious inactivity").

The borrowing motif is extended further as each chapter is headed by a Henry Fielding-type argument. Chapter One, for instance, purportedly is about *"The foundling on the priory steps—In which an ankle is sprained and a question asked—A pitcher is sent to the well and traded to the Braves—The long arm of coincidence rears its ugly head and in its hand is a hammer—An inkling about the foundling."* [17] Thus, Tom Jones (the foundling) is aligned with common aphorisms and sports references (the maxim of the pitcher taken to the well leads to citing the Braves baseball team). Similar statements precede the other chapters.[18] The range of allusions (literature, sports, politics, mythology, music, geology, religion, law, and so forth) is astounding. The references even sound as though they are connected, yet they are really a form of free association of Joycean stream of consciousness dimensions. As might be expected, the arguments are not related to the contents of the chapters that they introduce.

Essentially, the structure of *Parlor, Bedlam and Bath* is episodic. The plot, in contrast to the simplicity of Perelman's short magazine pieces, is convoluted—usually translucent, but with occasional surprising twists and numerous subplots. His other works tend to have simple story lines. In part this is because his shorter pieces generally are concerned with exploring only one subject, much in the manner of a one-line joke. The intricately entangled threads of the novel's plot, however, are certainly suited to a parody of classic eighteenth- and popular nineteenth-century novels. Chapter One, in the tradition of the eighteenth-century novel, for instance, begins the story by establishing the hero's family background in a tone similar to that of Lawrence Sterne's *Tristram Shandy*.

Naturally, the length of the book lends itself to contortions in the plot that could not be developed in a short story, but it is also likely that the possibilities inherent in a tangled plot appealed to Perelman for several other reasons. The numerous confusions permit Dickensian coincidences and humorous juxtapositions. Perelman found these situations amusing in themselves. Furthermore, the convoluted plot allowed the authors to string together a series of anecdotes on a number of dissimilar topics of the kind that Perelman usually wrote (each chapter is probably equivalent to a typical short story in length and treatment of the subject matter) but connected by the fact that all of them involve the novel's protagonist, Chester Tattersall.

Chester is not the amiable rogue or anti-hero that his predecessor Tom Jones was, but he is certainly not cut in the figure of a romantic hero either. The opening chapter helps establish the divergence from the figure of a heroic protagonist, and, of course, sets the humorous tone for what is to come. It begins by focusing not on Chester but on his father and uncle, as though the hero is not important enough to merit immediate attention. Furthermore, the information provided about his forefathers is not conducive to raising the reader's expectations regarding Chester:

Luke and Mameluke Tattersall were born just about the time that the Methodist Church was beginning to realize that a new devil, the Waltz, needed legislation. . . . [They] were born of the same mother, and, as far as anyone in St. Louis ever knew, of the same father. That was all they ever had in common. Luke spent most of his boyhood hanging the turkey from fences. . . . Mameluke was the kind of boy who was always ready to make up a fourth hand at jacks with the girls.   (pp. 11-12)

Luke (whose name seems to connote a lazy, ne'er-do-well type for Perelman, who uses it frequently in later works) turns out to be Chester's father. A newspaperman who picked up the drinking habit from his wife (she had what was called "a weak chest" and constantly consumed "amber-colored medicine in flat black bottles which were then sold openly to sufferers at corner hospitals"[19]) and who soon died after overdosing on "the specific" (by way of a fall from their third floor flat), proves a failure as a father. Mameluke, however, married money, and by the end of the chapter Chester is the beneficiary of his uncle's good fortune.

In Chapter Two Chester meets Cherry LaRue, the rental agent at the Endocrine Arms where he takes an apartment. Most of the chapter is devoted to describing the lavish suite of rooms and furnishings of the apartment. It is almost, as in many of the movies of the period, as though the authors are giving their imagination *carte blanche* and unlimited funds in decorating a dream house as a means of temporarily excising the stark world of the Depression that surrounds them.

Chester also meets Rolf Weatherbee, a melancholy young man who at the end of a year of married life "was beginning to wonder whether marriage wasn't a gamble. Perhaps the little woman standing beside him that morning in front of the minister had not been a Queen of Hearts but a three of clubs."[20] The Belmont Social and Pleasure Club, where Chester and Rolf meet, is the site for much of the novel's action—like the Sutton Club Hotel of Perelman's later life, it is a place where many characters come together for social pleasures. As was frequently the case with Perelman's cohorts, Luke and Rolf had been college classmates. And, presumably as was true with the authors' acquaintances, the work that Rolf was engaged in was as "obvious as a placard" because of his uniform: "black Chesterfield overcoat, derby hat, hard collar, regimental striped tie, and fraternity pin"—he sold either bonds or real estate.[21] The significance of superficialities, as well as their absurdity, in society is a constant source for Perelman's satire, and he delights in pointing out the inherent gap between arrogant pretentions and the reality of the insignificance and unimportance of what they are applied to. The kind of characters who are recipients of Perelman's disdain are the kind who would become objects of Holden Caulfield's "phonies" appellation in J. D. Salinger's *The Catcher in the Rye*.

Chapter Two also contains a comic element that Perelman used frequently, especially at the beginning of his career: the repetition of a phrase or line of dialogue. The amusement derived from this technique is based on an enjoyment with the sounds involved, possible even to the point of devaluing language in the way that Samuel Beckett does. In other words, the repetition and recognition of the sound becomes pleasing and more important than the arbitrarily assigned meaning of the words. This sort of repetition would become a popular technique with practitioners of the Theater of the Absurd twenty-five years later, though it has always been part of the comic repertoire. Related to the devaluation of language, yet emphasizing comedy's social orientation, is Perelman's placing of the words in the mouths of members of disperate social classes in a variety of circumstances. "There's a lot more drinking going on now than before Prohibition" is first uttered by a taxicab driver.[22] In a slightly altered version a "dark" elevator operator says, "They's a powerful lot of drinkin' goin' on these days . . . Yes, sir, moh'n befo' Prohibition," and additional repetitions are scattered throughout the novel.[23]

Chapter Three opens with a conversation, in a mode mocking Leo Tolstoy, between a horse and a pigeon who are observing Rolf. Having lampooned the upper classes, the authors throw a barb at the servant class while at the same time reminding the audience that the conversation is contained in a piece of fiction. "My husband is indisposed," Rolf's wife, Helen, informs the butler and the cook, " 'Please put him to bed.' And being servants of fiction instead of fact they obeyed.''[24] By keeping their audience aware that it is reading a book, the authors reinforce the feeling of emotional distancing that is necessary for humor, and they remind the reader that they are functioning within the established novel tradition, which again is one of the objects of their satire. American society receives a jibe when the action switches to a description of a parade in which the incongruity of an Irish holiday being celebrated by an American crowd composed of working-class European Jews and Italians in an upper-class WASP locale, if analyzed objectively, creates a sense of the ridiculous that fits Fielding's definition of humor as deriving from this source.[25] The description of the noise and bustle also is reminiscent of the depiction of a political rally in Dickens' *The Pickwick Papers*. The parade is relevant to the plot, too, for it is while he is watching it that Chester meets Lila Winter.

Other than developing the relationship between Chester and Lila in Chester's apartment, Chapter Four is notable for the authors' use of two of Perelman's favorite comic devices. First there is a passage that pokes fun at the stilted purple prose of popular melodramatic novels:

The girl's eyes were bright with tears as she realized what the morrow must bring; for must not Prince Danilo rejoin his regiment ere the cock crow? She alone amongst those heedless dancers knew sadness. But do not think she passed unobserved as her tear trickled down the front of Danilo's tunic. The old Capelmeister, dreaming over his violin, had taken in the situation at a glance, and at a signal from his capable wand, the enchanting bars of Lehar's immortal ''Merry Widow Waltz'' teased the toes of the frolickers. Thus an old man who had known love granted a tender reprieve to the blushing Bertha.   (p. 74)

This, to describe a present-day woman in a man's apartment! The Walter Mittyish, fanciful imaging of the hero is found throughout Perelman's writing. Throwing in an allusion to the world of music (or art or literature or sports or politics), ''Lehar's immortal Merry Widow Waltz,'' is typical of Perelman, too.

Following soon afterward is another ubiquitous element of Perelman's style, punning. The narrator observes that Chester and Lila kissed, or ''In another and simpler word intended for the high-school trade, they 'osculated.' '' Chester reacts to the narration and the sequence is begun:

"Now there's a word!". . . .

"What?"

"To osculate."

"It sounds as if it came from a Greek root," observed Lila hazily.

"I love Greek roots," commented Chester, "especially with drawn butter sauce and a parsley garnish."   (p. 75)

In the Plumbers' and Mechanics' Bridge and Whist Club bar in Chapter Five, Chester has just decided that he is in love with Lila when he meets Wendy and begins another amorous adventure. In Chapter Six the adventure continues, with some risqué word play. " 'Hold the baby and I'll make a coat!' boomed Chester . . . 'Or hold my coat and I'll make this baby,' offered Wendy, pulling up before a policeman,''[26] is followed by:

"Just a couple of lushes," observed Officer Reilly contemptuously as he raised the flask again. "I don't know what this city's coming to. *C'est un autre Sodome et Gomorrhe, par example!*"

"Isn't that the title of one of Proust's books?" queried the panhandler who had loaned Reilly the flask.

"Yes, and a fine book, too," said Reilly warmly. "Are you an admirer of Proust also? I've known him for years. Have you read 'The Sweet Cheat Gone'?"

"No, I've just gotten through 'Du Cote de Chez Swann' myself," blushed the modest panhandler. "Just a dilettante, you know."

"A fine fellow, Proust," commented Reilly. "We were in police college together."

"Which one?" interrupted the panhandler with a start.

"Which Proust?"

"No, which police college?"   (pp. 91-93)

Later, as Chester and Wendy are about to enter Chester's apartment building, one of the clues to the solution of the plot is introduced. Chester sees a gentleman who looks like Rolf leaving the building but decides that it cannot be his old college chum for "what would that much-married gentleman be doing coming out of an apartment house in the Village at four in the morning?"[27] As will be seen later, the term "much-married" is significant. Surprisingly, Wendy's reaction to the sight of the departing figure parallels Chester's. It is amusing that the same objection occurs to her as had occurred to Chester, as though he had spoken his thoughts aloud, but what is more interesting, and later even more salient, is that this stranger whom Chester picked up on the street apparently knows Rolf well. At this point, however, the Annual Exhibit of American Mustache Artists seems at least as imposing an event.

Chapter Seven does little to advance the plot—Chester's college club and Benny Green the reporter are the subjects—but it does contain a passage that would fit in a Marx Brothers movie by virtue of the illogical sequence of comments, the supposed autobiography, the corrupted Latin motto, and the cadence of delivery:

"Mr. Feinbloom is dead," said Chester slowly, "I just got a cable from Palestine. He has been eaten by Arabs. Repose to his ashes. Do not profane the dead. *De mortuis nihil nisi boom-boom*. I have spoken."   (p. 125)

This is followed by Chester's absurd outlining of his foreign adventures in Walter Mittyish/Captain Spaulding-like hyperbole and downright invention.

The next chapter similarly is notable more for a single element than for a plot movement or expression of socially significant issues. In a vein that will become identifiably Perelmanesque, the character of Roger Llewellyn Chicago McDuff, a Fuller Brush man, is introduced:

The door opened cautiously and a fantastic individual propelled himself slowly forward into the room. Although outwardly normal, the visitor gave the impression of having web feet. He seemed to be about thirty years of age and carried a battered valise in one hand. His face looked as if it had been slept in and his morning clothes gained nothing by having the gray striped trousers at least two sizes too large. . . . The caller looked doubtfully at Chester and the bottles, and apologetically began to back out.

"You wouldn't want any brushes," he said almost contemptuously. "What the hell would you be doing with brushes?"

"Who told you my name?" asked the salesman, open-mouthed.

"There it is on the lining of your hat," indicated Chester quietly. "Elemental, my dear McDuff, elemental! . . . Unless I am very much mistaken, late of the Indian Army, a retired major on half pay, I should say; smokes a fair Trichinopoly cheroot, has a slight limp in his left leg due to a saber-cut received at Peshawar during the Sepoy Mutiny and lives alone except for an elderly housekeeper in a semi-detached villa at Maida Vale."

"Have another brush," [McDuff] invited. "This one is for cleaning cats, dogs, parrots, ferrets, mandrils, stoats, shoats and animals of all descriptions. No dog is complete without one. It cleans without scratching, or if you prefer, scratches without cleaning. Give it to your wife, your sweetheart, your mistress. . . . This little brush will quiet the baby, make the iceman behave, and wind the clock. It saves time and trouble toil and tears."   (pp. 130, 136)

Perelman treats the exaggerations of Sherlock Holmes and those of modern advertising in the same manner, as though they are no different, which is his point. There is fun in the exaggeration, and no one should take it seriously. The playing with names (a city, Chicago, linked with the Shakespearian McDuff), the cataloging, the juxtaposition of common animals with uncommon ones, the attention to word sounds ("parrots" leads to 'ferrets," "stoats" to "shoats"), the easy verbal reversal that seems to be mathematically equatable but which is clearly not ("cleans without scratching" is very different from "scratches without cleaning"), and the panacea claims that indiscriminately extend from animals to wives/sweethearts/mistresses to babies to icemen and finally to clocks are all featured devices in Perelman's arsenal.

Chapter Nine details Chester and Helen's attendance at the Kid Chocolate boxing match. During the course of the evening, the couple becomes acquainted with a taxi driver who is writing a book titled *The Clutch*, based on his experiences as a cabbie, an usher "gathering material for a novel on prize-fighting to be called 'The Clutch,' " the boxer's manager who is writing a book called *The Clutch* that recounts a fight between Chocolate and Jack Dempsey (when Dempsey "was a featherweight"), and a group of policemen (who are labeled "gardenias of the law," which simultaneously reflects Perelman's delight in choosing the most expansive noun formations available and his proclivity for punning), each of whom is "busily engaged at his post blocking out his novel of conditions in Tammany to be called 'The Clutch.' "[28] The chapter ends with Chester and Helen in a haystack in New Jersey being observed by a pair of cows, one of which is "a Holstein by her seventh marriage" and one who is writing a novel on farm life entitled *The Clutch*. The running coincidence joke and the anthropomorphic animals are two more devices characteristic of Perelman's style.

In Chapter Ten the plot lines begin to come together as Chester and Rolf travel by train to Rolf's home for a rural weekend. Chester is thinking fleetingly of Helen, and Wendy and Lila have already become blurred memories, though obviously they have been brought back to the reader's mind when Rolf reminds Chester that he has never met Rolf's wife. Rolf goes on to confess that he had been married to a chorus girl briefly right after graduation. He also admits that he got a job for his ex-wife about a year ago and that he still sees her now and then. Nothing comes of these disclosures until the following chapter. As Chapter Eleven begins, it seems as though the authors are merely going to continue to lambast the lazy, surly, and sullen servant class, this time in the person of Sanford, the chauffeur who ignores his boss and ignores his duties with a minimum of grace. He proves to be poor driver, abusing the car, as would be expected, though he charitably decides not to knife Chester for asking him for help with the luggage.

Suddenly Chester is confronted with Rolf's wife, who turns out to be Helen: "Chester and Helen stood there while the color drained slowly out of his face and into hers."[29] Again, the twist of logic implying that there is a literal connection between their faces that permits blood to flow from one to the other is so obviously impossible that it creates a humorous tone.

The denouement continues as Chester is faced with more ironic revelations. First he finds out that Lila Winter is Rolf's sister, then he learns that Wendy is Rolf's aunt. The quiet stay in the country has turned into a Georges Feydeau farce.

In the final chapter Chester returns to his apartment in New York where he becomes entangled with Cherry. First, though, the authors delay things a bit by bringing Chester into contact with some of her friends, such as Edward Bulwinkle, the young inventor of blue dandruff. When they get back on track it is by having Cherry recite her history, beginning with a mock–mythic tale of how her father, whose name was Androcles, found a snake "clasping its hands in anguish as it writhed with pain." The father extracted the thorn and the snake followed him home where the family gave their new pet a saucer of fresh cream and a live chicken. "Why a live chicken?" Chester asks. "We had no dead chickens," said Cherry. "We were very, very poor."[30] The story of the snake is further extended toward absurdity in a manner reminiscent of several Robert Benchley sketches on the order of "Do Insects Think?" (published eight years earlier); there are other instances that reflect Benchley's influence on Perelman scattered throughout his *oeuvre*, in *Acres and Pains* and elsewhere. Cherry recalls how the snake later apprehended two burglars who had broken into the house.[31] Having established an affinity for each other, at least partly based on Chester's appreciation for Cherry's past, the two decide to opt for marriage and domestic bliss. One more revelation is forthcoming, though. Cherry must make a final confession so that there will be no secrets, and the secret that she reveals is that she eloped with a college boy but the marriage lasted only two weeks.[32] The circle has now closed and Chester has formally met Rolf's first wife. Chester can take no more and he leaps out of the window, so upsetting Cherry that she exclaims, "My word. . . . Almost seven o'clock! It's time I got some sleep."[33] All is not lost, though, for Chester was caught on a ledge, and when he climbs back into the room they embrace for "They have found their bluebird in the vale of heart's desire."[34]

As the foregoing illustrates, *Parlor, Bedlam and Bath* is meant to amuse, nothing more. There are no themes of great significance, no major insights into either humankind or society. There are satiric jibes throughout, to be sure, pointing out human foibles and societal foolishness, but it is evident that the authors never intend to delve below the surface of things, and it is the superficial that is the butt of their myriad jokes. For the casual reader, this is sufficient.

Although Perelman did later discuss the possibility of collaborating on a novel with his brother-in-law West,[35] after *Parlor, Bedlam and Bath* he abandoned the genre. It is probably just as well that this is so, for his style and content seem perfectly suited to the short story/essay format. *Parlor, Bedlam and Bath* is not composed in a grand, sweeping high style, it does not show a seriousness of purpose, and the subject matter is not timeless in any significant sense. Even a comic novel must go beyond mere entertainment if it is to have any literary significance (see some of the novels to which Perelman and Reynolds pay homage—*Tom Jones, Humphry Clinker, Tristram Shandy*). *Parlor, Bedlam and Bath* is filled with amusing scenes and a great deal of wit and word play, especially that which links incongruities as a source of humor, but nowhere is there any indication that the authors ever intended to go beyond this. Their style, choice of subject matter, and plot line by their very nature impose self-generated limitations. Puns, purple prose parodies, clichés, stock comic character types, light satire, attention to insignificant social foibles, awareness of art forms (constant allusions to), and a melodramatic plot compose the warp and woof of *Parlor, Bedlam and Bath*, just as they do in Perelman's short prose. Fortunately, the author excels at the smaller canvas provided by his forte, and he soon returned to expanding his talent in the short story/essay format, though it was not until seven years after the publication of *Parlor, Bedlam and Bath* that Perelman's next collection of stories, *Strictly from Hunger*, was published. In the meantime, the thirties were full of new experiences for Perelman; he was "seduced" to Hollywood by the Marx Brothers, where he worked on ten movies in ten years for Paramount and MGM, he wrote for Broadway, and he started writing for *The New Yorker* in 1934.

STRICTLY FROM HUNGER

When *Strictly from Hunger* (1937) was published, it was done by Random House, the company that would publish Perelman's next four books. The collection contains several of what are generally considered his earliest masterpieces: "Waiting for Santy" (a take-off on Clifford Odets); "Scenario" (one of his first parodies of Hollywood motion pictures, in which he runs together hundreds of B-movie clichés and lines of dialogue); "The Love Decoy" ("A Story of Youth in College Today"—complete with an improbable conclusion parodying Victorian novels), and "A Farewell to Omsk" (subtitled "The terrifying result of reading an entire gift set of Dostoevsky in one afternoon," this essay is not a reprint, being published for the first time in this anthology, though the acknowledgment section in *The Most of S. J. Perelman* reads "first appeared in the book, *Crazy Like a Fox*").

In the seven years since *Dawn Ginsbergh's Revenge* appeared, Perelman has matured both as a humorist and as a stylist. As a result of moving from *Judge*, his stories no longer follow that very short format, and he has time to develop his points more fully. In addition, his use of language has become much sharper, and his attitude toward his subject matter has lost most of the sophomoric tinge that is present in his earlier writing, though he still maintains an exuberant tone. The transformation is something like moving from the dance style of Gene Kelly to that of Fred Astaire. As time goes on, the style approaches elegance.

"Waiting for Santy" is a "playlet" in the manner of Clifford Odets (particularly his *Waiting for Lefty*, a drama about a union organizer). The scene is "The sweatshop of S. Claus, a manufacturer of children's toys, on North Pole Street."[36] As the curtain rises, seven gnomes are discovered making toys and complaining about working conditions. Riskin is the major instigator, describing the boss as "A parasite, a leech, a bloodsucker—altogether a five-star nogoodnick! Starvation wages we get so he can ride around in a team with reindeers!" In keeping with stereotyped characters and dialogue filled with leftist rhetoric, Ruskin is labeled a scab, stool pigeon, and company spy, Briskin is a fatalist, Panken is accused of having a slave psychology, and Rivkin is in love with the boss's daughter, Stella. Sanford (a.k.a. Sam) Claus returns from a visit to a medical specialist ("The biggest professor in the country . . . the best cardiac man that money could buy. . . . I tell you I was like a wild man"—the Yiddish phrasing and timing increase the humor[37]) with the news that his adhesions, diabetes, sleeping sickness, and decalcomania are forcing him to cut out chimney climbing, and, naturally, the day is saved when Claus appoints Rivkin as his successor and partner in the firm and blesses his relationship with Stella. The playlet ends happily with Claus's announcement that there will be a forty percent pay cut, a statement met by cries of joy and dancing by all but Riskin and Briskin, who go underground.

"The Idol's Eye," also included in this collection, is in many ways Perelman's best and most representative piece. The tale begins with the narrator, Clay Modeling, explaining how he and three others spent a weekend at the villa of a mutual friend, Gabriel Snubbers. Snubbers, who speaks with the pseudo stage accent of a stereotypical English major, has come into an inheritance and refuses to leave home; Gossip Gabrilowitsch, the Polish pianist, Downey Couch, the Irish tenor, Frank Falcovsky, the Jewish prowler, and the narrator have bicycled down from London to visit him.

Immediately Perelman introduces four of the literary devices that characterize his style: outlandish names, puns, understatement, and literalism. Perelman's first pun is delivered in the description of their arrival when Snubbers leads them up a "great avenue of two stately alms."[38] Understatement comes into play when the party discovers that the entire left wing of the house, incidentally containing Snubbers' aunt, has just burned down, but Snubbers dismisses the incident casually. This deadpan understatement, a common element in native American humor, serves as the basis for the major reversal that is developed later in the piece. Literalism, a variation on Fielding's concept of the ridiculous, is another source of humor, as when the host offers his guest "a spot of whiskey and soda," which turns out to be a drop of whiskey on a piece of paper that his "sleekly Oriental" servant, Littlejohn, shows them, and baking soda. The thread of conscious literalism that leads to nonsense runs through the rest of the selection as a counterpoint to the tale that Snubbers will offer and expect to be taken as accurate—which it is. First, the narrator responds, logically, to a suggestion that he drank the soda "like a little soldier" with the thought that he had never drunk a little soldier. Of course, the original statement had not been meant literally, but Perelman is making us aware of the ridiculousness of the simile and of assuming that words have arbitrary meanings or that they mean exactly what they say. Later, after Snubbers tells a dull story, Falcovsky grunts. When Snubbers' attention is drawn to Falcovsky, the latter merely proposes that grunting in front of a fire is part of the good life and he grunts several more times. Perelman then ties this bit of literalism back to that having to do with the spot of whiskey and soda by observing that "The baking soda was beginning to tell on Snubbers."[39]

This is following by a sequence that reflects Perelman's mental tracking

"I was going through some of my great-grandfather's things the other day . . . "

"What things?" demanded Falcovsky.

"His bones, if you must know," Snubbers said coldly. "You know, Great-grandfather died under strange circumstances. He opened a vein in his bath."

"I never knew baths had veins," protested Gabrilowitsch.

"I never knew his great-grandfather had a ba—" began Falcovsky derisively. With a shout Snubbers threw himself on Falcovsky. It was the signal for Pandemonium, the upstairs girl, to enter and throw herself with a shout on Couch. The outcome of the neckingbee was as follows: Canadians 12, Visitors 9, Krebs and Vronsky played footie, subbing for Gerber and Weinwald, who were disabled by flying antipasto.   (p. 32)

The train of thought is a kind of stream of consciousness taken to be an absurd extreme. One thought or image leads to another rapidly with no ascertainable linkage—the transitions are missing. A careful analysis shows that there is a natural relationship between some of the parts (the movement from the literal to the comic in the great-grandfather's vein/bathtub-vein/great-grandfather's bathing progression; the thought of pandemonium; the scoring of the altercation in sports terminology), but some have no apparent relevance and may have been thrown in purely because they are not relevant (a technique frequently employed earlier in the dadaist tradition and further developed in the Theater of the Absurd twenty-five years later).[40] The overall effect is to keep the reader off balance logically, and the random, fast delivery of lines and thoughts echoes the dialogue that Perelman scripted for the Marx Brothers.

The humorist's manipulation of logic and language also mirrors his amusement with and love of language. Language is fundamentally logical, while at the same time providing a basis for logic. But, as Perelman recognizes, the logic has been arbitrarily assigned; it is not innate. Therefore, language is vulnerable to alteration that fits within its own inconsistent rules, and Perelman plays with the sounds and even the look of words to produce humor. Logic and sound converge in puns, so he fills his works with them. For example, Snubbers begins the tale of his great-grandfather's adventures with a reminiscence that his ancestor "would rather fight than eat and vice versa"[41] (a contradictory set of premises). This caused him to become interested in cooking, and Snubbers' tale opens, "One night he was chaffing at The Bit, a tavern in Portsmouth." We are also told that during his travels to the Holy City of the Surds and Cosines, the great-grandfather lived on "the few ptarmigan which fell to the ptrigger of his pfowling-piece," whereby Perelman brings sight and sound together.

The story that continues is Snubbers' account, in detail, of how his great-grandfather managed to steal the huge flawless ruby that served as the eye of a temple idol. This is a plot straight out of the B movies and serials of the nineteen-thirties and forties, even to the particular of the dark face appearing at the window. The twist comes when Snubbers reveals the upshot of the case, that the movers had taken away his great-grandfather's piano because the old man had missed the last four installments. The final twist is an innocent, though human reaction of *reductio ad absurdum*: "And—and the ruby?" inquires one of the listeners. " 'Oh, *that*,' shrugged Snubbers. 'I just threw that in to make it interesting.' We bashed in his conk and left him to the vultures." Many of Perelman's endings do not match the level of his text, but this one certainly hits the nail on the head.

LOOK WHO'S TALKING

Perelman's fourth collection of essays, *Look Who's Talking*, was published in 1940. The twenty-four selections first appeared in *The New Yorker*, the *New Masses*, and *Broun's Nutmeg*. As is the case with several of his earliest collections, before his writing became more formulaic and while his juxtapositions and expressions were still fresh and inventive, *Look Who's Talking* contains a number of selections that are regarded as classics (though even in his last writings he maintained that special perspective on mundane subjects that reduces them to their essential ridiculousness and allows us to identify with his narrators, who are beset by the tastelessness and absurdity of the world about us). "Down with the Restoration," for example, starts out by establishing the author's expertise: "I haven't made a prediction since the opening night of *The Women* some years ago, when I rose at the end of the third act and announced to my escort, a Miss Chicken-Licken, 'The public will never take this to its bosom.' Since the public has practically worn its bosom to a nubbin niggling up to *The Women*, I feel that my predictions may be a straw to show the direction the wind is blowing away from." [42] He then goes on to make an astonishing prophecy: "One of these days two young people are going to stumble across a ruined farmhouse and leave it alone." The story that follows is a parody of those articles that fill the pages of magazines such as "The American Home-Owner": Mibs and Evan completely remodel a farmhouse for $51.18 with the help of one of a long line of handymen who appear in Perelman's writing and who are named Lafe.

Parody is one of Perelman's primary devices, and "Somewhere a Roscoe" provides an example of the sort of writing that leads the humorist to parody and shows its effect on him. Two years ago, he begins, he was "almost a character in a Russian novel," lying in bed for days and drinking tea out of a glass. [43] Then he picked up *Spicy Detective*, a pulp magazine, and his life changed dramatically, for he has been introduced to the Dan Turner series. The essay continues with excerpts from a number of episodes in the Turner saga. Turner, "the apotheosis of all private detectives," is forever finding himself in situations, Perelman notes, described in the same terms in story after story—though there are minor differences, as in the sound of gunfire. Guns always cough or belch "Kachow," "Chow-chow," "Ka-

chow,'' or simply ''Chow,'' and the victim is always a woman, usually well-endowed and dressed suggestively, often one who has an
oriental servant. A similar look at the science fiction genre is the basis
for ''Captain Future, Block that Kick!,'' and books about medical
practice written by doctors come under fire in ''Boy Meets Girl Meets
Foot.'' Perelman's eye, or ear, for vital stylistic elements is exhibited
in these selections and is certainly related to his ability to capture the
essence of another writer in his parodies. The fact that parody relies
on specific exaggerations melds nicely with Perelman's predilection
for exaggeration as a humorous device in his literary satires.

For Perelman, advertising is always open to parody, and in ''Tomorrow—Fairly Cloudy'' the author focuses on this topic. After describing some actual advertisements that he has encountered, for Knopf
books and Listerine toothpaste, he presents a scenario for an advertisement that portrays the profession at its worst.

In ''Mercy, the Cat's Got into the Budget,'' Perelman reacts to two
newspaper articles, a forerunner to his technique of placing reprints of
items (real or imagined) taken from newspapers at the beginning of a
piece. In this essay he is disturbed by the extravagance of the reported
monthly expenses of Elaine Barrie Barrymore and the Baroness Maud
von Leidersdorff. Perelman concludes that life can go on at a less
expensive level.

''Frou-Frou, or the Future of Virtigo'' is, as the title undoubtedly
indicates, an exposé of the author's love-hate relationship with the
''Why Don't You?'' column in *Harper's Bazaar*. It all began while
the narrator was ''reclining on my chaise lounge in a negligee trimmed
with marabou, reading trashy bonbons and eating French yellow-backed
novels,'' and started to look through *Harper's Bazaar*:

The first time I noticed this ''Why Don't You?'' department was a year ago
last August. . . . Without any preamble came the stinging query, ''Why don't
you rinse your blonde child's hair in champagne, as they do in France?'' . . .
''Why don't you,'' continued the author, spitting on her hands, ''twist her
pigtails around her ears like macaroons?'' I reread this several times to make
sure I wasn't dreaming and then turned to the statement of ownership in the
back of the magazine. Just because the Marquis de Sade wasn't mentioned
didn't fool *me*. . . . I slept across the foot of the crib with a loaded horse
pistol until the next issue appeared.   (pp. 47–47)

But, as the narrator warns, "Don't think it does any good to pretend there *is* no magazine called *Harper's Bazaar*." Obviously Perelman feels a need to warn his readers about insidious things such as this, based on his own experiences, because all too often, it is inferred, this rampant preposterousness would go undetected. By including minute, realistic details (the naming of the month—August), he establishes a sense of veracity supposedly intended to make the reader heed his warnings.

THE DREAM DEPARTMENT

In 1943, *The Dream Department*, containing twenty-five selections reprinted from *The New Yorker* and *Funny Bone*, followed *Look Who's Talking*. The volume is dedicated to his close friend and brother-in-law, novelist Nathanael West.

The first selection, "Counter-Revolution," returns to one of Perelman's favorite topic clusters—advertising, shoddy workmanship and merchandise, and the cavalier treatment of customers by sales clerks who insinuate that they would rather not sell anything to this particular *schlemiel* of a customer anyway. As shown above, from the very beginning of his career Perelman was preoccupied with the absurdities contained in advertising. "Advertisers in the thirties were giving themselves the most colossal airs," he has complained, "bombasting away about the creative importance of what they were doing."[44] This piece begins with an explanation of how the narrator came to purchase a bottle of Major's Cement and his incredulity upon reading the extended disclaimer that came with the bottle. Expect nothing and you will not be disappointed is substantially what it said, yet it also asserted that the user should grin and bear it and not make any disparaging remarks about the quality of the product to other potential buyers. Having established his conceptual background, the author presents a playlet about a "Mr. Average Customer" who tries to buy a Mackinaw but who seems to ask outrageous questions and to make unreasonable demands of the exasperated salesman: "Does this model come with pockets?"[45] The curtain falls with the clerk pouring acid on the merchandise as the floorwalker looks on approvingly. As usual, Perelman takes his notion to its extreme in order to demonstrate the full implications of what might normally be accepted as an unimportant inconvenience. It is exactly these minor irritations and what they reflect about the people who perpetrate them and about the people who allow them to continue without a whimper that occupy Perelman's interest. As an author, he not only relates his own experiences, reactions, and frustrations, but he simultaneously accomplishes the primary function of comedy in his satires—he points out society's foibles. The fact that we *let* people do these things is probably funnier than what they do.

Advertisements for the film version of Somerset Maugham's life of painter Paul Gauguin, *The Moon and Sixpence*, stimulates Perelman's mockery in "Beat Me, Post-Impressionist Daddy." The narrator claims to have unearthed some letters between the artist and his own father's barber (who lived in the family's bureau, which is where the letters were discovered). Following the lines of the advertisements, which distort Maugham's work by over-emphasizing Gauguin's passion for women, at least, Perelman notes, as it is displayed in the painter's journal (*Avant et Après*) and correspondence, these spurious letters are filled with provocative lines. Women will not leave him alone, he declares, pleading with him to abuse them: " 'I'm a strange little beast!' she cried. 'Beat me 'til your arm aches!' . . . 'what could I do? I bounced her around a bit, knocked out several of her teeth,' " but still he is "surrounded by hordes of beauties begging me to maltreat them."[46]

"To Sleep, Perchance to Steam" is a short piece about insomnia, enlightened by Perelman's own special brand of insanity: "I shuddered for approximately half an hour to relax my nerves, plugged a pair of Flents into my ears, and tied on a sleep mask. I probably should have waited until I got into bed before doing so, as I took a rather nasty fall over a wastebasket."[47] Perelman never lets us forget that we cannot make any assumptions or take anything for granted. "I read several chapters of Durfee's *Monastaries of the Rhone*," he informs us, "with no success whatever until I discovered I had forgotten to remove my mask." The series of events that seem to conspire to keep him awake—"the annual outing of the Clan-na-Gael," the wife upstairs beating her husband—recall the marvelous vegetable man sequence in W. C. Fields's *It's a Gift* (1934).

"Woodman, Don't Spare That Tree!" is a scenario that returns to the author's dismay at the projects of decorators, and "A Pox on You, Mine Goodly Host" presents Jiggs and Maggie types (the narrator's pseudo-persona metaphorically implied) trying to establish their credentials so that they can be served at Schrafft's. In spite of their attempts, they are rejected along with George S. Kaufman and Moss Hart in a vulgar display of vanity and pomposity by the management. Perelman finds pretentiousness ludicrous and by suddenly weaving Kaufman and Hart into his fiction he makes the arrogant conceit seem even more preposterous since nobody would treat the two playwrights in the manner that he suggests, yet the possibility that someone might, and for the picayune reasons that he describes, adds to the piquancy of his point. Finally, Perelman's self-disparagement enhances both the humor and his theme, for by reducing himself he shows us how puny his tormentors must really be to have been concerned with him in the first place, and he permits us to identify with his plight because everybody has been in the position of responding so adroitly to an insult: " 'That shrimp couldn't be a cat's bodyguard,' sneered his neighbor. I looked the speaker full in the eye. 'That's for the cat to say.' " [48]

The subject matters of "Our Unbalanced Aquariums" (sparked by letters to the editor of a tropical fish fanciers' magazine), "Button, Button, Who's Got the Blend?" (a scenario that results from exposure to a Hostess Cup Cake ad), "Caution—Soft Prose Ahead" (comments on publisher's notes regarding forthcoming books), "Kitchenware, Notions, Lights, Action, Camera" (about the personal appearances of film stars at department stores, with Perelman's fanciful illustration rendered in scenario form), "Hold That Christmas Tiger!" (decorations suggested by *Mademoiselle*, *Vogue*, and *House and Garden*), and "Smugglers in the Dust" (a scenario expanding on a blurb in *Variety* about visitors being smuggled into film studios) provide an idea of the range of topics that Perelman found suitable for attacking in *The Dream Department*. Not only was anything and everything fair game to him, but it usually proved to deserve the potshots that the author took, and he took those shots frequently.

CRAZY LIKE A FOX/THE BEST OF S. J. PERELMAN

Crazy Like a Fox was published by Random House in 1944 with a dedication to Laura and Abby Laura and reprinted as *The Best of S. J. Perelman*, dedicated to Robert Benchley, by Vintage Press in 1973. However, the publishing history of this volume is confusing. A note in *The Best of S. J. Perelman* indicates that the volume is merely a reprint with a title change, and in comparing a *Crazy Like a Fox* volume with the 1973 edition of *The Best of S. J. Perelman* I found them to be identical. Several of my colleagues insisted, though, that they had seen somewhat different versions, so I investigated further. As it turns out, there are, in fact, different versions of the books. Between these two printings an Armed Forces edition appeared (New York: the same year as the original publication). Garden City Publishing reprinted the book the next year, as did Heinemann in London. In 1951 Penguin Books, also in London, reprinted the volume too. All of the editions between the initial publication and 1947 appeared with the title *Crazy Like a Fox*. In 1947 Random House published the book under the title *The Best of S. J. Perelman* in their Modern Library series. The volume was later reprinted by Vintage Books (in 1973) as a reprinting of the 1947 *The Best of S. J. Perelman* edition.

Most of the selections were also collected in *Look Who's Talking, Strictly from Hunger, The Dream Department*, and *Keep It Crisp*. However, an amusing introduction purportedly by one Sidney Namlerep of 1626 Broadway, New York City—Namlerep is Perelman spelled backwards and the Broadway address was the location of Perelman's office—appears in some of the editions but not all of them. Even the stories included vary, with "Physician, Steel Thyself," "Pale Hands I Loathe," "Insert Flap 'A' and Throw Away," and "Farewell, My Lovely Appetizer" appearing in some editions but not others.

In the introduction Namlerep admits that Perelman deserves the kind of consideration accorded the feeble-minded and then tries to explain Perelman's writing first by describing the author's nature and background and then by examining samples of his craftsmanship. The man who has been responsible for "the most picayune prose ever produced in America" in a series of books "each less distinguished than its predecessor" has a disposition "so crabbed as to make Alexander Pope and Dr. Johnson seem sunny by contrast."[49] Physically, Perelman is a marvel—his mediocrity, his "Monument to the truly banal" has been accomplished "without the benefit of [a] brain," Namlerep reports. Other characteristics include "tiny pig eyes," the forehead of a Piltdown Man, a self-inflicted broken nose, and a barrel belly. Namlerep also informs us that Perelman's many allusions are merely the products of total recall, usually of unconnected events involving other people and barely related to his own narrow experiences. A "scavenger" who "plucks words out of context" and "ravishes them," the humorist is "patently devoid of talent" opines Namlerep, as demon-

strated in the "deplorable lapses of logic and decorum" found in that "gigantic kitchen midden" of a short story "Scenario."[50] There is a half-hearted attempt to excuse this execration because it was written "after extended servitude in Hollywood," but in this and other pieces Namlerep accuses Perelman of leaving behind him "a spoor of crushed and bleeding prose" while declaiming on his two "most dominant themes," money and women. "The damage he has done to the language is incalculable," clamors Namlerep and, foreshadowing Charles Schulz's Lucy, he declares that Perelman's only hope may be to "betake himself to that good five-cent psychiatrist he is forever prating about."[51] Most of the literary abuses that Namlerep attributes to Perelman, needless to say, are the very ones that Perelman makes fun of.

KEEP IT CRISP

By 1946, when *Keep It Crisp* was published, most of Perelman's work was appearing only in major magazines. This collection, for example, was compiled of twenty-five reprints from *The New Yorker* and *The Saturday Evening Post*.

The best known of these pieces is "Farewell, My Lovely Appetizer," a parody of Raymond Chandler's thrillers, especially those about hard-boiled private detective Philip Marlowe (featured in *The Big Sleep* and others). In the *Paris Review* interview Perelman admits his pleasure that Chandler has praised the piece in a collection of his letters, *Raymond Chandler Speaking*: "I ran across a very flattering reference he made to a parody of his work I had done."[52]

Perelman does, indeed, capture the feeling of the genre. The plot, except for minor details, could have been taken from any number of sources. Mike Noonan, at the Atlas Agency—Noonan and Driscoll ("but Snapper Driscoll had retired two years before with a .38 slug between his shoulders, donated by a snowbird in Tacoma"[53]), enters the "crummy anteroom we kept to impress clients," growls at his secretary, Birdie Clafflin, and is informed that a "looker," a Swede named Sigrid Bjornesterne is looking for him. When Sigrid returns they take turns concealing information from each other ("playing it safe until I knew where she stood") until she finally hires him to find out how the herring that she serves her husband is given its pinkish tones. After an adventurous afternoon, avoiding possible tails while ferreting out information, Noonan returns to his office where Sigrid is awaiting him, pistol in hand. Noonan, having determined that Sigrid intends to poison her husband with the herring, disarms her, refuses to be seduced, and calls the police.

A successful parody depends on more than just the plot outline, however, and Perelman's stylistic imitation is masterful. The first-person narration informs the audience throughout, and the slang and imagery are faithful to Chandler's style. The passage in which Noonan greets Birdie is a good example: " 'Well, you certainly look like something the cat dragged in,' she said. She had a quick tongue. She also had eyes like dusty lapis lazuli, taffy hair, and a figure that did things to me. I kicked open the bottom drawer of her desk, let two inches of rye trickle down my craw, kissed Birdie square on her lush, red mouth, and set fire to a cigarette."

A comparison of the above passage with the following selections from Chandler's *The Long Goodbye* demonstrates how well Perelman captures the mystery writer's style and condenses it to create an effective parody:

Her hair was a lovely shade of dark red and she had a distant smile on her lips and over her shoulders she had a blue mink that almost made the Rolls-Royce look like just another automobile. It didn't quite. Nothing can.

The attendant was the usual half-tough character in a white coat with the name of the restaurant stitched across the front of it in red. He was getting fed up.

"Look, mister," he said with an edge to his voice, "would you mind a whole lot pulling your leg into the car so I can kind of shut the door? Or should I open it all the way so you can fall out?"

The girl gave him a look which ought to have stuck at least four inches out of his back. . . .

She was slim and quite tall in a white linen tailormade with a black and white polkadotted scarf around her throat, her hair was the pale gold of a fairy princess. There was a small hat on it into which the pale gold hair nestled like a bird in its nest. Her eyes were cornflower blue, a rare color, and the lashes were long and almost too pale. . . .

"Please don't give up," she said in a voice like the stuff they use to line summer clouds with. . . .

I went down the stairs fast and crossed into the study and grabbed the bottle of Scotch and tilted it. When I couldn't swallow any more I leaned against the wall and panted and let the stuff burn in me until the fumes reached my brain.[54]

The secretiveness and violence of the detective persona, and the props of guns, cigarettes, whiskey, seedy characters, grimy locations, and beautiful women all fit the mold. Two amusing sidelights: when Sigrid throws in the bit about the tremendously valuable golden spintria coin "just . . . for glamour,"[55] Perelman is parodying his own device in "The Idol's Eye." When Sigrid asks where he learned her name, Noonan answers, "I haven't been a private snoop twelve years for nothing, sister." She reminds him that "It was nine last time," to which he replies, "It seemed like twelve till you came along." Fifteen years later Perelman uses virtually the same dialogue in an exchange between a detective and his female client in *The Beauty Part* thus creating almost a parody of himself.[56]

By and large, there are more thematic groupings in *Keep It Crisp* than there are in the average Perelman anthology. Among the recurring thematic concerns in this collection are hack writing, motion pictures, and the medical profession. "White Bimbo, or through Dullest Africa with Three Sleepy People" is a book review of Armand Brigaud's *Killers on Safari*. Perelman begins by establishing his credibility, referring to several authoritative texts on Africa—H. Rider Haggard, Dr. Livingston, Paul Du Chaillu, Cecil Rhodes. This is followed by bombastic prose and an unbelievable plot as Perelman summarizes a novelette supposedly taken from the pulp magazine *Jungle Stories* in another amusing display of his skill at burlesque. "Amo, Amas, Amat, Amamus, Amatis, Enough" takes on those pulp magazines that specialize in romance.

An amusing *Life* biography of J. P. Marquand by Roger Butterfield serves as Perelman's model for a pseudo-autobiography in "So Little Time Marches On." Tying clearly unrelated events together (Marquand's nervous feelings and the bombing of Pearl Harbor, for example) is an error that some biographers make; Perelman is not about to let such a thing go unnoticed, so he presents a description of his narrator's first conflict with his father: "He had been reading *The Private Papers of Henry Ryecroft* and had mislaid it. Fearful lest I might have eaten it, he invaded the nursery and demanded, 'Have you noticed any Gissing around here?' 'No, sir,' I replied submissively, 'but I saw you pinching Nannie in the linen closet.' He frowned thoughtfully and withdrew, leaving me prey to a strange uneasiness. Four days later, Italy declared war on Tripoli."[57] After similar incidents, the narrator reports, "Bosnia severed relations with Herzegovina," "Georges Carpentier climbed into the ring," "A society bridge expert named Joseph B. Elwell padded downstairs," Rudloph Valentino died, and "Frances 'Peaches' Browning sued for divorce." Perhaps there is a causal connection, perhaps not, but the warning signs are strong, Perelman indicates, and they must be paid heed to. In addition to the faulty *post hoc ergo propter hoc* logic, other characteristics evident in the account are the play on words (Gissing—kissing), the literary allusions, and college and show business milieu.

Parody and motion pictures blend in "How Sharper than a Serpent's Tooth" when a viewing of *Mildred Pierce* induces Perelman to conceive of a scenario in which divorcing parents are forced to reveal the source of their livelihood to their son. The dialogue between Mr. and Mrs. Milo Leotard Allardyce Du Plessis Weatherwax is again almost verbatim that spoken by the same characters in *The Beauty Part* in 1961. Show business is also the subject of the libretto in "Whatever Goes Up," and "Hell in Gabardines" uses the diary format to comment on the idea of concealed cameras espoused by Manny Farber, film critic for the *New Republic*. In another movie related piece, "Garnish Your Face with Parsley and Serve," Perelman moves from the use of a hypodermic that looks like a French bakery icing gun to a newspaper account of Hollywood personalities who use foodstuffs as cosmetics to a scenario for a radio program about a husband, his wife, a hostess in a rumba school, and food. In "Physician, Steel Thyself" film and psychiatry are brought together in the story of Sherman Wormser, psychiatric technical advisor at RKO studios.

The style of "Pale Hands I Loathe" diverges from Perelman's normal style. The tale of an office manager who has a hand fetish is told in short, stream-of-consciousness sentences to reflect the narrator's psychological disturbance. "Dental or Mental, I say It's Spinach" concerns a visit to a dentist's office and the relationship between fear and pain. The nature of advertisements found in *Vogue* causes the author to devise a *mise en scene* about an advertising agency in "Take Two Parts Sand, One Part Girl, and Stir," a standard Perelman approach to one of his pet topics. "No Dearth of Mirth—Fill out the Coupon!" explains how the writer became a member of the Fruit-of-the-Month-Club. In "The Customer Is Always Wrong" Perelman's characters demonstrate why Chicago has a scarcity of hotel rooms—management does not like visitors. Finally, as might be guessed, "Insert Flap 'A' and Throw Away" is the result of the author's trying to follow the directions for assembling a child's cardboard toy, an experience and response familiar to most of us.

ACRES AND PAINS

Acres and Pains, published in 1947, was the first of what might be called Perelman's few thematic collections (see also *The Swiss Family Perelman*, below). Instead of following the usual pattern of his books, which are merely anthologies of the best but unrelated essays written over several years, *Acres and Pains* is a collection of stories that, Perelman claims, are "the by-product of a dozen years of country living."[58] Parenthetically, *A Child's Garden of Curses*, a compendium containing *Acres and Pains* along with *Crazy Like a Fox* and *Keep It Crisp* was published in London by Heinemann in 1951.

Twenty of the twenty-one segments originally appeared in the *Saturday Evening Post*; the other was published in the *Country Book*. All are set on Perelman's farm, Rising Gorge, near Tinicum Township, Erwinna, in Bucks County, Pennsylvania.

The farm, located seventy-five miles from New York City, had belonged to Michael Gold, author of *Jews Without Money*. When he prepared to sell the property, Gold had mimeographed a description of the farm. "The farm consists of 83 acres of tillable land, twelve being in excellent timber," it began. Priced at $6,000, the property sounded attractive and reasonable:

The soil is rich Southern hillside land. There are fruit, nut, and persimmon trees, berry bushes, and a large garden. A creek flows through the meadow in front of the house, and several natural springs furnish a constant supply of fresh, clear, pure water. . . . There is a large dwelling house, five out-buildings, three studios and a large stone barn. . . . It is two miles from Frenchtown, New Jersey, where there are chain stores and shopping at cheaper than city prices. Erwinna is an old canal town on the Lehigh Canal, one mile from the farm. The Delaware River is one mile and a quarter away. There is fine swimming, canoeing, and fishing on these waters. . . . This is fine, hilly country, inhabited by old Pennsylvania Dutch farmers and a colony of well-known New York writers and artists. The farm is a mile away from the State Game Preserve and the hills are full of deer, pheasants, quail and other game."[59]

When Nathanael West acquired a copy of the description, he got together with the Perelmans, and on December 19, 1932, the three gave

Gold a $500 downpayment. The property was dubbed "Eight Ball" by West and the new owners "set out to improve it with paint, hardware, tools, and furniture liberated from the Sutton [Club Hotel]."[60]

Each segment of *Acres and Pains* deals with a specific aspect of country living, with topics ranging from neighbors to architects and remodeling, from swimming pools to maids, from milk cows to country doctors, from hoboes to dogs. Among the best sections is that on the vegetable gardening (Chapter Twelve), in which the trials and tribulations experienced by everyone who has tried to raise vegetables are recaptured—searching through seed catalogues. . . . , fighting to bring the plants to the point that they are "poking their heads through the lava and broken glass, just in time to be eaten by cutworms, scorched by drought and smothered by weeds."[61] Chapter Thirteen examines the country dweller's experience with solitude. In Perelman's world, though, solitude is in no way akin to that lauded by Thoreau at Walden Pond. Instead of revelling in marvelous thoughts, the inhabitant of Perelman's farmhouse cringes under the bed covers, joined by the family dogs, terrified by the unidentified creakings and whispers of noise that surround him at night.

These two chapters sum up the concept underlying *Acres and Pains*: rural life is not for civilized man. Nowhere in Perelman's trek back to nature does he discover the noble savage among the locals who continually take advantage of his pocketbook, gullibility, naiveté, and inexperience in things rural. Rather than a georgic, the author has produced a near diatribe. His idealized vision of life in the manor house is soon replaced by the reality of chiggers, dry wells, cracked walls, dying trees, termites, and mosquitoes. And, after nature is through with him, he must face neighbors who either laugh at his follies or take advantage of him or, most frequently, both.

The first line of this collection sets the tone for the attacks on rural philosophy that will follow: "If you can spare the time to drive sixty miles into the backwoods of eastern Pennsylvania, crouch down in a bed of poison ivy and peer through the sumacs, you will be rewarded by an interesting sight."[62] As usual, the Perelman characteristics are present. There is a juxtaposition of seemingly straightforward, serious exposition with the sudden twist—poison ivy. This leads to a new perspective on the subject as typical clichés are quickly reversed or scrutinized with an unflattering logic. And, finally, the reward is an "interesting" sight, not necessarily a pleasant one that would make the discomfort suffered worthwhile after all.

Written in the first person, the apocryphal anecdotes about commonplace adventures commonly end up with Perelman as the butt of his own joke. He portrays himself as a soft-headed sucker who has only the vaguest romantic conception of the life that he has adopted and this conception frequently comes back to haunt him when he misunderstands or grasps just a particle of the truth: "I started wearing patched blue jeans," he informs us, and "mopped my forehead with a red banana."[63] It was some time later that he realized he should have been using a red bandanna.

Another familiar element is present in an episode involving an architect when he refers to this nemesis as Sir Christopher Wren, an allusion to the eighteenth-century designer of St. Paul's Cathedral in London. In Chapter Six his mechanical misadventures might be attributed to his confusing stop-cocks with bushings and storage tanks with flanges. There is an echo of Benchley when he admits to "a slight headache caused by exposure to poisoned bourbon."[64] And, there is the ever-present play on words, as when he describes the outcome of an attempt to build a swimming pool, which ultimately has to be dynamited because it leaks and floods his neighbor's yard, becoming a haven for poisonous snakes, among other things: "When the dust finally settled, I had enough firewood for the next fifty years, most of it right inside the house where I could get at it. And when *I* finally settled, the man next door had a new front porch and a glass eye you couldn't tell from the other one."[65] The paralleling of seemingly good fortune, a fifty-year supply of firewood, with ingenious undercutting, it was blown into the house, is a favorite technique, too, as hyperbole and understatement sit side by side.

Perelman's definition of a farm is "an irregular patch of nettles bounded by short-term notes, containing a fool and his wife who don't know enough to stay in the city."[66] *Acres and Pains* illustrates the aches and pains that life in such an environment can produce. There are humorous passages throughout, as the proverbial Little Man confronts forces that he can neither control nor overcome. The volume has a more fictive ring to it, though, than do some of the later collections that focus on single topics, such as *The Swiss Family Perelman*. Perhaps this is because of a combination of the author's use of the kind of names usually associated with his pure fabrications (the attorney Newmown Hay, the real-estate agent Dewey Naïveté) and his apparent attempt to capture the essence of a series of experiences rather than accurately reporting on a specific event or making us aware of the foolishness of an advertisement. The book is filled with amusing concepts (all hired hands are named Lafe) and funny lines ("My wife and I were still knee-deep in a puddle outside our front door, exchanging shrill taunts and questioning each other's legitimacy, when our first visitor drove up"[67]). An interesting sidebar is that in March 1962, Perelman reported to *New York Times* correspondent Murray Schumack that a television series based on the book was being developed by CBS Television. The pilot, starring Walter Matthau and Anne Jackson had already been filmed, but there was some concern that sponsors might not be found.[68] Still, *Acres and Pains* seems to suffer from the artistic problem encountered by any writer of serial comedy—humor is difficult to sustain when confined to one subject over an extended period of time. Individually the pieces are funny, yet too many of them are similar to other selections in the book. In part, then, it may be that the variety of topics dealt with in most of Perelman's books is in itself sufficient to maintain a freshness in interest and tone that occasionally wanes here. It also may be that Perelman's humor is best savored a dollop at a time and that any of his collections is too much of a good thing when read at one sitting.

WESTWARD HA!

Westward Ha!, published in 1948, was the first of Perelman's volumes to come out with a Simon and Schuster imprint, the publishing house that would publish the humorist's last thirteen books—but whose publicity department a year and a half after the author's death professed to have no information on him in its files and was not even sure at first that Simon and Schuster had ever published any of his works. Perelman probably would not have been surprised by such a development.

All twelve of the selections in this collection were initially printed in *Holiday* and are considerably longer than the average Perelman essay. The subtitle, *or Around the World in Eighty Clichés*, gives a clear indication of the kind of fare to be expected. Perelman had published travel pieces before, but this was his first collection devoted entirely to his travel experiences, and together with *The Swiss Family Perelman* and *Eastward Ha!* it forms a sub-genre in his canon. Travel books have been around for centuries, but none were ever quite like these. The journey reported on in *Westward Ha!* was an around-the-world trip that the humorist undertook with Al Hirschfeld, the theatrical caricaturist from the *New York Times* who became Perelman's illustrator (one is reminded of Charles Dickens and George Cruikshank) and to whom the author was to dedicate several of his books, starting with this volume.

Not only is *Westward Ha!* the author's first travel book, it is also his best. The content is well balanced between providing insights into the writer himself, exploring the human condition through the metaphor of travel, and commenting on the locales visited, as when Perelman describes Chinwangtao in "The Flowery Kingdom." In other words, Perelman talks about Perelman in this collection within the context of what he sees and does in foreign places, whereas in later collections such as *Eastward Ha!* he is so interested in trying to be cute that his surroundings and adventures barely serve as frameworks for his dissertations. In *Westward Ha!* the anecdotes are complete in themselves; in *Eastward Ha!* the essays are about Perelman, and, as he says, "we could have had all this in the Bronx for a five-cent subway ride."[69]

Perelman's normal attitude toward himself is evident throughout *Westward Ha!*. He combines obviously unrealistic self-idolizing with self-deprecation, the first making him fair game for the second. In "Please Don't Give Me Nothing to Remember You By," the narrator describes himself thus:

A simple, unpretentious man of a grave but kindly mien, his gaunt profile blended the best features of Robinson Jeffers, Lou Tellegen, Pericles, and Voltaire. A keen, humorous eye sparkled above a seamed cheek which had been tanned a rich oleomargerine at the Copacabana and the Stork Club. His loosely woven tweeds were worn with all the easy authority of a man accustomed to go into a pawnshop, lay down his watch, and take his four dollars home with him. As he sat there, relaxed and skyborne, it was the type of subject that would have inspired Monet or Whistler to reach for his palette—the humble dignity of the wayfarer, the pearly effulgence of the clouds, the sense of perfect equilibrium between man and nature.[70]

To this he adds bits of biographical data dropped here and there at random, but in a constant flow (he was, for example, a pre-med student for two years). He continually makes himself the butt of his own jokes (in "Boy Meets Gull" he claims to have been "a deep-water sailor since boyhood," but subsequently he refers to "the man whose duty it was to drive the ship—the chauffeur or the motorman or whatever you call him"[71]), and he proclaims that he relishes a joke even at his own expense, yet, as when he is knocked down by the Prince Regent's Belgian shepherd (and note the attention to detail—it was not just an unidentified dog) in "The Road to Mandalay," he finds nothing funny in the situation: "What there was in my plight to provoke screams of laughter, I do not know. Possibly they had never seen a man on a dog before."[72]

Stylistically, too, *Westward Ha!* is superior to most of the travel pieces that follow it, with a few exceptions (such as the anecdotes that comprise "Dr. Perelman, I Presume, or Small Bore in Africa"—see *The Rising Gorge*). It is rich and compact, much in the manner of the dialogue in *Horse Feathers*. Instead of a few brilliant gems scattered through each piece, in the tales of *Westward Ha!* every line is either funny or building to a funny line—very little is mere filler or wasted verbiage. Much of the collection has the tone of a Marx Borther's movie: "In no time at all—five minutes—we were laughing and chatting away as though we had known each other five minutes."[73]

Perelman has demonstrated that he can write in a conventional, straightforward style, and the openings of most of the chapters in *Westward Ha!* are fairly traditional stylistically, though not for long, of course. For instance, "The Flowery Kingdom" begins "An early morning mist, periodically illuminated by the feeble rays of a wintry sun, shrouded the harbor of Chinwangtao as I thrust my head through our porthole on the *Marine Flier* and stared drowsily about me,"[74] and "Goodbye Broadway, Hello Mal-de-Mer" starts, "The whole sordid business began on a bleak November afternoon a couple of years ago in Philadelphia, a metropolis sometimes known as the City of Bleak November Afternoons."[75]

The writer's love for words, and even the sound of words, is manifest in his characters' names (Cass Register) and in the catalogues, whether of ports of call ("Samoa, the Figis, New Zealand, Australia, the Netherlands, East Indies, the Federated Malay States, Siam, Indo--China, India, Iraq, Syria, Palestine, Turkey, Egypt, the Anglo-Egyptian Sudan, British East Africa, the Belgian Congo, North Africa, France, Switzerland, England, and Ireland"[76]) or the cargo in the ship's hold ("phonograph records, sardines, jeeps, canned abalone, steam hammers, pencils, bulldozers, haberdashery, beer, railroad ties, telephones, clothespins, aircraft tires, after-shave lotion, quicklime, truck bodies, powdered milk, steel safes, quicksilver, electric ranges, newsprint, resin, plate glass, and dipilatories"[77]). Walt Whitman had nothing on Perelman in the use of this technique, and his love for the device goes beyond by-the-word payment considerations. The conglomeration of sounds and images produces an appealing richness of style.

Foreign languages also amuse the writer. In preparation for the trip he learns handy Malay colloquialisms on the order of "Boy, buy me tomorrow a chicken in the blackboard,"[78] and his proficiency and command of other tongues is invaluable at times, as when he breaks the ice on meeting the deposed Emperor of Annam by inquiring in fluent French "whether the pen of his uncle was in the garden."[79]

The humor in these selections primarily derives, as always, from Perelman's persona. He represents himself as a man who seeks good food (which he seldom finds even acceptable), drink (in large amounts), and women (who never submit), who is a little nervous, and who does not want to offend anyone (or risk physical harm) by pushing things too far or protesting too much. This allows him to keep things in perspective, especially when that perspective permits him to rationalize things to his own benefit: "I experienced what I am told is the customary sense of embarrassment at having a fellow-creature act as one's beast of burden" he recalls in "The Flowery Kingdom" regarding the ethical question of employing a rickshaw for transportation, "but mine was such a wiry specimen, weighing as he did well over eighty pounds and amazingly fleet for a man of sixty with tuberculosis, that I quickly overcame my compunctions."[80] His ever-present sense of the preposterous comes into play, too: "there was Hirschfeld's thirteen-month-old baby to be shipped west to be present at our sailing, though the poor thing was so backward it could not even speak English."[81]

"Goodbye Broadway, Hello Mal-de-Mer" details the first meeting between Perelman and Hirschfeld (who is pictured as having "a pair of liquid brown eyes, delicately rimmed in red, of an innocence to charm the heart of the fiercest aborigine, and a beard which would engulf anything from a tsetse fly to a Sumatra tiger. In short, a re-markable combination of Walt Whitman, Lawrence of Arabia, and Moe, my favorite waiter at Lindy's''[82]) and relates the genesis of their trip around the world in 1947.

''Please Don't Give Me Nothing to Remember You By'' sketches the first leg of their journey, a stopover in Los Angeles. ''Boy Meets Gull'' sees the two departing aboard the freighter *Marine Flier* with a play on words (''By a stroke of good fortune, the passenger scheduled to bunk with us had dropped dead the day before''[83]). In ''The Flow-ery Kingdom'' the travellers visit Chinwangtao (twice) and Shanghai. Hong Kong is the scene for ''Carry Me Back to Old Pastrami,'' with a side trip to Macao. ''The Road to Mandalay'' depicts a sojourn in the Malay state of Johore and recalls Perelman's introduction to the charming city of Bangkok, one of the few places in the world that he is enthusiastic about.

In ''The Back of Beyond'' the narration concerns Perelman's jour-ney to Penang and includes an anecdote about the kind of experience familiar to all, even if never exactly encountered: ''About four o'clock [in the morning, as the train sat in a station], someone outside flung in a banana peel which settled on my chest. My visit to the Pasteur Institute in Bangkok had made me a wee bit snake-conscious, and when I felt the clammy embrace, I naturally assumed a fer-de-lance was pitching woo at me. Fortunately, I had enough presence of mind to open my mouth and discharge a piercing scream. The signal pene-trated to the caboose, and hastening forward, the conductor extricated me from the washroom where I had barricaded myself.''[84] The under-standable assumption coupled with an understated presentation of the incident is a characteristic Perelmanesque device for evoking humor. Exaggeration in the guise of factual reporting is another favorite tech-nique found in this essay, particularly in relation to food: ''This was followed by a crisp morsel of the fish called *selangor* for want of a more scathing term, reminiscent in texture of a Daniel Green comfy slipper fried in deep fat.[85] Even the imagery suits the developing mood when Perelman proceeds by describing a garnish—''a spoonful of greenish boiled string and a dab of penicillin posing as a potato.'' In this tale, too, Perelman begins to pay attention to those travelling with him, something that becomes a major topic in his later travelogues. The chapter concludes with Perelman and Hirschfeld briefly in Cey-lon, buying American-made articles and trinkets at prices three times those at home, and then arriving in Bombay on the *President Monroe*.

"It's Not the Heat, It's the Cupidity" carries on in India, with the anticipated disappointment over the Taj Mahal turning into a moment of ecstacy. Its revelation "turned out to be one of the major emotional experiences of the entire journey."[86] It is interesting to note that the title of this chapter is a phrase that appeared in a film review of *Florida Special* for which Perelman had written the screenplay twelve years earlier.[87] In the review it is implied that the reviewer's initial positive reaction to the movie might have had more to do with the circumstances of the viewing than with the excellence of the product, though the rapid pace of the film was certainly appreciated. The author's reaction to the Taj Mahal seems sincere, in spite of the implied parallel.

"Bile on the Nile" includes descriptions of another group of passengers, this time on the *President Polk*, and then lands Perelman and his partner in Cairo, where the author begins to sense European influences. A visit to the interior of a pyramid and a viewing of the Sphinx in 119-degree heat are described in the first half of "Forty Centuries Look Down"; the second half reports on a bus trip through Italy. The narrative of the pair's adventures continues in "Seamy Side Up," set in France where ice cream cones become a prevalent image. Perelman's first exposure to England is also recounted in this chapter, which is interesting since he would return to London nearly a quarter of a century later to spend two years there. The English, he generalizes, "are all glib and all equally shallow."[88] He likewise finds that they have two other national characteristics, "courage and serenity." Something else that he admires in England is the comedienne Hermione Gingold, who would be in the cast of *Around the World in Eighty Days* nine years later.

Westward Ha! concludes with "Home is the Hunted." The voyage aboard the *Queen Mary*, snobbish passengers, arrival in New York, and the families' welcome home whirl by quickly. The narrative ends when, the following year, Perelman and Hirschfeld decline an offer to traverse the globe once again.

LISTEN TO THE MOCKING BIRD

The beginning of Perelman's third decade of publishing was marked by the publication of *Listen to the Mocking Bird* in 1949. This volume is especially notable because it features what the author calls his "nostalgia kick,"[89] the "Cloudland Revisited" series mentioned above. The importance of this *New Yorker* series of affectionate reminiscences about books and movies from Perelman's youth is underlined by the fact that the writer utilized this format twenty-two times in the short period of five years, from October 30, 1948 ("Into Your Tent I'll Creep," which is included in this collection), through October 10, 1953 ("Shades of Young Girls Among the Flummery").

"Into Your Tent I'll Creep" establishes the pattern for the series. Perelman introduces his subject, E. M. Hull's novel *The Shiek*, by explaining the circumstances under which he read it—as a Brown University sophomore, standing behind the counter of a cigar store where he was the night clerk. The occasion for writing this essay is Perelman's rereading of the novel twenty-five years later. He summarizes the plot and supplies quotes as specimens of the novelist's stylistic accomplishment. The conclusion drawn from sampling these passages confirms Perelman's suspicion: "the relief manager of a small cigar store in Providence about 1922 showed the most dubious literary taste of anyone I ever knew. To add to his other defects—he was shiftless, scheming, and transparently dishonest—he was an incorrigible romantic, the type of addlepate that, in later life, is addicted to rereading the books of his youth and whining over their shortcomings. Altogether, an unattractive figure and, I fear, a hopelessly bad lot. But then I suppose there's no point in being too tough on the boy. You can't judge people like him and Diana Mayo [the novel's heroine] by ordinary standards. They're another breed of cat."[90]

Among the other "Cloudland Revisited" reprints in *Listen to the Mocking Bird* are "Sodom in the Suburbs" (concerning Warner Fabian's novel about women, *Flaming Youth*), "Tuberoses and Tigers" (Elinor Glyn's *Three Weeks*, the story of a wealthy young Englishman "blasted by a searing love affair with a mysterious Russian noblewoman"[91]), and "Great Aches from Little Boudoirs Grow" (Maxwell Bodenheim's "erotic" novel of sexual scandal, *Replenishing Jessica*—though Perelman finds the work to have the "tension of high-speed oatmeal"[92]).

Other pieces in this volume bear some of Perelman's classic titles: "The Sweeter the Tooth, the Nearer the Couch" (a confrontation between Perelman, who is trying to protect a cache of candy in a hotel room in Penang, British Malaya, and the horde of tiny red ants that manages to wrest it away from him), "Don't Bring Me Oscars (When It's Shoesies that I Need)" (a calamitous home movie filming session—the announcement of which is met by his wife's usual enthusiasm: " 'A really crackpot notion,' she admitted, confusing the word with 'crackerjack' "[93]), "Danger in the Drain" (a mock nineteenth-century detective story), "Methinks He Doth Protein Too Much" (food imagery as applied to a female love object, literally), and "Stringing Up Father" (a playlet about business competition between a father and son).

THE SWISS FAMILY PERELMAN

The Swiss Family Perelman, like *Westward Ha!*, is a collection of travel articles. Published in 1950, *The Swiss Family Perelman*'s twelve chapters chronicle a trip taken by the author, his wife Laura, their twelve-year-old son Adam, and ten-year-old daughter Abby, across the United States by train and then, after a short stopover in Hollywood, on to Honolulu, Manila, Hong Kong, New Guinea, Bali, Bangkok, India, Istanbul, Rome, Nice, Paris, London, Dublin, Denmark, Germany, and back to New York.

The stories, first published in *Holiday*, are dedicated to Ted Patrick and illustrated by Al Hirschfeld. The tales begin *in medias res* in "Rancors Aweigh" as the family is aboard the *S. S. President Cleveland* out of San Francisco and bound for Hong Kong. There is a flashback in "Low Bridge—Everybody Down" to explain how they arrived in San Francisco, and then in "The Wild Blue Yonder" they are back on shipboard. Starting much like a normal narrative with straightforward description and exposition, the account soon becomes typically Perelmanesque. It fits into the category of personal adventures that the author occasionally writes about (often when detailing his travels), embellished by his unique style and personality—frequently exposing himself as the source and object of his humor. Along the way Perelman manages to acquire a talking mynah bird in Siam,[94] suffer through several bouts with fellow travellers who are decidedly anti-American, undergo a number of unpleasant (though usually funny) incidents, and meet a "chemically blond" French *chanteuse*. When he finally returns home in "The Roaring Traffic's Boom" ready to settle in for an extended stay, he is informed by the superintendent that his apartment building is scheduled for demolition at the end of the month.

The Swiss Family Perelman does not sustain the level of humor and style found in much of the author's other works (perhaps because it is too formulaic, perhaps because the author was inhibited by his family's presence). Although the volume was well received, it seems staged and not light and instantaneous when compared with some of his other work. It reads as though he wrote under the pressure of a deadline and not at a free and leisurely pace. But, as in everything he does, there are moments, lines, and images that carry us happily along. Like Woody Allen's work, which is greatly influenced by Perelman, some of his writing is rather bland until one of these moments appears. There are elements in common with his other writing, naturally, and one of these is the wondrous mixture of references and allusions to all areas of life, some familiar and some pretty esoteric, often juxtaposed with one another. Taken at random, the following is merely a sampling from this rich trove that provides an added dimension, one of those small, extra fillips that simultaneously characterize and set apart Perelman's particular style and brand of humor: Guy Fawkes, Major Andre, striptease artists Georgia Sothern and Ann Corio, *Tabacco Road*, Lytton Strachey, singer Perry Como, musician Cozy Cole, Trotsky, Lorna Doone, poet Rupert Brooke, comic strip characters Maggie and Jiggs, *Terry and the Pirates*, Allessandro Volta, the Gallup poll, Emil Zola, Shiller, Himmler, Lizzie Borden, Carlsberg and Bols beers, the Abby Theatre, Gauguin, the *Harold Tribune* and *Le Figaro*, Teddy Tetzlaff, Ken-L-Ration dog food, actress Nita Naldi, existentialist Jean-Paul Sartre, Rabelais, Alfred Hitchcock, Teddy Roosevelt, Thomas Dewey, Henry Luce, *Quo Vadis*, Orson Welles, Don Quixote, Anna Magnani, Emil Jannings in *The Last Laugh*, Jean Gabin, Gregory Peck, Abe Burrows, and a number of sports figures.

THE ILL-TEMPERED CLAVICHORD

In 1952 *The Ill-Tempered Clavichord* was published. With the exception of "Young as You Feel," reprinted from *Redbook*, the twenty-three selections first appeared in *The New Yorker*.

Five of the pieces are part of the "Cloudland Revisited" series, already discussed in connection with *Listen to the Mocking Bird*. Among the other "sportive" essays in the collection are "A Girl and a Boy Anthropoid Were Dancing," which deals with one of the writer's most beloved subjects, striptease dancers, and a digression on bravery, "Up the Close and Down the Stair," in which the narrator proves his sensibility in staying out of scrapes ("when the Princess Pats stood at

Passchendaele in '17, I was damned careful to be twelve yers old and three thousand miles to the rear''[95]), only to be caught in an embarrassing situation when he mistakes a neighbor dumping trash for a burglar. As an aside, the "Princess Pats" line is repeated by the author in the Zinsser interview seventeen years later.[96] Perelman was never shy about repeating good lines, and he borrowed from himself as frequently as he did from others. Additional evidence of this habit is found in "The Hand that Cradles the Rock." Based on a biographical portrait of Fleur Fenton Cowles, directress of *Look, Quick*, and *Flair*, this piece is another of those scenarios that the *feuilletoniste* (French for "a writer of little leaves"[97]), as Perelman designates himself, transfers almost directly to *The Beauty Part*, now only nine years in the future. The episode deals with the editor's (Hyacinth Beddoes Laffon) handling of the yes-men who surround her, though the character of Lance is not incorporated here.

"Nesselrode to Jeopardy" begins with a supposed excerpt from a *Times* news story. This is one of Perelman's most frequently used techniques, and some critics have complained that it is a little heavy-handed and that he employs this stratagem too often, but it is effective. In this piece the narrator becomes involved in an international attempt to track down the source of contaminated hollandaise sauce, told somewhat in the mode of Eric Ambler.

"Chewies the Goat but Flicks Need Hpyo" is a movie treatment designed to appeal to the "gustatory as well as the visual instinct."[98] The intent is to make fun of theater owners' efforts to prod audiences over to the concession stand for popcorn and other goodies, and Perelman sees film as a perfect medium for this endeavor and for his mockery as well. During a feast scene, he suggests, why not insert dialogue on the order of "Thanks, Baroness. . . . And, speaking of matters edible, the fans watching this need not fall prey to the green-eyed monster, for adjacent to the chairs they will lamp a pleasing selection of mint drops, chocolate creams, and candied apples to beguile themselves stomach-wise."[99] Again Perelman has extrapolated a trend to the point of its logical absurdity.

In "Personne Ici Except Us Chickens" Perelman uses a magazine advertisement to get his narrator and a gullible neighbor to Europe on a wild-goose chase. Imagined Russian agents become involved, and the author's thoughts leap about illogically, in the manner of some of his early works. He winds things up with a sort of reversed *deus ex machina*—the husband suddenly appears: " 'Name of a name!' exploded Grimalkin. 'Why have I never heard of this husband before?' 'Ze exposition was too extensive to plant 'is existence,' she hissed." [100]

"A Hepcat May Look at a King" is a libretto that purports to reveal how the King of Thailand, along with the Shah of Iran, came to write the music for a Michael Todd review.

PERELMAN'S HOME COMPANION

Perelman's Home Companion was published in 1955. Although this volume is subtitled "A Collector's Item (the Collector Being S. J. Perelman) of 36 Otherwise Unavailable Pieces by Himself," most of the selections in this volume were, in fact, reprinted from *Look Who's Talking* and *Keep It Crisp*. There is nothing sufficiently new, either thematically or stylistically, that warrants special attention in this collection.

THE ROAD TO MILTOWN

The Road to Miltown, or Under the Spreading Atrophy was published in 1957. It was published simultaneously in London (at least thirteen of Perelman's books have been issued by British publishers, primarily Heinemann), but under the title *Bite the Bullet*, since English readers would not be likely to recognize the reference to an American tranquilizer. Of the thirty-four pieces, thirty-one were reprints from *The New Yorker*, two were from *Holiday*, and one was new.

"Who Stole My Golden Metaphor?" is the new piece included in the anthology. In it, Vernon Equinox (a name Perelman resurrects for *The Beauty Part*) is cast as an artist upset because Truman Capote has plagiarized a metaphorical concept that he had used in describing himself. "I said I was about as tall as an Osage bow and just as relentless," Equinox asserts. Capote's rendition, as applied to himself, was "I'm about as tall as a shotgun—and just as noisy." Perelman is not adverse to mixing in a few metaphysical similes in a narration about metaphors, as when he recalls, "I guess his eyes *are* really heated, though. . . . The only time I ever saw him, in the balcony of Lowe's Valencia, they glowed in the dark like a carnation." [101] The detail of location is again used to lend credibility so that the reader at first slips right over the fact that, even if eyes seem to glow, carnations do not.

Another piece that will eventually be incorporated into *The Beauty Part*, at times word for word, is "De Gustibus Ain't What Dey Used to Be." April Monkhood's apartment decorations are the initiating premise, but it is Cyprian Voles, not Lance Weatherwax, who enters as the would-be lover, and instead of talking on the telephone with her former husband, Sensualdo, as in the play, in this version the husband passionately sweeps her out of the apartment (as she admits, "To kiss anyone else is like a mustache without salt"[102]) while Cyprian stands by rigidly, disguised as a hitching post.

The non-seduction of an Amazonian actress, called Audrey Merridew for reasons of discretion the narrator asserts, is the topic of "And Thou Beside Me, Yacketing in the Wilderness." Perelman's stance of being misused by women is imparted in his typical fashion. He comes close to achieving his lascivious desire with members of the opposite sex ("for nine tumultuous hours, her destiny and mine were interwoven. . . . [but] we never even progressed to the point of lacing fingers"[103]), though when the first blush of attraction is knocked off and he suffers at their hands, he is always more than a little relieved to have escaped without anything more serious having taken place than a blow either to his ego or to his romanticizing nature.

Harper's Bazaar, another of the writer's favorite targets, comes under fire again in "The Saucier's Apprentice." Delivered in the style of a B-movie Interpol detective story (hearkening back to the "Nesselroad to Jeopardy" hollandaise sauce caper in *The Ill-Tempered Clavichord*, and earlier pieces), the essay follows the determined efforts of the narrator and Inspector Marcel Riboflavin to track down the source that polluted a sauce bearnaise served at Maxim's in Paris. The enigma is solved with the revelation that the perpetrator was gathering material for a magazine article. Coincidentally, she also turns out to be the Inspector's wife.

"This Little Piggy Went to Market" traces the meanderings of a coconut turned into a cosmetic cream. The tale is told from the coconut's point of view, naturally, in memoir form.

"The holley had a trot-box! . . . I mean, the trolley had a hot box" are the first words spoken in "I'll Always Call You Schnorrer, My African Explorer."[104] The interchanging of initial letters is appropriate, for the essay recounts the narrator's first exposure, in 1916, to the Marx Brothers, then a vaudeville team performing in Providence, Rhode Island. From this introduction the narrative jumps to the early

1950's when the storyteller is invited by Groucho to visit him on the RKO lot in Hollywood, where he is filming *A Girl in Every Port* with William Bendix and Marie Wilson. The dialogue could easily come from a Marx Brothers movie:

> "Gravy, gravy!" shouted Groucho. "Everybody wants gravy! Did those six poor slobs on the *Kon-Tiki* have any gravy? Did Scipio's legions, deep in the African waste, have gravy? Did Fanny Hill?"
>
> "Did Fanny Hill what?" I asked.
>
> "Never mind, you cad," he threw at me. "I'm sick to death of innuendo, brittle small talk, the sly, silken rustle of feminine underthings. I want to sit in a ballpark with the wind in my hair and breathe cold, clean popcorn into my lungs." (p. 629)

One can almost see Groucho leaning backwards on a divan, eyes closed, brushing the hair back on the sides of his head, as he delivers this speech.

Among the other selections anthologized are ten "Cloudland Revisited" reprints.

THE MOST OF S. J. PERELMAN

In 1958 *The Most of S. J. Perelman* was published. Dedicated to Perelman's wife, Laura, the majority of the 120 pieces contained in this collection originally appeared in *The New Yorker*, with some from *Holiday*, *The Saturday Evening Post*, the *Country Book*, *College Humor*, *Contact*, and *Life*. In addition, there is an introduction by Dorothy Parker, based on a piece that she had written for the *New York Times Book Review*. Several of the selections first were published in earlier volumes (*Crazy Like a Fox* and *The Road to Miltown*), but with the exception of one piece that had not been published previously, all of the selections in this volume (including the whole of *Acres and Pains* and *Westward Ha!*) had already appeared in book form, so there is no need to discuss the content. In fact, the sampling represents twelve of the writer's fourteen books published to that time (omitted are *Dawn Ginsbergh's Revenge* and *Parlor, Bedlam and Bath*)—and only five more were published later—so it serves as an excellent source for introducing Perelman's prose. The one piece never before published is "The Pants Recaptured," a modern version of an event in

Marcel Proust's life, told as a story about a Broadway producer and a book bound in a pair of men's underpants.

THE RISING GORGE

Published in 1961, *The Rising Gorge* was dedicated to Al Hirschfeld, Perelman's perennial illustrator. Most of the thirty-four selections, never before published in a book, originally appeared in *The New Yorker*, with a sprinkling collected from, *Holiday, Redbook, This Week Magazine*, and *What's New*.

By now Perelman's style has matured to the point that it is well-wrought, but it has lost much of its frothiness. "Call and I Follow, I Follow!" for instance, concerns the narrator's meeting with an old flame in London (he reminds her that he used to bear a resemblance to Warren William) and the basic premise is similar to that used in other pieces, but the words no longer convey a light, fey touch as the density of the author's style gives the selection the feeling of being crowded with words. The "mindless jargon" advertised on the inside of the dust jacket is present; it just does not flow as quickly anymore. The sprightliness of Perelman's youth has been replaced by a sense of self-assuredness.

Still he continues, refusing to be limited and exercising his skills in a number of ways. The next selection, "Eine Kleine Mothmusik," its title alluding to Mozart's "Eine Kleine Nachtmusik," starts with a supposed news release from the *Times* of London and is constructed as a series of letters exchanged between Perelman and his dry cleaner. Clearly the two actually communicate very little, and the humor arises in the misunderstandings that develop. In "Dial 'H' for Heartburn" the author adopts the persona of a young woman (taking us all the way back to *Dawn Ginsbergh's Revenge*). The title is a play on the Alfred Hitchcock film, *Dial M for Murder*. "Is You Is or Is You Ain't, Goober Man?" is an "exposé" of Mr. Planters Peanut, written as a playlet.

"Dr. Perelman, I Presume, or Small-Bore in Africa" is a collection of seven stories revolving around the writer's East African travels with typical Perelmanesque bits, as when he reveals his concern about the possibility of meeting a Mau Mau terrorist patrol with the understated line, "I casually extinguished my cigarette in the wild-current jam." [105] Again, the attention to irrelevant detail is one of those elements that give Perelman's writing its piquancy: the casualness of his putting out the cigarette is made absurd by the way he puts it out, and this is emphasized by his mentioning the kind of jam used. Jam is funny enough, but naming the jam reinforces the ridiculousness of the whole situation (he is not likely to have noticed such a minute detail under the circumstances), just as the ordinary act of his trying to get dressed suddenly takes on a comic aspect when he admits that his movements were somewhat impeded because he did so with "one foot braced against the bathroom door." As might be expected, very little of Perelman's account is concerned with describing the scenery, native customs, or anything of the kind, although place names are dropped freely. Instead, the concentration is on Perelman and his tribulations, as well as the foibles and weaknesses of his fellow human beings encountered along the way. The human element in this travelogue is especially important as a source of humor. When Perelman takes into account emotions and actions familiar to us all, whatever his setting, he is at his best. One night, for example, he reports that he was awakened by the sound of an African machete, a *panga*, hammering on his door. When no one enters, he rationalizes that the occupant of the room above his (an "odd crotchet" he imagines) must have dropped a rather large pipe on the tile floor—the act of rationalizing, however incredible the rationalization, is very human, as is his reaction the following morning when he realizes that there is no room above his but dismisses this discovery because the sun is now shining and the birds are singing. The sudden reversal is there, but it is tempered and as a result subsides from horror to humor.

Similarly, Perelman's deft use of language increases his comic content. His similes ("my neck gave off a creak like a New Year's ratchet and I hastily withdrew it into my shell") have become more subtle in expressing his points, and a gentle sense of understatement has replaced the obviousness of his earlier pieces. It is a different kind of humor that results, but it is first-rate humor. More aware of his craft as a writer and less concerned with being funny, he is clearly a writer in control of his medium.

CHICKEN INSPECTOR NO. 23

Chicken Inspector No. 23 was published in 1966. Eight of the thirty-three selections contained in the collection come from a comprehensive variety of sources (*Holiday*, *The Saturday Evening Post*, *TV Guide*, *Diplomat*, and *Venture*), but following the normal pattern, the majority of the pieces included first appeared in *The New Yorker*, so it is appropriate that the volume is dedicated to William Shawn, the editor who was Ross's replacement.

The content and style are typical of Perelman's canon, as a brief representative sampling demonstrates. "Are You Decent, Memsahib?" is an "autobiographical" account of how a young beauty from Scranton, Pennsylvania (stage name, Sherry Muscatel), performs such a tasteful act of striptease that she turns the head of Lam Chowdri, an Indian maharaja from the state of Cawnpone who is currently attending Harvard. They are soon married, and, in order to be near his wife all of the time, Chowdri renounces his title. A Parsee lawyer named Mr. Nuroddin is sent to fetch Chowdri home, but the heroine's charms quickly turn his head too, and he becomes an ardent courter. In short order Uncle Nooj, the regent, arrives to extricate his nephew and lawyer from the narrator's wiles, only to fall for her himself. The story ends with Sherry treating them all as servants. At the other end of the social scale, and closer to home, is "Reunion in Gehenna," which is about the forty-second reunion of a Dropsical High School senior class.

"Palette and Tureen: Notes for a Life of Marc Grosgrain" begins by relating how a textile designer from J. C. Phrensy, "a firm of nationwide chain stores," [106] is called upon to be creative. After a herculean effort, her achievement is labeled perfect by the company's vice-president. Echoing the sentiments of *The Beauty Part*, the lady asks, "when you use the term 'perfection' . . . do you mean it in the Chinese sense of perfect philosophical balance, or in the Christian context, which implies a hint of martyrdom? Or . . . are you asking whether you can stamp out five million of these abortions and fob them off on the housewives of America?" [107]

Taking this as his point of departure, Perelman writes a life-and-times-of-the-artist account about a man whose hand-painted ties are drawing crowds to the Museum of Modern Art where the ties are on display amidst counters "piled with cut-rate shirts." [108] This "informal biographical sketch" goes on to detail how Grosgrain perfected his craft (being tripped over by waiters who spill food on his ties) and concludes that his art work is "practically eternal." The pompous, self-important artist who is really only a fake has been one of Perelman's favorite targets from the beginning of his career.

"Nobody Here 'cep' Us Riffraff" is prefaced by an excerpt from the London *Observer* that takes notice of Americans in London who pursue literary celebrities. In the format of a diary written by a female English literature major three years out of Wellesley, the piece traces the young woman's misadventures as she seeks the famous and uncovers the phony. And the phonies seek only sex and money from her.

"Walk the Plank, Pussycat—You're on Camera" is based on a premise derived from television actor Nick Adams' announcement to his wife on national television that he was divorcing her. Perelman presents a television script contrived to take advantage of the exploitative nature of certain types of programming and of the audience's desire to exercise its innate voyeuristic tendencies through public exposure.

"Sex and the Single Boy" examines the development of a startling thought in the mind of a twenty-five year old bachelor: women may be human beings. This is one of the few instances in Perelman's writing where a direct political-social comment is made. The author frequently points out in a humorous way how people tend to treat other people as though they are not human beings, but generally these observations are made within a context that makes them seem universal yet not personal—the insensitivity of department store clerks, the refusal to take responsibility for patently false statements and merchandise that is too shoddy to be able to live up to their claims on the part of advertisers, the pompous attitudes of high society and those in the arts, and so forth. In this piece the author has confronted a more basic social issue and he has done so relatively straightforwardly.

In "A Soft Answer Turneth Away Royalties," Perelman once more turns to an exchange of letters to make his point. This time he lampoons both publishers and authors. He also demonstrates the strength of his convictions in typically Perelmanesque fashion: "For a moment, I thought of vindicating my profession dramatically with a right cross to the man's jaw, but it occurred to me that he might vindicate his with a right cross to mine, and I forbore."[109] Other selections reveal more of the humorist's persona too. A needle that might have been sewn inside a baking chicken along with the dressing is the plot device used to initiate the narrator's self-exposure of his own failings in "Eat, Drink, and Be Wary." "Samson Shorn, or the Slave of Love" records Perelman's imaginary amorous exploits in an autobiographical context. Among his fantasies is a relationship with Elizabeth Taylor, who is attended by a Welsh actor whose name Perelman has difficulty remembering; it is Bolton, Benton, Buxton, Brompton, or Brixton, he thinks.

"The Sweet Chick Gone" is Perelman's way of making fun of anthropomorphic tales such as *Born Free* and *Ring of Bright Water*. The narrator of the story is a White Leghorn hen. Another animal-point-of-view piece is "Muddler on the Roof," presented in the form of a letter addressed to the editor of the English journal *Country Life* by an American ground hog (resident of a burrow on the land of one "S. G. Prebblemen" in rural Pennsylvania). The rodent has read letters to the editor in recent issues referring to hedgehogs and wishes to set the record straight on some of the readers' misconceptions. As might be expected, he also has some things to say about the strange human that he observes sometimes.

Perelman's acquaintanceship with Buster Keaton is the subject of "The Great Stone Face." He did not write many articles of this kind, but they are noteworthy for their warm, admiring tone, comparatively direct style of reporting, and the interesting tidbits of information provided about his subjects (Jimmy Durante, Fred Allen, Nathanael West, and Dorothy Parker were his other subjects).

"Goodbye Broadway, Hello Mr. Square," the last essay in the volume, is an expression of Perelman's attitude toward and experiences in New York City, beginning with his first trip while a senior at Brown University and through his residence there after leaving college and during the early years of his marriage—until he purchased his farm in Pennsylvania. His desire to return to the "indefinable bouquet of monoxide . . . to be trampled on again in the subway crush, to be spurned by headwaiters, fleeced by tradesmen and iced by theatre brokers" is clear: "not as long as *I* can help it, Charlie."[110]

The point of these plot summaries, as indicated above, is to show the wide range and variety of topics that Perelman still finds deserving of his attention after thirty-seven years of writing. While not so outrageously funny as the earliest collections, *Chicken Inspector No. 23* is more consistently amusing than several of the writer's later works. In it he is still reporting, incredulously but with good humor, on those incredible and unexplained experiences that everyone occasionally has. "Even a magpie, and a slovenly one, would have been dismayed at the sight that confronted me," he states in "Samson Shorn, or The Slave of Love" in describing his own attic: "Since 1952 when I had left the place in apple-pie order, some vandal has been systematically creating a replica of the Paris Flea Market. Piles of moldering luggage I had never seen before lay stacked against the eaves; the floor was strewn with an appalling mulch of old fly screens, Victrola records, lamp shades, tennis rackets, overshoes, hotwater bottles, and Ayvad's Water Wings.''[111]

BABY, IT'S COLD INSIDE

Perelman's next collection is even further removed from the type of merriment seen in his early writings. The author's first book since 1966, *Baby, It's Cold Inside* was published in 1970. Of this collection, all but six of the thirty-two pieces originally appeared in *The New Yorker* from 1961 through 1969 (the others come from *Holiday*, *TV Guide*, or *Venture*).

It may be significant that Perelman dedicated this book, his eighteenth, to J. D. Salinger, for in some ways the selections it contains reflect a kind of loss of innocence, a continuation of the maturing, perhaps, that was beginning to become apparent in *Chicken Inspector No. 23*, published four years earlier. The sixties were a time of national unrest—Vietnam, college sit-ins, political assassinations (President John F. Kennedy in 1963, Robert Kennedy in 1968, civil rights leader Martin Luther King in 1968)—and this collection reflects the decade in both form and content. Perelman's point of view has changed; he is no longer the madcap, freewheeling blithe spirit of the 1930's and 1940's, or even the middle-aged Perelman of the 1950's, looking back on fondly remembered books and films from his youth to point out that they were often ridiculous and frequently not as good as they should have been, yet whose reminiscences contain an almost paternalistic fondness for the exuberance, recklessness, and occasional personally significant high points of these books and films—much like his own writing at the time. Instead, in *Baby, It's Cold Inside*, Perelman's perspective is more tempered. Playing with the popular song title, ''Baby, It's Cold Outside,'' the writer does not focus so much on the exterior but instead becomes more introspective in his tone. There is still satire, still amusement and amazement at human failings, but the outrageously absurd connections of ''The Idols' Eye'' and the language of *Westward Ha!* are gone. The pieces are amusing, but there is an undertone of seriousness; we no longer laugh aloud while reading them. Somehow the author's personal involvement seems to have diminished, and he looks upon his material with a somewhat sadder and wiser detachment than had come through heretofore.

Three pieces demonstrate this late-period Perelman. In the opening selection, "Anna Trivia Pluralized," the protagonist is found in Dublin where he hears an anecdote about James Joyce from a friend who is going to use the story in a book on Joyce. During the course of his stay in Dublin, the protagonist hears the same tale repeated in confidence several times, and it is clear that for some time the owner of the pub where the story originated has been selling it on a purportedly exclusive basis to all who are interested.

In "And, in the Center Ring, That Stupendous, Death-Defying Daredevil . . . " the narrator recalls being enthralled by the acrobatic expertise displayed by trapeze artists in the movie *Variety*. The typical Perelman trademarks are present. Remembrance is involved, a movie is the stimulus that weaves throughout (he recalls "vividly" scenes of the "breathtaking" "wizard of the flying rings" that "induced a lifelong adoration" [112]), there are literary references (*The Moon and Sixpence, The Green Hat, The Sun Also Rises*), unsupported Mittyesque imaginings ("a couple of secret agents trying to pass themselves off as Swiss businessmen" [113]), foreign language bits ("*eine wilde Gansejaged*"—a wild goose chase [114]), outrageous names (Tubby Funkhouser), and the quick turn based on juxtaposing elevated language with clichés or slang ("a college classmate I had rigorously avoided as a drip"). As the story progresses, the protagonist is introduced to the female aerialist whose act he has been rhapsodizing over. He is disillusioned, for not only is she broad shouldered, her account of the performance has nothing to do with art or discipline. Her focus, she reveals while on the high trapeze, is money—the cost of the rope used to swing her back and forth. As the narrator and the friend who arranged to introduce him leave this meeting, they discuss the breaking of illusion, as when the friend went through "fire and water" to meet Picasso only to find the artist preoccupied with the expense of camel's hair brushes. When a limousine carrying Sophia Loren passes them, though, the despondent friend is suddenly ready to gallop after her— "I'd go through fire and water to meet her. . . . A person like this could change your whole life, give you a new perspective." [115] An adolescent hope still lives in mankind's breast.

In the final selection, "Thunder Under the Kalahari, or, Aliquid

Novi Ex Botswana?'' we return, by way of a supposed news filler from the London *Times*, to a 1940's B-movie plot. In this case the protagonist finds himself drawn into a murder mystery. At lunch in a hotel dining room on the southern coast of England, he meets an elderly gentleman who is bothered by the sight of truffles and mentions of Bechuanaland. When a ''tall, ravishing brunette'' visits him in London three weeks later, he learns that the old man, her uncle, has been murdered by a poisoned arrow. There follows an improbable, though perfectly conventional, series of events that leads to the discovery that the young woman's father and uncle had promised to make an African tribe rich by marketing their truffles but betrayed the tribe by selling out to a European combine. Needless to say, the pygmies seek revenge and the story's hero manages to subdue the rampaging Bushman who committed the murder and then is ready to settle down to live happily ever after with the niece (whose figure ''narrowly missed being voluptuous''[116]) when he meets an attractive manicurist.

In her assessment of *Baby, It's Cold Inside*, Eudora Welty notes, ''Back of some of these pieces, and not very far, lies deep sadness, lies outrage.''[117] This may be true, especially compared to the early collections, but she is probably more accurate when she continues, ''What an achievement Mr. S. J. Perelman makes today, that out of our own sadness and outrage we are brought, in these little leaves, to laugh at ourselves once more.'' There may be more stories such as ''To Err Is Human, to Forgive, Supine,'' in which revenge is extolled, but there are also light-hearted pieces like ''The Skin You Love to Watch,'' which takes the BBC and the University of Florida to task for their unliberated and unimaginative handling of nudity.

One possible reason for reviews of the later collections being as complimentary as those written about the author's best work, done primarily before the late 1960's, is that the anthologies are published several years apart and reviewers are not satiated. Another reason may lie in the competition—with Thurber and others like him gone, there was virtually no one else writing this kind or quality of humor for much of the second half of Perelman's life.

VINEGAR PUSS

In April, 1970 Laura Perelman died. A few weeks later Perelman sold their farm and in October he moved to London. The move, as he had told *Washington Post* reporter Myra MacPherson a month before he left, was an attempt to escape from "insanity and violence," "twice breathed air," the current political climate (from "the co-author of the Mundt-Nixon bill . . . to every hard hat and red-neck in the country"), and incivility, but "The fact that I think it's volcano time in this country is not responsible for the move, though I'm just as appalled as everyone about the conditions." [118] More important, he said, "I've reached the point where I regard my existence as an artichoke, and I'm stripping away the outer layers." "I've had all the rural splendor I can use," he reported, "and each time I get to New York it seems more pestilential than before." On the other hand, he found life in London more "rational": "The obvious good manners and consideration of people there toward each other may be only selfish, but it's good enough for me." Besides, he explained, "they still have a taste for eccentricity." In addition, the English, like Perelman, admire "clean hair and couth," and "The older person is respected always much more there. The English still cleave more to values and traditions of the past. In America the youth cult is pushed more and more to the forefront." And, finally, he finds that the English are "mad for" his favorite stylistic device, punning.

These comments reveal a lot about the man who wrote *Baby, It's Cold Inside*. Apparently he has been finding himself more and more an outsider in contemporary America. There does not seem to be any great bitterness present, but he does not belong anymore, either; he is "no longer at ease," in Eliot's words. Yet, it was also important to him that the interview contain a disclaimer: "I'd be grateful if you stress the fact that I had contemplated this move three years ago. It's really an unemotional plan . . . I hate the word expatriate. I plan to remain a non-resident of the United States and return as frequently as possible. I'll get the air mailed newspaper from here. I'm very far from being a Nathan Hale." For someone whose upbringing and career in so many ways epitomize American life, these sentiments seem appropriate.

Within two years Perelman was back in New York, stating that he had been sated by British couth: "I found myself surrounded in Kensington by stiff-backed Anglo-Indian women living in genteel penury, stalking out three or four times a day to buy one egg or one lemon— a condition that can only be described as tight-assed." He was hungry for New York rye bread.

Early in his English sojourn Perelman set out on an eighty-day world tour. The idea was for *The New Yorker* to publish his Phileas Fogg-like travel journal in serial form and then for Simon and Schuster to reprint the account as a book. The next volume published, *Vinegar Puss* (in 1975), included thirty-one selections from *The New Yorker, Travel and Leisure* ("Nostasia in Asia"), *Holiday, McCall's,* and *Escapade.* Among these were the six pieces grouped under the subtitle, "Around the Bend in Eighty Days."

The first anthology that Perelman published after his return from his two years in London, *Vinegar Puss* was well reviewed, as usual, but it is not up to Perelman's standard level. There are funny lines, puns, and so forth, but as with his other volumes published at this time it lacks the liveliness of the author's early writing. Perelman is clever, as always, yet his writing in this collection is more stolid than most of his previous work; he is amusing but seldom funny, and there is nothing new thematically or stylistically. For instance, in "Hail, Hail, the Ganglia's All Here," the eleven-year-old hero is named S. G. Pefelman, an obvious play on his own name, but the story of how young Pefelman solves a problem that has been baffling police simply is not very funny. In "Missing: Two Lollopaloozas—No Reward," Perelman returns to a device and a theme used before but with less verve. The story is prefaced by a blurb, ascribed to *Variety*, about an actress in India who is being sued for having walked off the set in the middle of filming thirteen pictures. The Perelman character, with pertinent references to Noel Coward, Laurence Harvey, Barton MacLane, and others, meets the actress, Shasta Allahjee, in Bombay, a woman with the face of a nineteen-year-old Ava Gardner mixed with a dash of "an Oriental Catherine Deneuve" and a body that makes Elke Sommer look like "a dried-up old prune" in comparison.[119] The combination of very current and somewhat past references is effective, and the narrator's blatant attempts to impress Miss Allahjee are amusing and in the same vein as many of Perelman's earlier premises with the everyman underdog scurrying to overcome the obstacles that stand between him and his idealized and unreachable object of desire. As is to be expected, in the end, although he has managed to save her from the evil clutches of the pursuing producers and at the same time establish her as a world-wide star of the first magnitude, all through a single stroke of genius, she rejects him.

"Mad About the Girl" depicts the narrator's infatuation with gorillas, particularly a young female named Quarta. ''Whenas in Gilt My Julio Goes'' (the title is a play on a Robert Herrick poem title) describes the efforts of an American hypnotist to obtain a quantity of cloth that has gold thread woven through it. The narration has the flavor of a Victorian melodrama, and part of the humor derives from the author's conscious parody of the form by forcefully drawing his audience's attention to the conventions:

''Forgive me, Highness,'' Geraldine apologized. ''I was merely contributing some exposition to help the reader identify us—the sort of thing a housemaid is usually discovered prattling over a flower arrangement when the curtain rises.''

''In that case, I withdraw the rebuke,'' said the Prince graciously. ''But what is this? A young person, his cheek mantled by a hectic flush, has just entered, bearing a tray laden with a dozen or so hard doughnutlike discs, heavily varnished and garnished with a fishy pink-and-white substance.''

(p. 170)

''The Machismo Mystique'' is a collection of tales about both famous and unknown exemplars of the concept of machismo. It is neither very funny nor enlightening, and it does not compare well with ''Sex and the Single Boy'' which appeared in *Chicken Inspector No. 23*.

''Around the Bend in Eighty Days'' is a series of tales about how Perelman and his companion, Sally-Lou Claypool (a 6'11'' beauty from Memphis) came to try to retrace Philias Fogg's route as described in the Verne novel fifteen years after the movie version was shot. ''Disquiet, Please, We're Turning!'' has a few high spots: Candide Yam, Todd's beautiful Chinese secretary; the exemplification of Todd's miserliness; the description of the events during the six-week location shooting in Spain and later an incident in Paris. ''New Girdle, with Lots of Support'' explains how Perelman's discovery of factual errors in Verne's story stimulated his interest in the trip (and points out that there was no hot air balloon in the original tale; Todd borrowed the balloon episode from another Verne story, *Five Weeks in a Balloon*). It also describes the writer's selection of his travelling companion. ''The Turkey Trot: One Step Forward, Two Steps Back'' details the first leg of the trip (to Rome) and provides insight into the nature of Sally-Lou, who, when Perelman discourses on the ''vanished glory of the Ottomans,'' admits that cushioned footstools turn her on, too.[120]

By and large, the series is a fairly straightforward account, embellished by Perelman's perspective and unique reactions, but it is not even as funny as *The Swiss Family Perelman* was, as similar in content as the two travel series are. One of the more interesting aspects of "Around the Bend in Eighty Days" is, fittingly, the large number of cinematic allusions it contains. A brief list includes John Huston, *The Treasure of Sierra Madre*, Joel Cairo (the Peter Lorre character in the 1941 movie version of *The Maltese Falcon)*, Ava Gardner, Julie Newmar, Ray Milland, Vera Hruba Ralston, *The Front Page*, Anna May Wong, Jane Russell, William S. Hart, Erich Von Stroheim, Errol Flynn, George Sanders, *Barbarella*, Modesty Blaise, David Niven, Gloria Swanson, Cecil B. DeMille, and Cary Grant.

EASTWARD HA!

Eastward Ha! (1977) was the last of Perelman's books to be published in his lifetime. Another collection of travel pieces, the major part of the text originally appeared in *Travel and Leisure*. Basically a catalog of impressionistic views as opposed to a descriptive travelogue, the nine chapters that comprise the book relate Perelman's experiences on his last trip around the world.

While preparing for the nine-month trip, Perelman was interviewed by Israel Shenker. In the interview he disclosed some facts about his background as well as some details about his travels in general. He was going to begin his eleven-country tour in London, "to get some worthless advice from people who've been where I'm going," then travel to Scotland because he had "been a caddy at age 11," with the trip winding up in "the most barbarous of all—Los Angeles." [121] Along the way he will go to Russia, since "There are some ancestral dachas I'd like to visit, nothing palatial, mind you—these are simple, unassuming 50-yard dachas." Moreover, in his youth, he explains, "one always used to see one's female relatives [wearing 'a handerchief (sic) knotted at the four ends' as a headdress], dunking themselves ponderously in the surf. That's my Proustian memory, and all I need to recapture it is a glass of tea with raspberry jam at the bottom, a cube of sugar clenched between my teeth."

He also recounted plans to visit Israel because a former Minister of Information (Moish Pearlman, no relation) kept telling him not to until "things settled down," and Hunja (in northwest Pakistan near where the borders of Pakistan, China, and India meet), which he prepared for by reading Justice Douglas's book *Beyond the High Himalayas*.

Among the travails that he faces while travelling, Perelman singled out several. "My problem has always been overweight baggage," he noted. Now that he is alone (his earlier accounts of battles with epic amounts of family luggage in *The Swiss Family Perelman* come to mind) this includes a "large suitcase, large handbag, and baby Hermes. That's the closest you can get to a toy typewriter, and it's commensurate with the significance of the whole journey. I've already discovered it's too small to allow room for corrections, and it only types in Swiss francs."[122] Speaking of Swiss francs, money is another of his bugaboos, for his bank no longer issues letters of credit, and he dislikes travellers' checks (if they do not get lost, they are too bulky). Laundry, too, is a source of irritation—"The traveller is a prisoner of his laundry. . . . You spend your time waiting for the laundry to return." And, hotel rooms are another pitfall that await the traveller: "the prototypical hotel room is French—with striped wallpaper, a smell of hair oil from some previous inhabitant, and heavy drapes from some previous regime—a place into which daylight never penetrates. With luck there's a table shaped like an irregular trapezoid, deeply beveled, and the wrong height for one's typewriter."

Unfortunately, as if this were not enough, the trip also meant that Perelman had to decline an invitation to be the Grand Marshal of the Commencement Day procession at Brown University. Shenker describes the invitation as a "boyhood dream," and although Perelman speaks disparagingly of other grand marshals (such as IBM's Thomas Watson) and makes light of the thought of wearing "a silk hat" on a "blindingly hot and humid" day, still, he claims, "This is the signal honor, as I will say in my letter to the president of the university, which I must regretfully decline."

Scotland is the setting for the first adventure, and "Looking for Pussy" contains a number of Perelman's trademarks. For example, the expected puns are present, there are cinematic allusions and references to other literati (recalling certain exploits of Thurber and Beerbohm), and the narrator adopts the stance of a man whose constant admiration for the ladies is unreturned and whose desires remain unrealized: "I felt I could lean on her shoulder should I ever need support. But that, of course, was academic since I never got her number. Perhaps it was because the moment she'd seen me, she instinctively got mine."[123] In

"Paris on Five Dolors a Day!" he traces his meanderings through the City of Light—meeting an old friend, having his fortune told, being on board a sinking sightseeing boat. "The Millenium, and What They Can Do with It" takes place in Russia (Moscow, Kiev, Leningrad), and contains a typical Perelmanesque exchange:

> "I am what Puritans scornfully call a womanizer. It's sort of a lay preacher."
> "You revere women?" she asked puzzled.
> "I worship the ground they walk on," I admitted. "Not the women, you understand, just the ground they walk on."   (pp. 45-46)

"The Nearer the East, the Shorter the Shrift" details the writer's trip to Istanbul and then on board the *Ankora* on a voyage to a Greek isle in search of a tailor to deepen the pants pockets of a suit that he had bought there while passing through the previous year. A five hour conversation with one of his favorite authors, Isaac Bashevis Singer, highlights Perelman's visit to Israel, as described in "Unshorn Locks and Bogus Bagels" (which is also about a barber and a gentleman who wears a ceramic bagel on a chain around his neck). Perelman's obviously respectful attitude toward Singer contrasts interestingly with the throwaway lines that repeatedly pepper his writing and reflect his love for Conan Doyle and his dislike for the "hacks" like Irving Wallace and Harold Robbins who are frequently mentioned in passing. "The Vinter Buys the Rolls Nobody Eats" recounts the sights in Iran. In "Rosy and Sleazy, or Dream and Reality in Asia," the traveller relates the changes that he sees that have taken place in Bangkok since his visit to Thailand in 1947 (and fondly reported in *Westward Ha!*) and then skips lightly through Malacca and Hong Kong, where he feels the freedom not to do the things customarily incumbent upon tourists. Perelman also writes about Malaysia in this section, with Penang being singled out as one of the few places in all of his travels that he finds attractive and unchanged and that consequently receives sympathetic, affectionate treatment. There is a quick swing to "To One Cup of Java, Add One Snootful of Tahiti," and the book concludes with "Back Home in Tinseltown" and the author's stay in Los Angeles.

The style of *Eastward Ha!* is much more relaxed than that of its immediate predecessor, *Vinegar Puss*, published two years earlier. It may be that the greater distance in time from his wife's death or revisiting foreign locales that he had enjoyed previously had a calming effect. Whatever the cause, he seems to be pressing less, not trying as hard as he had been, and this style is better suited to the themes and topics of his later writing. At the same time, though, his sexual allusions and double entendres are more harshly worded in his later writing. It is not that they were not obvious before, just that the manner of expression was more metaphorical. As with most of his travel writing, the pieces are designed not to map out the history of the local sights but rather to catch the national flavor in what might be called a montage. A series of similar episodes, largely romantic imaginings à la Walter Mitty and revolving around airline stewardesses on flights between countries, serve as a unifying character line for Perelman's narrator persona. On the serious side, his essays include occasional passing social commentary and he incidentally describes some points of interest in connection with plot development (almost always located in major cities), but Perelman's prime concern, is as usual, Perelman. He is still his own best subject, and it is often difficult to distinguish between reporting and fiction in the tales of his peregrinations. They are built around fact, but they also contain exaggeration that supplies us with the essential reality instead of a superficial, photographic reality. Accidents, mishaps, scraps, emotional reactions, relationships with his fellows (usually other travellers)—these are Perelman's subjects; how he sees himself vis-à-vis the world around him. When he reacts, he is reacting for us, as we would probably react in the same situation.

THE LAST LAUGH

In 1981 Simon and Schuster published a posthumous collection of Perelman's pieces. Entitled *The Last Laugh*, the volume contains seventeen selections in Part One that had been published in *The New Yorker*, with Part Two containing four essays that comprise the finished portion of *The Hindsight Saga* (although editor Paul Theroux talks about three chapters, four are included). There is also the "Introduction" by Theroux referred to previously. Theroux suggests that at this point the only things left uncollected are Perelman's letters, though *That Old Gang O' Mine* proves that there are minor pieces still floating around, and in collecting material for *S. J. Perelman: An Annotated Bibliography* I located several later works that apparently have gone unnoticed since their journal publication. The letters now have been published too.

Since this anthology presumably reflects Perelman's most mature writing, a little extra time will be devoted to examining the volume's contents to show how many of the stylistic devices that became the author's trademarks in his earliest compositions are still present in his final publications.

The first article, "And Then the Whining Schoolboy, with His Satchel," is another of those selections that pay homage to the novels that the humorist read in his youth and which he feels somehow influenced him or made his life more pleasurable. He begins the story be setting the scene: "four o'clock of a late-February afternoon in 1919" in Providence.[124] As is his wont, Perelman includes a number of fictitious-sounding names connected with activities that have no bearing on his tale. Morris Schreiber, Azouf Harootunian, Walt Zymchuck, Edward Gipf, and Mrs. Anna Rubashkin of Central Falls are all involved in improbable and unrelated events; one is reminded of the circumstantial-history parody in "So Little Time Marches On" (*Keep It Crisp*). Also present is the catalogue, in this case beginning with a list of the odors that issue forth from a well-known bakery, scents of "cakes, pies, cookies, twists, and rings, its chocolates, caramels, mints, and nougats, and the syrups and garnishes employed in its parfaits, smashes, cabinets, and banana splits that travellers have been known to leap from trains passing through the Union Station, three blocks away, and squander their patrimony there with no thought for the morrow."[125] The elegant adjective with which he starts ("the ambrosial smell"), and the exaggeration with which he concludes the image are typical of Perelman's favorite figurative devices.

Similarly, the description of an incident regarding a stockroom clerk who "embezzled a quantity of jabots, altered the labels on their boxes, and sold them to unsuspecting French Canadians as sabots"[126] contains several characteristically Perelmanesque turns. First, there is the author's attention to detail (naming the firm where the clerk—and note that he signifies a "stockroom" clerk—is employed, for example). Second is his enjoyment of the sound of words—the name of the firm (ridiculously called "the Pussy Willow Ruching Corporation"), the similarity between "jabots" and "sabots." Third is the usage of the fairly esoteric (and, paradoxically, wide-ranging) vocabulary, as epitomized by "ruching" (from ruche, which *The American Heritage Dictionary of the English Language* defines as "A ruffle or pleat of lace . . . used for trimming women's garments"), "jabots" (frills or cascading ruffles down the front of a shirt), and "sabots" (wooden shoes). Fourth is the fact that the humor of the situation depicted depends on the reader's knowing these definitions, for it consists of mistaking ruffles for shoes. And, fifth is the amusing ridiculousness that is demanded by implying that such a mistake could be made, although it might be funnier to picture someone with shoes hanging down the front of their shirt than imagining them wearing ruffles on their feet in place of shoes.

Having spent a little over one-seventh of the article on these preparatory asides, Perelman is now ready to engage his plot. The story is "really" about how the English teacher in his sophomore year in high school caught him plagiarizing from those novels that he so loved. The teacher, Miss Cronjager, has a figure evocative of a "coryphée," another esoteric term (this time from ballet and linked by Perelman to advertising), so when she invites her pupil to meet her at the above-described bakery (with the detail of the name of the establishment, Gibson's, appended), he is glad to do so. During the discourse between the two, Miss Cronjager comments that the essay that he wrote for an autobiographical assignment includes numerous details that seem familiar to her. Might his account of his early life among the lobster fishermen off the coast of Maine reflect some acquaintance with Rudyard Kipling's *Captains Courageous*, for instance? And, perhaps, his adventures at the Admiral Benbow Inn and hiding in an apple barrel, his stay on a cotton plantation in Dixie where the family retainer was named Uncle Cudgo, his experience in the Texas Panhandle (which the author reminds her was not so atypical, as she would know if she had read *Riders of the Purple Sage* or *The Winning of Barbara Worth*), and his meeting with Owen Johnson's "fabled character," "Doc Macnooder the Tennessee shad, and so forth," might have something to do with the fact that at fifteen (Perelman's age in 1919) he had "managed to squeeze in quite a lot of reading." [127] There are other literary allusions, to the call of the Yukon, Rarotonga in the South Seas, *The Arabian Nights' Entertainments*, Dr. Fu Manchu, Allan Quartermain, Leatherstocking, Sax Rohmer's Nayland Smith, and Craig Kennedy, the Scientific Detective. Inserted are occasional bits of actual autobiographical information that make the tale both more personal and more credible—such as the author's age and the name of his high school (Classical) in Providence. The story ends with the admission that the essay unaccountably received a grade of D-minus.

"One of Our Stagecraft Is Missing" tells how the author read a story in *Variety* about Liberace ("a great, gorgeous peacock who shed enchantment on our lives"[128]), who had opened a new night club act at the Las Vegas Hilton which culminated in his flying off stage and into the wings suspended by wires. This leads Perelman to reminisce about an occurrence during the autumn of 1943 when the company of *One Touch of Venus*, under the direction of Elia Kazan, was readying for its Boston tryout. At one point in the play, Venus causes Gloria Kramer, the protagonist's fiancée, to vanish, and Perelman recounts the problems involved in achieving the effect of her vanishing from the audience's sight while she is in the middle of the stage. A magician was hired, and he created an illusion for this purpose, but the young woman who played the role of Gloria literally vanished at the dress rehearsal in the Colonial Theatre. Supposedly, after all of these years, Perelman runs into the actress at Macy's, and she explains what happened; she had been kidnaped. Again, the fanciful story contains enough real details to give it a sense of verisimilitude.

The premise behind "The Frost Is on the Noggin" is even more far-fetched. Perelman sets up the story by telling about a conversation that he once had with Dashiell Hammett, "a former Pinkerton employee who'd switched to writing for the pulps,"[129] about tailing people—Hammett was conspicuous, "for his height, emaciation, and snow-white thatch." This conversation is linked to a story in the London *Times* about a shoplifter who stole frozen chickens by concealing them under his hat. From these two elements Perelman fashions a tale about how he stumbled on Abe Lincoln performing the same feat at Nussbaum's Gourmeteria in New York City and applied his intellect to solving the problem of how the thief managed to get away without the frozen fowl causing "syncope, from cerebral anemia."[130]

The story is not particularly funny, but it does illustrate some of the humorist's thought processes. To begin with, the title is a play on the title of the James Whitcomb Riley poem, "When the Frost Is on the Pumpkin." The story has nothing to do with the theme of Riley's poem, but "pumpkin" is sometimes used as a slang expression for "head," as is the word "noggin." Thus, pumpkin begets head begets noggin. The story is concerned, if concerned is the appropriate word, with the effect of cold on a person's head, so the title fits.

Basically, if we accept that an article appeared in the London *Times* reporting the incident that Perelman describes, then his thinking must have been: given this action, is there any way of counteracting the effects of the cold, thus permitting the shoplifter to accomplish his goal? The story reflects a possible, albeit improbable, solution to this intellectual puzzle. Along the way the humorist alludes to films ("retrieving gold falcons"), Shakespeare ("knew a hawk from a handsaw"), actors (Faye Dunaway, one of his modern favorites, and Raymond Massey), popular fiction (Jacques Futrelle's *The Thinking Machine*), pipes (a Dunhill) and tobacco (Latakia), areas of New York City (Third Avenue, Gramercy Park, Second Avenue), American cities (Philadelphia, Hagerstown, Richmond, Raleigh, Knoxville, Columbia, Macon, Savannah, Miami, Zanesville, Altoona), Arthur Miller, and food (kippers, broilers, beef pie, cheesecake, novy, whitefish, Maatjes herring, bagels, wonton soup, Chinese snow peas, water chestnuts, halvah, goose liver, chicken wings, butterball turkeys).[131] He also displays a knowledge of nineteenth century clothing (his quarry wore a Prince Albert and a "silk hat of the type known as a tile"), throws in a couple of foreign phrases (*"ruat caelum," "coup de theatre"*), and manages to include the brand names of several products (Stouffer's and Sara Lee).[132] The encyclopedic knowledge and the inclusion of accurate details lends to the believability of the piece, but they also become stylistic elements to be treasured in themselves. In addition, since the article is purportedly about detecting, Perelman's dialogue contains detective novel jargon: " 'Reach for the sky.' . . . I herded him. . . . He lamped [saw]. . . . In my mitt. . . . The jig was up. . . . He'd buy it. . . . 'You the buzz?'. . . . 'This your pad?'. . . . 'What's bugging you?'. . . . 'You're breaking my heart,' I growled. . . . 'Keep your hands on your lapels. That way nobody gets hurt'. . . . 'I wasn't born yesterday'. . . . 'tailing me'. . . . 'figured the odds'. . . . 'how did you tumble?' "[133] The style has become ingrained in his writing, even when the result is only mediocre.

"Zwei Herzen in die Drygoods Schlock" begins with a quotation by dress designer Diane Von Furstenberg in the *Los Angeles Times* and then turns into the scenario format. As is true about most of Perelman's scenarios, this one is not very funny. Although some critics rate several of the scenarios among his masterpieces ("Waiting for Santy," "Counter Revolution," "A Farewell to Omsk," "Nesselrode to Jeopardy"), possibly many of the scenarios are generally among the writer's less successful efforts because they are pure dialogue and do not allow for setting up punch lines as in his prose pieces, or because they do not convey the quick thrusts of wit as well, or maybe it is because they involve absolutely fictitious characters and the Perelman persona is absent. The only noteworthy points in this piece are Perelman's vocabulary ("anarchistic frocks," "must have seemed a frump," "these habiliments"[134]), which is spiced with a number of Yiddish terms ("schmottas," "ignatz," "shiksa"[135]) a typical practice when he writes about the clothing trade, and he does so with some regularity, and a couple of literary allusions, the most amusing being in the form of a character's name—Ricky Tichitavsky, after the Kipling tale. There are occasional foreign phrases ("Selbstverstandlich") and plays on words, as when Charisma claims to have "sprung from the proudest loins" and Ricky understands her to have said that she "sprang from a pride of lions."[136] And, there is an infrequent flash of Perelmanesque/Groucho Marxish dialogue:

Yes, I mingle with crowned heads as naturally as a duck takes to water, like a baby loves its rock-and-rye. Is there a pheasant drive across the Tweed, a boar hunt in Styria, a gala at Bad Ischl, a champagne party aboard a dahabeah on the Nile? Wherever the *jeunesse doree* convokes, wherever fun is at its maddest, look for me there, the cynosure of all the men, the envy of all the women. Tell me—do you find me attractive?   (p. 43)

"The Joy of Mooching" purports to relate how fillers in the *Times* and the *Jerusalem Post* about Monza, Italy, and especially in relation to a recently published book entitled *How to Make Begging Pay*, lead the author to an adventure as a neophyte beggar. The piece is not exceptional.

On the other hand, "Recapture Your Rapture, in One Seedy Session" is an example of the journalist's strong suit, a cogitative piece in which he reflects on the glorious cultural artifacts of his past. The strength in this cinematic memoir, and a concurrent solidness of style at times missing in his less personal ruminations, again comes from the fact that ultimately Perelman is writing about himself. Moreover, the informal essay style that he utilizes, an anecdotal approach conveyed in a light, entertaining, and personal tone, is perfectly matched with the enlightening thoughts that he is sharing with his reader. The style is not ponderous or condescending. It is not even consciously funny. It is conversational, as though the reader were an old friend being acquainted with some new facts.

The essay begins as is customary with a reference to an article in a newspaper. The author states that although he does not want to antagonize the *New York Review of Books* or the *Times* (London) *Literary Supplement*, he feels that it is his duty to discuss the "Steinberg Theory." What is this theory? That Proust's madeleine in *Remembrance of Things Past* was actually a matzo ball. Calling on such authorities as L. Ron Hubbard (former science fiction author and founder of Scientology), Jeane Dixon (an astrologist), and William Safire (a syndicated newspaper columnist) to corroborate his own contention, Perelman asserts that "one's own skein of memory often starts unwinding under similarly mundane circumstances." [137]

Using this thought as his starting point, Perelman remembers the performances of Valentino and Nita Naldi in *Blood and Sand* in 1922. Furthermore, he "was struck by an awesome thought: I was probably the only surviving member of the Rhode Island audience that witnessed the original screen version of *Anna Karenina* in 1916." [138] From this reflection he moves to a series of plot synopses that he finds in a 1913 issue of the *Cinema News Property Gazette*. The plot lines of *The College Chaperon, The Story of Lavinia, Luggage in Advance*, and others, cause him to comment on the "birth of a new art form" and to wonder about the thoughts of the audience that was witnessing the birth. [139] This leads to a comment on the deficiences of modern films, among these being the deliberate suppression by the movie makers of "some vital ingredient" that is the key to understanding the film.

"Under the Shrinking Royalty the Village Smithy Stands" ironically portrays an author waiting in his publisher's anteroom, perhaps a circumstance more apropos than Perelman might have guessed, in light of Simon and Schuster's forgetful nature. The story about a publisher who has taken up horseshoeing as a profession so that he can afford to publish only what he wants to, and who turns down the author's proposals on the basis that they will become commercial successes, has little to recommend it.

"To Yearn Is Subhuman, to Forestall Devine" puts the writer in the role of a screenwriter who worked in Hollywood during the Golden Age of the thirties. Because of this background he is asked to offer some advice to the nephew of an acquaintance. Perelman uses a bit of a variation in this selection; rather than the author whose imagination is stimulated by a news article, it is the nephew, an aspiring young filmmaker, who is energized. Like the publisher in the preceding piece, though, the young man despairs of creating a commercially successful picture. Perelman decides not to disabuse him of his misconcepts about the "tremendous burst of creativity" in Hollywood in the thirties or at the Round Table in the Algonquin Hotel at about the same time, since at his "back I seemed to hear a Turkish steamer hurrying near" [140]—a play on a line from Andrew Marvel's "To His Coy Mistress," a poem about the passage of time. Instead, the former script writer confirms the neophyte's theory, taken in part from Tobe Hooper (director of *The Texas Chain Saw Massacre*), that "the motif is more important than what happens on the screen." [141] The upshot is that instead of making a full-length documentary about jeans in which jeans are never shown, the young man takes a job in Korvettes' shipping room, much to his uncle's pleasure.

"All Precincts Beware—Paper Tigress Loose!" details, in detective-genre fashion, the capture of a young woman (another Faye Dunaway look-alike), "a she-devil, maddened by who can say what dark neurotic compulsion, dedicated to undermining the very foundations of stationery as we know it today." [142] As the man who might be called Mr. Answer Man ("Who Killed Cock Robin? Who was the Dark Lady of the Sonnets? What was S. S. Van Dine's real name?" [143]), the protagonist is asked by Interpol, through the New York Police Department, to solve the case of a woman who sells large amounts of paper products wholesale "without even a retail license." [144] In spite of his incompetence—he does not even know that the woman in his company is the culprit even though she fits the description and tries to sell him a warehouse full of memo pads—the story's hero aids in her arrest. In describing the culprit, Perelman repeats a formula that he uses frequently: it turns out that she is not Faye Dunaway but instead she is "another cupcake, equally a goddess. The face was a pastiche combining elements of Corinne Griffith, Olga Baclanova, and Mary Astor." [145]

In "Methinks the Lady Doth Propel Too Much" Perelman relates an anecdote about Alma Mahler (the wife of the composer, she had liaisons with the writer Franz Werfel, Walter Gropius, and the painter Oskar Kokoscka—"a lady whose fame rested on the fact that four headliners rested on her," as the humorist puts it[146]). The anecdote is paralleled by a news release in the *Times* about a woman who has invented a swimsuit that makes the wearer look like a mermaid. The story proceeds to tell how the narrator (Henry Knifesmith), who used to be one of the Katzenjammer Kids, while on vacation on Martha's Vineyard meets a young woman wearing one of these outfits and trying to pass herself off as a mermaid. The narrator exhibits no fondness for the island's inhabitants, but the reference to the newspaper comic strip is developed amusingly.

Professor Gideon Titmarsh of Rexall College in Ohio is the identity of Perelman's persona in "Scram! You Made the Pants Too Short." The tale is written in reaction to a review of a book on the Bloomsbury Group that appeared in the *Times* (London) *Literary Supplement*. The section of the review that stimulates the author's imaginative process is a comment that novelist/critic E. M. Forster wore his trousers three inches too short. Amidst references to the Marquis de Sade, T. S. Eliot (fittingly, "The Lovesong of J. Alfred Prufrock"), James Joyce, and Tom Stoppard (*Travesties*), the storyteller takes us on a tour of London, filled with place names and geographical details ("Away we whizzed past the V.A. and the Brompton Oratory, into the turbulence of Knightsbridge, through the underpass at Hyde Park Corner, and along Piccadilly"[147]), as he tries to track down an illusive pair of pants that he needs to recover in order to test the veracity of the reviewer's statement regarding the length of Forster's inseam.

Amusingly, Perelman inserts a jibe at the National Endowment for the Humanities, mentions his honorary Litt.D. and the freshman trigonometry class that he flunked in 1921, is referred to as a "schnorrer," and corrects a tradesman who is unaware that Coleridge and Cavafy are dead. At the tale's denouement the narrator exclaims, "Well, dog my cats," a phrase previously spoken by Groucho Marx.

The battle of the sexes, stimulated by exposure to daytime television soap operas, is the subject of "Meanness Rising from the Suds." According to *American Film* and *True* magazines, the image of men as portrayed on *Another World, Days of Our Lives, As the World Turns,* and *Somerset*, is one of "gutless and/or villainous boobs." Feeling that he is neither of these, the narrator is put to the test when a female acquaintance of his who stars in a network show agrees to go to lunch with him. Despite his well-planned attempts to do everything right, everything goes astray because of her "Typical feminine behavior": "They eat a spoonful of yogurt when they're alone, but when you're buying, man, its like Thanksgiving." [148] The outcome of this adventure is that not only is the hero rejected but he finds himself pilloried in the actress's series in the figure of a new character introduced for comic relief.

"Is There a Writer in the House?" speaks to the question of deteriorating craftsmanship in the modern world, even in the field of writing. In this piece Perelman primarily is concerned about the attribution of authorship when the name that appears on the published product may have very little to do with whoever created the product. Ghostwriters, secretaries, secretaries' roommates, and so forth, may actually have contributed more to the work published than the so-called author did, a condition that the humorist labels "mass authorship." [149] The most amusing segment of this piece is in the opening exchange between the narrator and a representative of a publishing house who wants to engage him in this practice. "Just answer me one question," says the first man, "Is one hour of your time worth five hundred thousand dollars?" "Yes," responds Perelman's persona, "and I've already wasted a bundle on you."

An anecdote about Perelman's youthful enthrallment with Jimmy Durante opens the piece "As I was Going to St. Ives, I met a Man with Seventeen Wives." (Interestingly, Durante had written a dust jacket blurb for *Dawn Ginsbergh's Revenge*.) This admiration is connected with a (London) *Times* story about a 117-year-old man who had been married seventeen times, and, naturally, the combination results in a scenario about an old man engaged to a young woman. Contemporary references (to Plato's Retreat, a sex club in New York City), the use of current slang ("grotty," an English slang term meaning grotesque), the names of the *dramatis personae* (including Bonanza and Wolfram Frontispiece, Farkrimter, Dass Is Kein Kint, Wheatena), the unwillingness to suspend disbelief ("the audience knows all that. Farkrimter and I planted it in the exposition," Frontispiece explains), and another allusion to Eliot's "Prufrock" ("On Bailey's Beach you will hear the mermaids singing each to each") are typical Perelmanesque elements found in the work. [150]

"Wanted: Short or Long Respite by Former Cineaste" is a series of vignettes that explore some of the reasons for Perelman's sixty-five-year-long fascination with motion pictures. "Still avid for whatever nuggets might turn up in the sludge,"[151] he talks about the spring of 1935 when he was employed for a brief time by the Warner Brothers-First National studio in Burbank, and about the McCarthy era's effect on Hollywood as related to actor Keenan Wynn who was threatened by an MGM executive with blacklisting if he did not name the industry people whom he had encountered at Hollywood Anti-Nazi League meetings (anti-nazi, it seems, in the thinking of the period had to mean pro-Communist). Wynn struggled for several days, professing to have an extremely poor memory, when suddenly he opined that he thought maybe Dore Schary had been there. Along with Louis B. Mayer, Dore Schary was, as Perelman puts it, a suzerain, and the interrogator "went livid. 'What the hell, kid,' " he told Wynn, "If you can't remember, you . . . can't . . . *remember*!"[152]

Perelman also repeats a fantasy wish, that he could have been a fly on the wall observing an intriguing and significant conversation between major figures in the world of art or politics. In this case he recounts some time after it happened an opportunity that he had to hear about one such meeting in Hollywood between two famous poets, one of whom was e. e. cummings. According to cummings, the other poet claimed that Hollywood had turned him into a "whore." "But, of course, that was just a metaphor." Perelman comments, "I worked in the place. They never made any of us wear kimonos."[153] It is interesting that in a piece in which he starts out talking about "nuggets," Perelman's vignettes all show Hollywood in a bad light.

"Portrait of the Artist as a Young Cat's-Paw" begins, surprisingly, with a reference to Joyce scholarship. Soon, though, the article becomes a tale about how the narrator was so taken by the aerialists in the film *Variety* (described in some of his earlier writing) when he was a young cartoonist, that he took a trip to Europe and was subsequently used to bring a bed through customs in New York without duty being assessed. Oh shipboard enroute to Cherborg, the author met two young "lovelies," whom he describes in his normal fashion, and he includes a short passage that in tone and clustered details delivered without punctuation are fittingly reminiscent of Joyce:

"Well Mr. Protheroe it's too sweet my son's about to be married in New York and I bought him a bed at the Galeries Lafayette or Le Printemps I forget which but I have the receipt right here in my bag there look at it just forty dollars now to ship it would take months and months but since you're going over it won't be a bit of trouble to declare it just hand them this receipt I'll arrange everything with the store the bed'll be loaded on the ship Stanley will be waiting on the pier God bless you Mr. Proskauer for understanding a mother's heart full of overflowing gratitude.   (p. 135)

The final piece in Part One of *The Last Laugh* is "One Order of Blintzes, and Hold the Flimflam." As the final example of Perelman's nonautobiographical prose, it is disappointing. The short story takes place in Cooper's Dairy Restaurant, a seamy establishment in an even seamier neighborhood, New York City's lower East Side. While reading an anthology by Simenon over a bowl of borscht, the author, Jud Kluckhorn, is confronted by a con man who offers him an opportunity to become a member of a consortium that owns a collection of French furniture and works of art. By reversing the spelling on one of the consortium members' names, Kluckhorn exposes the other as one of a "goniff of swindlers." [154]

As is true of many of Perelman's short stories that are based purely on imagination—that is, from the conception itself—the piece is not as humorous as those in which more of the writer's own experiences come through. When he is talking about himself, or castigating a segment of society, Perelman is on solid ground; this proves true throughout his career. When he is writing primarily to amuse, the result is not always as felicitous, even though some of his most successful efforts (e.g., "The Idol's Eye") fall into this category.

Contrary to some of the other selections in *The Last Laugh*, *The Hindsight Saga* is an example of Perelman at his best. A project that he talked about off and on for several years, it is simultaneously similar to and different from most of his other writing. The four segments published as "Fragments of an Autobiography" in this volume include "The Marx Brothers," "Nathanael West," "Dorothy Parker," and "Three Little Photoplays and How They Grew." In an interview he had announced that he planned to entitle his autobiography *Smiling, the Boy Fell Dead*, but he abandoned this title when a play with the same title opened shortly thereafter.

The tone, style, and anecdotal approach in these essays are much the same as found in numerous pieces that preceded them, especially the travel accounts of *Westward Ha!*, *The Swiss Family Perelman,* and

Eastward Ha!. The fact that they are autobiographical does not represent a significant departure, either, for, as has been amply demonstrated, much of the humorist's writing grows out of an autobiographical basis—the first selection in *The Last Laugh*, "And Then the Whining Schoolboy, with His Satchel," is just the latest example of many. At the same time, this autobiography is not quite as autobiographical as the run-of-the-mill autobiography is. In the West and Parker selections, for instance, the material included has more to do with them as subjects than it has to do with Perelman, though much of what he recounts occurred in his presence, and both what he reports and his attitude toward it give us some insight into the humorist himself. The one thing that is missing from these pieces that is present in almost everything else that he wrote, including to some extent the travel articles, is the extension from fact into imagination. Normally Perelman moves beyond an initiating incident to a slightly exaggerated bit of fiction that makes a satirical point through extrapolation. This is how things happened, he says, and if we look at the next logical development as it might happen to some *schlemiel*, S. G. Pefelman, let us say, then we see how everyday events are fraught with imminent peril. In these four segments he is simply doing forthright reporting; he is recalling people and the things that happened to them that involved him. The whole point of the exercise is to provide information, not to use that information as a starting point for making a satirical comment on some social foible. There is no doubt that the writer's attitude toward his subjects is clear, and this is certainly not merely incidentally so, but his attention is focused only on these specific people and incidents rather than on seeing how they relate to some matter that transcends them.

Since Perelman's involvement with the Marx Brothers as the screenwriter for two of their early films, *Monkey Business* and *Horsefeathers*, is dealt with in Chapter Two, and since "The Marx Brothers" piece describes the events and, to some extent, the relationship between the author and the brothers during the making of these movies, the material in this article will be discussed in Chapter Two as part of the examination of Perelman's work in Hollywood. The material in "Three Little Photoplays and How They Grew" fits into the same category, and it, too, will be considered in the next chapter.

"Nathanael West" recounts West's sojourn as manager of the Sutton Hotel on New York's East Fifty-sixth Street. The Perelmans moved into the hotel in the latter half of 1932 when Perelman's play, *Sherry Flip*, "slid into the vortex." [155] At the time West was working on his second novel, a work based on letters shown him several years earlier by a woman who wrote the advice-to-the-lovelorn column for the *Brooklyn Eagle* and to whom he had been introduced by his brother-in-law for that purpose. The novel was *Miss Lonelyhearts*.

The article is not a day-by-day account of its subject's life but rather captures the essence of the man through assorted revelations about his activities. Perelman discusses West's literary likes and dislikes, the influences on his writing, and his taste in clothes and women. He also describes West's venture with William Carlos Williams and Robert McAlmon as coeditors of *Contact*.

Because of West's sympathy for aspiring writers, the Sutton was filled with literary hopefuls. Perelman met one of these in an elevator and was asked for advice: "The housekeeper told me you had a big hit on Broadway. I'm scripting a play too, on a Biblical theme, but I got stuck in the second act, in the obligatory scene. Could you recommend a good book or construction, or would you advise me to go back to the Bible?" [156] Perelman used the stairs thereafter.

From non-writers Perelman turns to talking briefly about genuine writers who were inhabitants of the hotel then—Lillian Hellman, Norman Krasna, Dashiell Hammett. About each he reveals a small piece of information regarding their first efforts at writing. Another acquaintance of West's who also wrote was Michael Gold, identified as Mark Silver, and thus Perelman segues into a short recapitulation of how the Bucks' County farm, complete with a "monumental barn . . . larger than the cathedral at Chartres," came into their possession. [157] Included are stories of why George S. Kaufman had come not to purchase the property just before West and the Perelmans did, and how the Perelmans struggled to raise their half of the $500 deposit; finally West had to talk the owners of the Sutton into buying a baby grand piano that was an heirloom from Laura's family. A long passage details the new owners' work to convert the place into a liveable home, a description that reflects Perelman's frustration with the farm, but even more so his love for it:

For the next couple of months, every ounce of energy the three of us could summon—along with whatever paint, hardware, tools, and furniture West could liberate from the hotel short of downright larceny—went into making the farm habitable. The self-deceit of landowners is proverbial, but we reached new heights; we became artisans as well, installing pumps and plumbing, wiring the house, and even, in a Herculean spurt that left us crippled for weeks, implanting a septic tank. All these furbelows, being makeshift, constantly tended to remind us of our inadequacy. Water pipes we had painstakingly soldered would burst their seams in the middle of the night, with a roar like Krakatoa, and drench us in our beds. Tongues of blue fire licked our homemade electrical conduits; half the time we reeled about with catastrophic headaches, unaware that the furnace needed escape vents to discharge its burden of coal gas. Each weekend was a turmoil of displacement. Groaning like navvies, we trundled barrows of shale to and fro, unrooted and redistributed trees, realigned fences, and changed the entire topography of the place. The vogue for Pennsylvania Dutch artifacts had not yet become general, and there were quantities of dough trays, dry sinks, horsehair sofas, Victorian wig stands, and similar rubbish available around the county to any fool who confused himself with Chippendale. We invariably did, and spent endless nights in a haze of shellac dust, scraping away at some curlicued gumwood commode to bring out the beauty of the grain.   (p. 170)

Just as everyone was about to settle in the next spring, the Marx Brothers asked Perelman to return to Hollywood to write their next movie. Perelman was not overjoyed: "Somewhat less than radiant at the thought of being sucked into the millrace a second time, I hesitated, but the long financial drought had sapped my resistance."[158] This last point was the crucial one. Financial difficulties (as described in "The Marx Brothers") plagued the author at this time, and when the returns of West's *Miss Lonelyhearts* fell short of expectations due to problems with his publishers (the first went bankrupt soon after the novel appeared, and although a second firm reissued the book, the delay devastated its potential sales) the trio had to scramble. Perelman admits that "It seemed a cruel irony to be cheated of the rustic joys we had labored to achieve, and yet, if we were ever to enjoy them, a spell in the Hollywood deep freeze was unavoidable."

Throughout the article, Perelman's tone is light, and his anecdotes are amusing in themselves, but basically his approach is direct reportage. While he employs many of the same techniques and devices found in his other writing, when used in this piece they are a natural part of his style or meant to enhance his point instead of being employed merely for humorous effect. Again, this produces a much more solid style than found elsewhere in his work, and the article itself has a feel of reality about it that obviously has to be kept out of some of his short stories and primarily inventive essays.

Dorothy Parker "was already a legend" when Perelman met her in the autumn of 1932, he recalls in the relatively short article about her. They met at a pre-rehearsal cocktail party given by the producer of the revue *Sherry Flip*. The meeting was not very promising, for when they were introduced Parker had complimented him highly, yet almost immediately an atmosphere of animosity was established when Perelman did not find her suggested titles for the still unnamed play appropriate. Parker's reaction to this rejection by an upstart author was a verbal attack, and Perelman never wanted to meet her again. The next evening, however, he received a dozen "magnificent roses" from her, "accompanied by a note steeped in remorse." This was, he says, "the beginning of a friendship that survived thirty-five years." [159] The use of the word "survive" emphasizes the difference between Parker and Groucho Marx, with whom Perelman also had a stormy relationship, for all three were bright, witty satirists who could easily ruffle one another's feathers, but the friendship with Groucho did not survive.

The next time that Perelman met Parker was when they were both on the Coast. "Dottie" and her husband, Alan Campbell, were co-writing screenplays (Perelman later worked on an MGM film with them), but she "detested"Hollywood and she envied the Perelmans for the farm in Pennsylvania that they spoke about so glowingly. Soon after the Perelmans returned to Bucks County, the Campbells arrived to see if they could find something suitable in what was becoming a small artists' colony (Kaufman, Moss Hart, Perelman and West, and a few others had acquired homes in the general area). Perelman then describes the farm-hunting expedition engaged in by the two couples that resulted in the Campbells becoming neighbors. Much of the piece is reminiscent of the selections that were gathered for *Acres and Pains*.

The Last Laugh contains material similar to that produced by Perelman throughout his career. Some of it is quite humorous; some of it fails. The material reflects the author's virtuosity and his catholic interests. The style is sure and mature and contains all of the major ingredients that he developed and refined over fifty years. Finally, though, it is *The Hindsight Saga* that elevates this volume to among the very best of all of Perelman's collections. Possibly because he was so intimately involved with his subject matter there is more strength in these articles than in some of his other work. It is a shame that he

did not find time to write more of what would have been a fine autobiography and a fitting capstone for his career.

NOTES

1. Jay Martin, *Nathanael West: The Art of His Life* (New York: Farrar,
Straus, and Giroux, 1970), p. 74.

2. S. J. Perelman, *That Old Gang O' Mine* (New York: Morrow, 1984),
p. 133. N.B.: As a matter of convenience, in this and all of the collections of
Perelman's work that follow, I generally have dealt with individual articles in
the order in which they appear in the volume on the assumption that this
arrangement will make it easier for the reader to follow my path through each
volume than if I simply talked about the pieces in a random order. Occasionally, and it should be evident from the context when I am doing this, I will
treat a group of stories that are thematically or stylistically related as a category, but since Perelman typically employs a scattergun approach (all imag-
inable subjects are targets and the same techniques are used throughout fairly
indiscriminately), this does not occur with great frequency.

3. Ibid., p. 136.

4. Ibid., pp. 15–16.

5. Ibid., p. 71.

6. William Cole and George Plimpton, "S. J. Perelman," *Writers at
Work: The Paris Review Interviews, Second Series* (New York: Viking, 1965),
p. 244.

7. S. J. Perelman, *Dawn Ginsbergh's Revenge* (New York: Liveright,
1929), p. 14. Interestingly, there is some confusion about the spelling of
Ginsbergh. Although it is spelled with an "H" in the book, dust jacket blurbs
on some of the author's subsequent volumes omit the "H."

8. Ibid., p. 14.

9. Ibid., p. 11.

10. Ibid., p. 12.

11. Ibid., p. 13.

12. Ibid., p. 87.

13. Ibid., p. 93.

14. Ibid., pp. 124–25.

15. Reynolds (1902–1965) wrote for the *New York Times* and the *New
York World Telegraph*. Among his many books on war is *Britain Can Take It*
(1941) and his biographies included volumes on the Wright Brothers and Winston Churchill.

16. The copy in which this is written is in the University of Wisconsin
Library collection. The person to whom it was addressed is not further identified.

17. S. J. Perelman, *Parlor, Bedlam and Bath* (New York: Liveright, 1930), p. 11.

18. Further examples include "Moses washes himself of Israel Hands. . . . What the Tartar saw through the keyhole—exit Heywood Broun" (Chapter Two), "The 'Pequod' sights in the White Whale. . . . In which our heroine breasts the waves and vice versa—Bertha writes Goethe a letter" (Chapter Three), "Phileas Fogg befogs Passepartout. . . . A short history of poltroonery—Enger Von Moltke, mouthing" (Chapter Four), "Leopold Dedalus meets Stephen Bloom. . . . Inspector Lestrade bolts his lunch and shoots his bolt—The owl on the battlements" (Chapter Five), "The message to Garcia. . . . We proceed inland from Mombassa" (Chapter Six), "The feast of Ramadan. . . . Under the Beerbohm tree" (Chapter Seven), " I meet Lady Brett. . . . Tinker to Evans to Chance" (Chapter Nine), "Moussorgsky springs full-blown from the head of Zeus, hoist by his own petard. . . . I Bury a banana, Holmes amd Brandeis dissenting" (Chapter Eleven), and "We move to a house without closets. . . . Temple Drums. . . . Exit the glorious rouge" (Chapter Twelve).

19. Perelman, *Parlor, Bedlam and Bath*, p. 14.

20. Ibid., p. 38.

21. Ibid., p. 39.

22. Ibid., pp. 46–47.

23. Ibid., p. 48.

24. Ibid., p. 54.

25. Ibid., pp. 56–57.

26. Ibid., p. 74.

27. Ibid., p. 91.

28. Ibid., p. 101.

29. Ibid., pp. 151, 154, 156–57, 161.

30. Ibid., p. 193.

31. Ibid., pp. 228–29.

32. Ibid., p. 229.

33. Ibid., p. 238.

34. Ibid., pp. 239–40.

35. See Martin, p. 251.

36. S. J. Perelman, *The Most of S. J. Perelman* (New York: Simon and Schuster, 1958), p. 3. I have used this volume for quotation purposes rather than using *Strictly from Hunger* and several other collections because of its accessibility and because it contains selections over such a wide range of time in Perelman's career.

37. Ibid., p. 4.

38. Ibid., p. 31.

39. Ibid., p. 32.

40. See Ring Lardner's nonsense plays of the 1920's, for example, and Lucky's speech in Samuel Beckett's *Waiting for Godot* or the early plays of N. F. Simpson and Harold Pinter.

41. Perelman, *The Most of S. J. Perelman*, p. 33.

42. S. J. Perelman, *Look Who's Talking* (New York: Random House, 1940), pp. 3–4.

43. Ibid., p. 13.

44. William Zinsser, "That Perelman of Great Price is Sixty-Five," *New York Times Magazine* (January 26, 1969): 76.

45. Perelman, *The Most of S. J. Perelman*, p. 27.

46. Ibid., pp. 20–21.

47. Ibid., p. 35.

48. Ibid., pp. 56–57.

49. S. J. Perelman, *The Best of S. J. Perelman* (New York: Random House, 1947), p. ix.

50. Ibid., p. x.

51. Ibid., p. xii.

52. Cole and Plimpton, p. 244.

53. Perelman, *The Most of S. J. Perelman*, p. 191.

54. Raymond Chandler, *The Long Goodbye* in *The Midnight Raymond Chandler* (Boston: Houghton Mifflin, 1971) pp. 419, 492, 497, 596.

55. Perelman, *The Most of S. J. Perelman*, p. 194.

56. See Chapter Three for an extended discussion of Perelman's borrowings from himself in this play.

57. Perelman, *The Most of S. J. Perelman*, p. 236.

58. Ibid., p. 127.

59. Quoted in Martin, p. 200. This account is repeated in Perelman's "Nathanael West" in *The Last Laugh*. (New York: Simon and Schuster, 1981), pp. 161–70.)

60. Ibid.

61. Perelman, *The Most of S. J. Perelman*, p. 149.

62. Ibid., p. 129.

63. Ibid., pp. 136–37.

64. Ibid., p. 142. See again Benchley's "Do Insects Think?" for example, in *The Benchley Roundup*. Edited by Nathaniel Benchley (New York: Harper and Row, 1922), pp. 44–45.

65. Perelman, *The Most of S. J. Perelman*, p. 144.

66. Ibid., p. 139.

67. Ibid., p. 152.

68. Murray Schumach, "Perelman Tries Series for TV," *New York Times*, March 1, 1962, p. 27.

69. Perelman, *The Most of S. J. Perelman*, p. 346.

70. Ibid., p. 319.

71. Ibid., p. 328.

72. Ibid., p. 348.

73. Ibid., p. 311.

74. Ibid., p. 332.

75. Ibid., p. 310.

76. Ibid., p. 313.

77. Ibid., p. 330.

78. Ibid., p. 316.

79. Ibid., p. 342.

80. Ibid., p. 335.

81. Ibid., p. 314.

82. Ibid., p. 312.

83. Ibid., p. 327.

84. Ibid., pp. 355–356.

85. Ibid., p. 356.

86. Ibid., p. 367.

87. See "At the Rialto," by J.T.M., *New York Times*, May 29, 1936, p. 15.

88. Perelman, *The Most of S. J. Perelman*, p. 387.

89. See Zinsser, p. 76.

90. Perelman, *The Most of S. J. Perelman*, p. 202.

91. Ibid., p. 280.

92. Ibid., p. 407.

93. Ibid., p. 270.

94. The mynah bird became a resident of the Bucks County farm, along with numerous dogs and other animals. At one time Perelman even tried to obtain a gibbon, having realized that the span of his barn was exactly equal to the span required by a swinging gibbon, but he never managed to acquire such a pet.

95. Perelman, *The Most of S. J. Perelman*, p. 433.

96. Zinsser, p. 27.

97. Cole and Plimpton, p. 248.

98. Perelman, *The Most of S. J. Perelman*, p. 496.

99. Ibid., p. 497.

100. Ibid., p. 506.

101. Ibid., p. 568.

102. Ibid., p. 513.

103. Ibid., p. 529.

104. Ibid., p. 624.

105. S. J. Perelman, *The Rising Gorge* (New York: Simon and Schuster, 1961), p. 99.

106. S. J. Perelman, *Chicken Inspector No. 23* (New York: Simon and Schuster, 1966) p. 24.

107. Ibid., p. 25.

108. Ibid., p. 26.

109. Ibid., p. 90.

110. Ibid., p. 255.

111. Ibid., p. 122.

112. Perelman, *Baby, It's Cold Inside* (New York: Simon and Schuster, 1970), p. 225.

113. Ibid., p. 226.

114. Ibid., p. 227.

115. Ibid., p. 230.

116. Ibid., p. 248.

117. Quoted in *Current Biography* (New York: H. W. Wilson, 1971), p. 321.

118. Myra MacPherson, "Perelman's Wit Becomes an Anglo-File," *Washington Post*, October 18, 1970, Sect. E, p. 4.

119. S. J. Perelman, *Vinegar Puss* (New York: Simon and Schuster, 1975), p. 12.

120. Ibid., p. 47.

121. Israel Shenker, "S. J. Perelman," *Publisher's Weekly* 20 (May 19, 1975): 90.

122. Ibid., p. 91.

123. S. J. Perelman, *Eastward Ha!* (New York: Simon and Schuster, 1977), p. 17.

124. S. J. Perelman, *The Last Laugh* (New York: Simon and Schuster, 1981), p. 19. There is an interesting comparison in book prices: Perelman's first book, *Dawn Ginsbergh's Revenge*, sold for $2, this volume listed at $12.95.

125. Ibid., p. 20.

126. Ibid.

127. Ibid., pp. 22–25.

128. Ibid., p. 27.

129. Ibid., p. 34.

130. Ibid., pp. 34, 35, 36, 37, 38, 39.

131. Ibid., pp. 36, 37, 38.

132. Ibid.

133. Ibid., pp. 38–39.

134. Ibid., p. 40.

135. Ibid., pp. 41, 45.

136. Ibid., pp. 42–43.

137. Ibid., p. 55.

138. Ibid., p. 56.

139. Ibid., p. 59.

140. Ibid., p. 74.

141. Ibid., p. 75.

142. Ibid., p. 80.

143. Ibid., p. 81.

144. Ibid., p. 85.

145. Ibid., p. 82.

146. Ibid., p. 87.

147. Ibid., pp. 99–100.

148. Ibid., pp. 106–7.

149. Ibid., p. 114.

150. Ibid., pp. 117, 120, 121.

151. Ibid., p. 123.

152. Ibid., p. 127.

153. Ibid., p. 129.

154. Ibid., p. 143. "Goniff," properly spelled *gonif*, a variation of *ganef*, is a Yiddish slang term meaning thief or scoundrel.

155. Ibid., p. 162.

156. Ibid., p. 164.

157. Ibid., pp. 166–67.

158. Ibid., p. 170.

159. Ibid., p. 173.

2

Filmscripts

At around eleven, the period in his life that Perelman regarded as "without question my formative education" when he began reading the popular fiction mentioned so frequently in his own writing, he was also exposed to this second major influence in his artistic development, the movies.[1] These two sources, the novels and the films, were later remembered fondly in the author's "Cloudland Revisited" series discussed previously.

The impact of other writers on Perelman's perceptions, subject matter, and style has already been touched upon. The influence of films on the writer's work is suggested by the fact that when *New York Times Magazine* interviewer Zinsser visited the author in his New York City studio in 1969, he noted that it contained a photograph of silent screen actress Jetta Goudal, who was described as "the great crypto-Eurasian vampire of all times," by Perelman.[2] The humorist went on to explain that he "was also successively in love with Corinne Griffith . . . Priscilla Dean, Aileen Pringle and Nita Naldi."[3] Perelman has categorized himself among the "inveterate movie-goers" of his college days,[4] and the constant references to and similies centering on pictures and Hollywood stars that infiltrate his writings, as well as the scenario format that he sometimes adopted and those essays and stories directly concerned with these subjects, are further evidence of how the writer came to see as though with a camera's eye, perceiving events as if they were unfolding in a movie script.

In the early 1930's something happened that affected Perelman greatly for the rest of his life. Groucho Marx had written the dust jacket blurb for *Dawn Ginsbergh's Revenge* ("From the moment I picked up your book until I laid it down, I was convulsed with laughter. Some day I intend reading it.") and although Perelman was a relative unknown, the Marx Brothers, who "were feverish to get into radio," Perelman recalls, "detailed me and Will B. Johnstone, another comic artist, to contrive a program. We had a conception of them as four stowaways immersed in the hold of a trans-Atlantic liner, and there our invention stopped. They said, 'This isn't our radio show, it's our next movie.' They took us up to Jesse Lasky in the Paramount Building, and three weeks later we were barreling westward on the Chief to write 'Monkey Business.' "[5]

Perelman describes his first meeting with Groucho Marx in more detail in the segment from *The Hindsight Sage* (contained in *The Last Laugh*) entitled "The Marx Brothers." While attending the stage production of *Animal Crackers* in October 1931, Perelman had sent a card backstage expressing his admiration for Groucho's work. Shortly after the second act curtain rose, he received a note requesting that he go backstage after the performance, which he did eagerly:

Once, however, we had exchanged cordialities—a bit awkward for my wife since Groucho was clad only in his shorts—he breezily confessed to an ulterior purpose in his invitation. One of the networks had latterly been entreating the Marxes to appear in a radio series, and he wondered if I could be cozened into writing it. Flattering as I found his esteem, I was frankly overwhelmed.

"I—I wouldn't know how to begin," I faltered. "I've never worked on a radio script."

"Neither has Will Johnstone," admitted Groucho. "He's the fellow we'd like you to collaborate with. . . . I can't imagine two people worse equipped for the job, but there's one thing in your favor. You're both such tyros you might just come up with something fresh."[6]

Johnstone was a staff member of the *New York Evening World* who had a "fund of newspaper stories." A "jovial, exuberant chap in his late fifties, a raconteur,"[7] he had become involved with the Marx Brothers as the author of *I'll Say She Is*, which had been the Marxes' first Broadway success. Apparently he and Perelman got along well, though after a few sessions together they had nothing more concrete than "a misty notion that the Marxes might be characterized as stowaways aboard an ocean liner."[8] According to Hector Arce, Harry Granet supplied a screenplay treatment based on the same idea (*The Seas Are All Wet*) and also a comic sketch called *College Daze* (possibly the forerunner of *Horse Feathers*).[9] Perelman never commented on this allegation.

Perelman and Johnstone met the four brothers at the Astor to talk about the script. While Perelman's writing may be full of commotion, he seems to have needed a semblance of structure about him when he worked, as indicated by his need to keep an office in New York City, and a fairly spartan office at that. The Marx Brothers never sat still, and in retrospect this characteristic may have been more bothersome to Perelman than he was willing to admit at the time. As he describes it, Groucho spoke at length about his stockmarket losses, Chico kept running to the telephone to place bets, and Harpo table-hopped all over the dining room, discommoding any attractive woman who gave him a second glance.[10]

At length Johnstone managed to relay to the brothers the premise that had been worked out. To the authors' surprise, the Marxes responded enthusiastically. "Listen," said Groucho, "You fellows have stumbled on something big. This isn't any fly-by-night radio series—it's our next picture."[11] Within half an hour the brothers, "Pinioning our arms, . . . hustled us across the street into the office of Jesse Lasky, the head of Paramount Pictures. There was a short, confused interval brim-full of references to astronomical sums of money, contracts, and transportation to the Coast, inexplicably for our wives as well. We were to entrain for Hollywood within the week, it was tempestuously agreed, to write the screenplay."[12]

So began an association with Hollywood that Perelman detested. He readily admits that the sole motivation for his connection with Hollywood was money—"and the characters who ran the celluloid factories were willing to lay it on the line." Perelman's financial status was not healthy at the moment. The magazines for which he worked were feeling the effects of the Depression, and officials at his bank "hinted delicately" that perhaps he might "like to transfer to some bank that had facilities for handling smaller accounts. Maybe I didn't need a bank after all . . . merely a mattress or a loose brick in the fireplace."[13] Groucho's invitation was the first step toward solvency; Perelman was to work for over five months on the *Monkey Business* project at a salary of $500 a week. (The price paid for the Pennsylvania farm, $5,000, provides a standard for the buying power of the dollar at the time.) But, Perelman remembers the Hollywood experience as tawdry at best: "After all, it was no worse than playing the piano in a whorehouse." [14] In his 1963 *Paris Review* interview, Perelman expressed his impression of the city and the industry:

a dreary industrial town controlled by hoodlums of enormous wealth, the ethical sense of a pack of jackals, and taste so degraded that it befouled everything it touched. I don't mean to sound like a boy Savonarola, but there were times, when I drove along the Sunset Strip and looked at those buildings, or when I watched the fashionable film colony arriving at some premier at Grauman's Egyptian, that I fully expected God in his wrath to obliterate the whole shebang. It was—if you'll allow me to use a hopeless inexpressive word— *degoutant*.   (p. 252)

Elsewhere Perelman has talked about the hypocrisy that abounds in Hollywood. Perhaps Hollywood is a fitting locale for all types of hypocrisy, since it is in the business of manufacturing images, but Perelman found the disparity between "Hollywood life" and "reality" a constant source of provocation, taking an almost moralistic stand against it. "There is an air of false prosperity out here," he wrote, "that makes news of breadlines and starvation unreal." [15] Furthermore, "The noble piety of the Hollywood folks, as they immersed themselves in the plight of the migratory workers and the like was pretty comical. One couldn't fault them for their social conscience, but when you saw the English country houses they dwelt in, the hundred-thousand-dollar estancias, and the Cadillacs they drove to the protest meetings, it was to laugh." [16] Interestingly, it is from this period throughout the 1930's when he lived intermitantly in such a "hideous and untenable place . . . populated with few exceptions by Yahoos" that Perelman's loss of a sense of innocence and the resultant slightly bitter cynicism in his writing seem to derive.

Perelman's relationship with the Marx Brothers is also an interesting phase in his life, and one that he views ambiguously. On the one hand, Perelman has been quoted as saying "I'm sure that knowing Groucho Marx has meant a great deal," in a context in which he was expressing admiration for Robert Benchley and Dorothy Parker and admitting how important and helpful they were in his career. [17] The first five Marx Brothers films are generally considered their best, and

Perelman scripted two of those, the third (*Monkey Business*, not to be confused with a 1952 Cary Grant movie with the same title) and fourth (*Horse Feathers*). On the other hand, Perelman has expressed a real distaste for his experience with the Marx Brothers on occasion:

As far as temperaments and their personalities were concerned, they were capricious, tricky beyond endurance, and altogether unreliable. They were also megalomaniac to a degree which is impossible to describe. . . . I did two films with them, which in its way is perhaps my greatest distinction in life, because anybody who ever worked on any picture for the Marx Brothers said he would rather be chained to a galley oar and lashed at ten-minute intervals than work for these sons of bitches again.[18]

J. A. Ward's article, "The Hollywood Metaphor: The Marx Brothers, S. J. Perelman, Nathanael West," provides some insight into why the humorist may have reacted so violently to his days in Hollywood and his connection with the Marxes. Ward sees Perelman's highly emotional reaction primarily as a result of a conflict in personalities, with Groucho epitomizing the attitudes represented by those villains that the Perelman persona continually battles. As Ward says, "The Perelman protagonist finds Marx Brothers monkeyshines intolerable— intolerable because irresponsible. . . . Brashness is funny in Perelman, and funny in the Groucho manner, though Perelman's perspective is invariably that of the victim."[19] Given Perelman's severe comments about Michael Todd after working on the script for *Around the World in Eighty Days* twenty-five years later, though, his statements may also reflect a conflict between an artistic sensibility (the writer) and those who have the power to determine the shape of the final product (the Marx Brothers controlled their films as surely as Todd controlled his).

While Perelman and Johnstone worked on the screenplay for *Monkey Business*, the Marx Brothers played the London Palladium. According to Perelman, "when they got back they summoned us for a reading of our script. They came with their lawyers and accountants and masseurs and dentists—23 people, plus Zeppo's Afghans and Chico's schnauzer—and I read for 85 minutes in absolute silence. At the end Chico said, 'Whaddya think, Groucho?' Groucho took the cigar out of his mouth and said 'Stinks!', and they all got up and walked out. So we started again, and in 1932 the picture was done and was a hit.''[20] There are several other versions of the episode in print, and they are all remarkably similar in detailing the unpleasant event. Hector Arce repeats the story in *Groucho*,[21] as do Paul D. Zimmerman and Burt Goldblatt in *The Marx Brothers at the Movies*,[22] both renditions being based on Perelman's comments in *Show* magazine[23]; the most complete description is found in ''The Marx Brothers'':

Six weeks from the day we had begun work we were notified that the deadline was looming. The troupe was back in the country and about to converge on Hollywood, and we were to read the screenplay to them, *viva voce*, the following Friday night at the Roosevelt Hotel. . . . We decided to salt our pages with as many technical movie phrases as we could, many of which we only half understood. We therefore went over the action line by line, panning, irising down, and dissolving, painstakingly sandwiched in Jackman and Dunning shots, and even, at one point, specified that the camera should vorkapich around the faces of the ballroom guests. Neither of us, of course, had the remotest notion of what this last meant, and it was years before I discovered that it derived from a special-effects genius named Slavko Vorkapich. . . . The onus of reading aloud a 126-page script weighed heavily on both of us, so we flipped a coin and I, to my despair, was elected. Half an hour passed without any sign of the quartet, during which I twice urged my colleague to abandon the whole enterprise and leave by the fire escape, but his dentures were chattering so loudly that he did not hear me. . . . The first auditors arrived—Papa Marx, the progenitor of the band, accompanied by a fellow pinochle player. Our whiplash, Mankiewicz, turned up next, in company with his brother Joseph, then a rising screenwriter at Paramount. They were followed by Zeppo and his wife, who brought along a stately brace of Afghans they had purchased in England. The dogs had eaten the upholstery of a Packard convertible that afternoon and were somewhat subdued in consequence, but they looked intimidating, and they took up a position near my feet that boded ill. Harpo now strolled in with a couple of blond civilians he had dined with, and close on his heels the Chico Marxes, leading a scrappy wirehaired terrier which immediately tangled with the Afghans. In the midst of the tohubohu, Groucho and his wife entered; I supposed that thirteen constituted a quorum and made as if to start, but was told to desist—other guests were due. These, it proved, were three gagmen the Marxes had picked up in transit, each of whom was to furnish japes tailored to their respective personalities. Behind the gagmen came *their* wives, sweethearts, and an unidentifiable rabble I took to be relatives, and last of all several cold-eyed vultures obviously dispatched by the studio. When I counted noses and paws before ringing up the curtain, there were twenty-seven people and five dogs confronting me. . . . I could not have experienced worse panic as I stammered forth the setting of our opus. Destiny, whatever its intentions, had never supplied me with forensic gifts. . . . The incredible folly of my position, the temerity of a virgin scenarist hoping to beguile a hardened professional audience, suddenly overtook me. I became faint, and the roar of a mighty cataract like the Zambesi Falls sounded in my ears. Striken, I turned to Johnstone for succor, but cataleptic fear had seized him too; his face, the color of an eggplant, was contorted in a ghastly, fixed smile like Bartholomew Sholto's in *The Sign of the Four*, and I thought for one horrid moment he was defunct.

I had not proceeded very far before I began to sense a distinct change in the mood of my listeners. At first it was pliant—indulgent, so to speak—and there was an occasional polite ripple. This soon ceased and they became watchful—not hostile as yet, but wary. It was as if they were girding themselves, flexing for trouble they knew was inevitable. Then, by slow degrees, an attitude of sullen resentment stole into their faces. They had been betrayed, lured away from the klabiatsch and easy chairs by a will-o'-the-wisp promise of entertainment, and they grew vengeful. *Some* of them got vengeful, that is; the majority got sleepy, for by then I had stopped inflecting my voice to distinguish one character from another and had settled into a monotonous lilt like a Hindu chanting the Bhagavad Gita. I spared them nothing—the individual shots, the technical jargon, our colorful descriptions of sets and characters. At times my voice faded away altogether and I whispered endless pages of dialogue to the unheeding air. All the while, Johnstone sat with his eyes fixed alternately on his palms and the ceiling, patently trying to dissociate himself from me. Not once did he or anyone else bid me take respite or a glass of water. The whole room—exclusive of those who were asleep, naturally—was watching a man hang himself with a typewriter ribbon, and not a finger was lifted to save him. When I finally cracked "Fade Out" at the end of my ninety-minute unspectacular, there was no sound except the stentorous breathing of the dogs.

   After an aeon, Chico stretched, revolved in his chair, and addressed Groucho. "What do you think?" he growled.

   With the deliberation of a diamond cutter, Groucho bit the end off his cigar, and applying a match, exhaled a jet of smoke. "It stinks," he said, and arose. "Come on." As he stalked toward the door, he was engulfed in a wedge of sycophants hissing agreement and post-mortems.[24]

The three gagmen who were present have been identified as Arthur Sheekman, Nat Perrin, and Solly Violinsky.[25] Apparently at the time it was common practice for young men right out of college, often Ivy-leaguers, to submit ideas to well-known comics or studios and then be hired to assist in this manner. Perelman himself, of course, was still in his late twenties. In an interview with Richard J. Anobile, Perrin sympathetically corroborates Perelman's account:

Now, any reading, especially of a comedy script, is a pretty traumatic experience. It is difficult, even with a good script, to get a good impression from a reading like that. . . . Comedy is one form of writing that needs absolute continuity. Perelman read the script. He's a rather high-strung man and he's a stutterer. If he wasn't a stutterer, then he was a bad reader. I don't think it would have helped too much if he was a good reader. After a few pages a listlessness spread throughout the room. Then there was some dog annoying everybody. . . . Altogether, I think it was one of the most dismal and embarrassing evenings I've ever spent.

I doubt that the script was anywhere near as bad as the general impression of it from that reading. The Marx Bros. were a tough audience. They weren't given to listening. Especially Groucho, who was more accustomed to talking. It was asking an awful lot of them to sit there and listen for two hours.

How did Perelman react to this?

I think he was relieved when the reading was over. No matter what the reception was, he was just glad to get the hell out of there! And, of course, he realized that it was only a first draft, a general idea. I don't think Perelman and Johnstone would have written a treatment. . . . probably there was a lot more in that script that was salvageable than was apparent from the reading. But I don't think anyone went back to that script. It was about prohibition and bootleggers. Just the basic premise was used for the final picture.[26]

Amusingly, in light of this horrifying event, Andrew Sarris claims that "The limiting factor of the Marx Brothers is their failure to achieve the degree of production control held by Chaplin . . . Keaton and Lloyd."[27] If left to their devices, Sarris implies, the Marx Brothers might have done better: "The Marx Brothers often had to sit by in compliant neutrality while the most inane plot conventions were being developed." Sarris's word choice is deliciously ironic, given that first reading. He goes on to single out *Monkey Business* in particular because it "suffers from a studio-grafted gangster intrigue in mock imitation of the gangster films of the time." The incomparable Margaret Dumont has added about the brothers, "They never laughed during a story conference. Like most expert comedians, they involved themselves so seriously in the study of how jokes could be converted to their own style that they didn't even titter while appraising their material."

In any event, the Perelman/Groucho "feud" appears to stem from this incident. Over the years the two men said some harsh things about one another, to the point that Perelman refused to discuss the subject with Cole and Plimpton, insisting, "I've dealt exhaustively with this particular phase of my life."[28] Some of his comments have been touched on in passing during discussions of various prose articles in the last chapter.

Although Groucho, too, became more reticent in his later years, there were times when he lashed out at Perelman savagely. He harped primarily on two themes: one, that Perelman could not write for the "barber in Peru," and two, that the writer was proud, aloof, and arrogant, pretending that scripting for the Marxes was below him, but quick to take all of the credit once the films became hits.

When Groucho spoke about Peru, he meant Peru, Indiana, signifying that Perelman's writing was inaccessible to the masses. Perelman recalls, " 'What'll this mean to the barber in Peru?' [Groucho] was wont to complain whenever he came across a paticularly fanciful reference. The barber, in his mind, was a prototypical figure . . . a Midwestern square . . . whose funny bone the Marxes sought to tickle."[29] According to the author's analysis, "I knew that he liked my work for the printed page, my preoccupation with clichés, baroque language, and the elegant variation. Nevertheless, I sensed as time went on that this aspect of my work disturbed him; he felt that some of the dialogue I wrote for him was 'too literary.' He feared that many of my allusions would be incomprehensible to the ordinary moviegoer, whom he regarded as a wholly cretinous specimen."[30] It is interesting to note that on paper Perelman and Marx dealt with the same subjects in very similar styles. *Groucho and Me*, for instance, is filled with an amazing number of literary allusions, many of them from the same sources that appear in Perelman's writing.

When Groucho wanted to be nasty, though, he was nasty with gusto. Anobile recorded the following in an interview with Marx:

At first [Perelman] claimed that he practically had nothing to do with [*Monkey Business*] and then when he saw that the Marx Bros. were successful he went around saying that he wrote the whole thing. But there were other writers involved, like Will Johnstone and Arthur Sheekman. Herman Mankiewicz was involved, too. . . . But Perelman wasn't a nice man. He was a very funny writer for the *New Yorker Magazine* but I don't see much of his stuff in there now.   (p. 147)

Later the interviewer (in italics) again talked with Groucho about the relationship:

He wasn't very good for those films. He was a funny writer and could write great stuff for *The New Yorker Magazine* but not for our pictures.

I saw MONKEY BUSINESS recently and there is no doubt that Perelman left an indelible stamp on that film. A lot of the puns are pure Perelman. It was quite a funny film.

I didn't say he didn't work on it, only that there were other writers working on the film. . . .

You mentioned that you occasionally worked with the writers. Did you work with Perelman at all on the script of MONKEY BUSINESS?

Very little, very little. In the first place I hated the son of a bitch and he had a head as big as my desk.

But don't you feel that Perelman made a significant contribution to the films?

I'm sure he did, but so did the other writers.

I've spoken to Perelman. He seems very bitter about the fact that most people overlook everything he has done, with the exception of the Marx Bros. films. He won't talk with me because he is "bored to tears with the Marx Bros." Yet he is probably one of the greatest humorists in America.

Is that so? Does that include Benchley and fellows like that? He wrote one play with Ogden Nash and it was a flop.

Did you ever have any disagreements with Perelman over the material in the films?

I don't remember. Whatever I thought was good we kept in and whatever I thought was lousy we took out. . . .

I can't believe that you hated Perelman way back when he was doing those scripts for you. Weren't you friends with him in New York?

Yeah. . . . He was condescending to me and the other writers.

He read the script to a room full of people and before he knew it he found himself working with other writers. Do you feel that the other writers may not have been up to Perelman's ability?

Perhaps, but just because you're better you don't have to be a son of a bitch.

I'm sorry I keep harping on this but there's something wrong here. You admit that you were good friends with the man in New York. You thought highly of his work. He became a writer for two of your films, yet you insist that at the same time you hated the man. I get the feeling that something that happened later has clouded your recollection about the man during this early period.

He was not a playwright. He could write a funny line.

He must have written many funny lines for MONKEY BUSINESS.

I don't know, I'd have to see the film again to identify his stuff.

Well, I'll arrange a screening. It seems strange that all these people who couldn't work with Perelman ended up working with him again on HORSE FEATHERS.
Well, I didn't hate him. I didn't hate him until much later and I still hate him!. . . .

I liked him originally when he was writing pieces for *The New Yorker*. I've read all his books, so I must have liked him. But I don't think he was a good writer when it came to the movies. I thought he was one of the best humorists in America, along with Benchley and Thurber.   (p. 173)

Clearly there was a deterioration in the relationship between Perelman and Marx to the point that it finally became absurd. Groucho reminisces in still another conversation with Anobile:

As for Perelman I will admit that I had a great admiration for the man and for his talent. But then things changed.
Did you ever find him condescending towards you?
No, I was a big star. We once did a show together in London. It was a talk show moderated by the best critic in London [Kenneth Tynan]. . . . He thought it would be great, having both me and Perelman on his show. It ended up being the dullest fucking interview there ever was. Perelman was trying to outdo me and we both stunk.   (p. 202)

Even Perelman has found the whole sequence of events a bit bewildering. In "The Marx Brothers" he relates, "My own relationship with Groucho was, in a sense, a baffling one. I loved his lightning transition of thought, his ability to detect pretentiousness and bombast, and his genius for disemboweling the spurious and hackneyed phrases that litter one's conversation."[31] And, in "I'll Always Call You Schnorrer, My African Explorer," he reports receiving a long-distance call from Groucho in Hollywood inviting him out to the Coast to watch the filming of *A Girl in Every Port*, a movie released twenty-one years after *Monkey Business*. Perelman was happy to go.

Having found the constant commotion, anarchy, selfishness, and power of the Marx Brothers unsettling, Perelman stayed away from them for a while, and over a period of time he probably began to feel that he had been abused. This feeling begins to show up in his writing, and, as is often the case, once it is in writing it may seem more of a strident, personal attack than it was meant to be. Nat Perrin came close to the truth of the matter in his interview with Anobile when he was asked whether he detected any sign of bitterness on Perelman's part when other writers were hired to work on the *Monkey Business* script:

My impression was that he didn't seem at all bitter. His attitude seemed to be, "Well, okay, we took a flyer at it and now others are brought in." He was quite willing to work on the script and seemed to take it all in stride.

Groucho does feel strongly about Perelman and I can understand this. It seems to be due mainly to one or two articles written by Perelman. I think these articles may have clouded Groucho's vision on the subject of MONKEY BUSINESS. I do remember that the revisions on MONKEY BUSINESS started from page one and in the end Perelman had made his contribution and it is possible that that contribution is more than Groucho may give him credit for. Groucho was not in the room when Sheekman and Perelman were rewriting that script so he could scarcely isolate each man's contribution. . . .
What did he write that may have angered Groucho?
I can't remember exactly what Perelman wrote but it was most unflattering in, as I recall now, a more or less personal way. I was shocked when I read it because I had always felt there was a very warm personal feeling between them. . . . I had mentioned it to Groucho and had no idea how hurt, angry and bitter he was about it. I felt indignant about the article myself.

(pp. 213–14)

Despite these varied incidents, Marx, like Perelman, ultimately stated that things were never as bad as they had been made out to be. In *The Groucho Phile* he points out that in the late 1930's he belonged to a group in Hollywood that regularly met at Lyman's, across the street from the Hollywood Brown Derby and called itself the West Side Riding and Asthma Club; the title of the club was supplied by Perelman. Other members of the group included Robert Benchley, Donald Ogden Stewart, Charles Butterworth, Charles MacArthur, Ben Hecht—and Perelman. Finally, Groucho published a statement designed to put things in their proper perspective: "In recent years the press has concocted a feud between S. J. Perelman and me, but no such feud ever existed. Sid has often been asked about writing for the Marx Brothers, and I have often answered questions about his contributions to our films. What Sid and I both agree on is that he is a great writer with a brilliant comic mind that did not always mesh well with the lunacies of the Marx Brothers."[32]

It may be, then, as the Marx Brothers were rediscovered in the

1970's, when sufficient time had passed to make them not just entertainers but classics, that Perelman drew some writers' interest because of his previous association with the brothers, and attention was focused on what he considered a fairly minor part of his career to the exclusion of the rest of his writing. This circumstance would have produced some rather waspish retorts after a time, and given reporters something to seize upon and exaggerate. Two items from *Groucho and Me* support this contention. In one place Groucho includes Perelman in a select group of writers of wit, George S. Kaufman, Mark Twain, and G. B. Shaw being the other three of the quartet named.[33] This is high flattery. Equally high acclaim is expressed in the book's dedication:

> For What It's Worth
> This Book Is Gratefully
> Dedicated
> To These Six Masters
> Without Whose Wise and Witty Words
> My Life Would Have Been Even Duller;
> Robert Benchley
> George S. Kaufman
> Ring Lardner
> S. J. Perelman
> James Thurber
> E. B. White

Returning to Perelman's involvement with *Monkey Business*, it should be pointed out that it is difficult, if not impossible, to assess the exact contribution of a screenwriter to the finished cut of a film. The director especially, and to some extent the editor (not named in the credits in this case), cinematographer (Arthur L. Todd), and actors are all involved in shaping the product. With this seventy-seven minute Marx Brothers film the difficulty of determining who was responsible for what is compounded by the fact that some of what appears on film started out simply as a premise, and the brothers improvised while the cameras were turning. Furthermore, Arthur Sheekman is credited with writing "Additional Dialogue" for the picture. Sheekman tells an amusing story that gives some idea of what working with Perelman might have been like:

I was collaborating with S. J. Perelman on MONKEY BUSINESS. We had a difference of opinion on a line.

He said, "If you repeat that, I'll throw you out the window," whereupon, somewhat theatrically, I'll admit, I rose from my chair and walked to the window.

"I thought I'd make it easier for you."

This bit of youthful bravado was not a demonstration of courage. I knew for a fact that Perelman had never thrown anyone out of a window and I was reasonably certain that I was not going to be the first.

Besides, the window was on the first floor.[34]

Others who worked on the picture, as mentioned before, were Violinsky, who was paid handsomely for contributing one line to the film, and Perrin. Violinsky and Perrin arrived after Perelman had begun the script, and they stayed for about ten weeks, until about the time that shooting on the movie started. Perrin, at $1,500 a week (three times Perelman's reported salary), admits that he "was just a gag man" who "got a crack at doing some of the little scenes."[35] The movie also contains an in-joke. In one scene a girl says to Groucho, "Ever since I have been married to this man I have lived a dog's life," and Groucho responds, "Maybe he got a dog license instead of a marriage license." Arce points out that this line was originally spoken by Al Shean in his act years earlier.[36] Besides being an entertainer, Shean was also the Marx Brothers' uncle. Perelman's main co-worker, though, was Johnstone, about whom he talks in "The Marx Brothers." "An undisguised foe of Prohibition," Johnstone amazed Perelman with his ability to work while under the influence of applejack.

Perelman and his wife disliked Hollywood from the beginning. "I have been downcast in Piccadilly," the author confesses, "chopfallen on the Champs Elysees, and *doloroso* on the Via Veneto, but the avenues themselves were blameless. Hollywood Boulevard, on the contrary, creates an instant and malign impression in the breast of the beholder. Viewed in full sunlight, its tawdriness is unspeakable; in the torrential downpour of the rainy season, as we first saw it, it inspired an anguish similar to that produced by the engravings of Piranesi."[37] "Do we really need the money this much?" his wife asked.[38]

The Perelmans settled into "a modest duplex in a bungalow court" amidst garish furnishings and a hodgepodge of stereotypical Los Angelenos. At the studio Perelman and Johnstone worked in an office in "a ramshackle warren of tan stucco that housed thirty or forty other scribes''[39] under the supervision of Herman Mankiewicz, a hard-drinking gambler who was to produce the picture and about whom Groucho speaks very disparagingly in *Groucho and Me*.[40]

One of the collaborators' first experiences at the studio was when they were called into Lasky's office and told that the Marx Brothers had cabled from London demanding that they be fired—even though the Marxes had not seen a bit of their work yet. The writers were assured that this type of action by the actors was to be expected and by and large to be taken with a grain of salt. In spite of these inauspicious beginnings, Perelman and Johnstone managed to create a creditable filmscript.

Monkey Business (Paramount) was the first Marx Brothers film that was not an adaptation of a stage play. It premiered at the Rivoli in New York City at 10:30 on the morning of September 19, 1931. Besides Groucho, Harpo, Chico, and Zeppo, the movie, directed by Norman Z. McLeod, featured Thelma Todd (as Mrs. Alkie Briggs), Ruth Hall (Mary), Tom Kennedy (Gibson), Rockeliffe Fellowes (Big Joe Helton), Harry Woods (Alkie Briggs), Ben Taggart (The Captain), Otto Fries (Second Mate), Evelyn Pierce (Manicurist), and Maxine Castle (Opera Singer). Frank Tuttle was originally scheduled to direct the picture, but script revisions brought delays and McLeod was given the assignment, his first as a solo director (he had previously co-directed the undistinguished *Finn and Hattie*). Todd was seen as a possible replacement for Margaret Dumont, who had played Groucho's foil on stage and in previous films.

Most of the action has to do with the hijinks of the four brothers on the ship. Their discovery as stowaways living in barrels in the hold leads to a sequence of chase scenes, but soon they are no longer pursued (no reason is ever given for this), and they become embroiled in a second plot. Big Joe Helton is taking his daughter, Mary, back to the States for a party. Helton, a former gang boss who has been in prison, is sought out by Alkie Briggs, a new gang leader who wants Helton's approval so that there will be a consolidation of the mobs. Helton will have nothing to do with Briggs or his threats. Briggs forces Groucho and Zeppo to join him so, naturally and purely by accident, Chico and Harpo are enlisted by Big Joe as body guards. Soon the Marxes are faced with another dilemma: how to get off the ship without passports (it is never explained how they got this far without them). Zeppo manages to acquire the passport of another traveller, French singer-actor Maurice Chevalier, and the four brothers take turns trying to impersonate Chevalier by singing his "nightingale" song. Once on land the four attend Mary's party where Alkie appears and kidnaps the heroine. A free-for-all in a bar ensues as the brothers save Mary from Briggs' evil clutches, and Mary and Zeppo are united.

Zimmerman and Goldblatt claim that "The whole of *Monkey Business* could be played, with slight alterations, on the stage." But, the significance of this statement may have been overlooked by these critics for these alterations are all-important; they are what distinguish the film from a play. "The film contains scenes in which close-up and chase are part of comedy. Settings switch quickly. . . . The characters no longer declaim to some phantom audience beyond an invisible proscenium arch. Their gestures are less baroque, knowing that the camera is sensitive to smaller responses. On balance, *Monkey Business* is conceived of and executed as a moving picture in the literal sense of the word. The camera can no longer sit on its hindquarters and absorb the action; it must chase madly after the Marxes."[41]

Reviewers enjoyed the movie. Sid, the writer for *Variety* (October 13, 1931), calls it "the usual Marx madhouse with plenty of laughs,"[42] though Harry Evans of the original *Life* laughs at Paramount for paying $5,000 for the dog-license joke.[43] The *New York Times* reviewer, Mourdaunt Hall, finds that the picture "can stir up boisterous laughter," applauds Perelman and Johnstone for their writing, discusses the "mirthful incidents" in the film, and is surprised that "The most atrocious puns pop up from all sides and somehow or other they have the desired effect."[44] Ten years later, Winston Churchill wrote in his memoirs, "news arrived of the air raid on London [the heaviest of the war to that date, involving 1,200 German bombers]. There was nothing that I could do about it so I watched the Marx Brothers in a comic film [*Monkey Business*]. . . . I went out twice to inquire about the air raid and heard it was bad. The merry film clacked on, and I was glad of the diversion."[45]

Still, there is nothing very exciting cinematically about *Monkey Business*. The titles are run over a series of rolling barrels and the first shot is an establishing shot of an ocean liner at sea. Everything is pretty traditional and unimaginative. Most of the shots are medium shots, with very few two shots or close-ups, the camera seldom shoots from anything other than a static position and a straight-on angle (even in the chase scenes movement generally is achieved with cuts rather than with tracking or pan shots), transitions are abrupt (no wipes or dissolves), there are few special effects and even lighting and sound receive no special attention. By and large, the Marx Brothers strut their stuff and the camera merely records the action. Parenthetically, although the filmscript for *Monkey Business* has been published, a note to that edition points out that "no original scripts were available," and that "the versions presented . . . were built up from a dialogue continuity provided by Universal City Studios Inc., amplified with material gained from a shot-by-shot viewing of each film." [46] A comparison of the page from the original script included in *The Marx Bros. Scrapbook* (p. 163) with the same scene in this edition (pp. 8–9) shows that they are not exact duplicates. To be as accurate as possible, I have relied on my own shot-by-shot examination of the film rather than the published version of the screenplay, and thus all quotations are taken from the film itself.

Typical Marx Brothers business runs throughout the movie. Groucho leers and tangos on a bed; Harpo never talks except with his taxi horn, he chases blondes, puts his leg in someone's hand, and plays a harp solo; Chico plays the piano with his index finger pointed like a gun and misuses language. There are constant sight gags: Harpo stands in front of a sign on a restroom, covering up the W and O in WOMEN, with the expected brouhaha resulting; Groucho walks in a crouch; Harpo pursues one girl down the stairs and another one up; when his brothers are chased around the salon, Harpo waits until they have run a circle before he jumps in (looking forward to the marvelous mirror scene in *Duck Soup*); there is a Punch and Judy show and Harpo's mask; a woman gets out of a desk chair and Harpo is revealed lying beneath her—though there is a double reversal when he gets up and another man has been lying beneath both of them; Harpo and Chico give the mate a shave, cutting first one side of his mustache ("a little snoop") and then the other while trying to get the sides even until they remove the entire mustache.

What is most likely to be Perelman's handiwork, though, are the comic lines of dialogue and puns that often follow one another so fast that it is hard to keep up with them—the timing is a major source of the humor. Sometimes the lines grow out of one another, sometimes they are unrelated by logic. This is the kind of thing that Perelman does well, working with short humorous bits that require no real development, and the Marx Brothers are perfectly suited to delivering the madcap dialogue. Examples abound. For instance, Groucho asks the ship's captain who sneaked into his stateroom at three in the morning—which is quickly turned into a complaint because no one did. The captain threatens to have the stowaways put in irons, and Groucho replies that he "can't. It's a mashie shot [playing on the word irons and putting it into an entirely different context, golf]. It's a mashie shot if the wind is against you and if it isn't, I am," again turning the meaning around. Groucho is also interested in a situation where there are "more women than you can shake a stick at—if that's your idea of a good time." His dealings with women are never successful, though always full of hope and innuendo, much like the Perelman narrator. As Groucho says, "Love flies out the door when money comes innuendo." He also claims that his lawyer is shy—a shyster. Lusting after Thelma Todd, he pleads, "I wish you'd keep my hands to yourself," and later, at the party, he invites her to pass out on the veranda with him or to "lodge with my fleas in the hills." To prove his intentions, he grabs her and declaims, "I've known and respected your husband Alkie for many years, and what's good enough for him is good enough for me."

This dialogue is similar enough to lines in Perelman's prose pieces that it can be assumed that he was the author. When he collaborated with Ogden Nash on the Broadway plays *One Touch of Venus* and *The Beauty Part*, authorship was harder to guess at, in part because there was much less of this kind of dialogue. Too, it has been claimed that Marx Brothers' humor is more appreciated by men than women, whether because of the sex roles displayed or the disruption of logic is unclear, and Perelman's humor frequently exploits these same characteristics whereas Nash's humor develops from a more conventional base.

One element that transcends all three, Perelman, the Marxes, and Nash, is the pun. Most of the intellectual puns are delivered by Groucho; most of the others come from Chico. One, combining sight gags and the concept of literality, comes when Chico measures the officer's rapidly disappearing mustache in the shipboard barbershop scene and declares that the right side is still a foot too long; Harpo pulls out a hatchet and offers to chop off the officer's foot. There is also an abundance of sound puns: Groucho mentions that Columbus was looking for a shortcut, Chico claims that he likes "strawberry shortcut"; Groucho talks about a sailing vessel, Chico says, "Sure, I can vessel," and whistles a tune to prove it; when Groucho talks about mutiny, Chico sets him straight—''No mutinies at night,'' only on Saturday and Sunday afternoons; when the bad guys have been corralled in the barn, Chico observes that ''it's better to have loft and lost.'' Incidentally, Groucho's pretended radio broadcast of the big showdown fight in the barn is reminiscent of the running narration describing the combat in ''The Idol's Eye.''

Released the year after *Monkey Business*, Perelman's second Marx Brothers script was *Horse Feathers* (Paramount). The sixty-eight minute long feature opened at New York City's Rialto on August 19, 1932. Again directed by Norman McLeod and starring the four brothers and Thelma Todd, along with David Landau (Jennings), Robert Craig (The Biology Professor), James Pierce (Retiring President of Huxley College), Nat Pendleton (Mac Hardis), Florine McKinney (Peggy), E. J. Le Saint, and E. H. Calvert, this film is in much the same vein as its predecessor, but it is cinematically more interesting. Bert Kalmar and Harry Ruby, who had written the songs for the Marx's *Animal Crackers*, were signed to work on the filmscript with Perelman. Other names also associated with the writing were Sheekman, George Marion, Jr., and Harry Sweet. Ray June was director of photography.

One of the crew who was a holdover from *Monkey Business* was the producer, Mankiewicz, about whom Groucho speaks as disparagingly in *The Groucho Phile*, and *The Marx Bros. Scrapbook* as he does in *Groucho and Me*.[47] Mankiewicz had collaborated with Orson Welles on *Citizen Kane* (it has been said that he actually wrote most of the script) and was known as a witty writer, but Groucho felt that the man was no longer reasonable, and he explicitly pictures the producer as spending most of his time drinking, womanizing, playing cards with B. P. Schulberg (Paramount's general manager), and generally terrorizing the three innocent young writers recently imported from the East. According to Groucho, an ordinary meeting between Mankiewicz and the writers began when the producer awakened from his afternoon nap:

Around four he would wake up and bellow for his three timid writers who had been sitting in the outer office for hours, apprehensively awaiting for his summons. . . . He would then reluctantly read whatever dialogue the writers had sweated out that morning. After he read the scenes he would shake his head, look at the three writers pityingly and resume shaking his head. Then there would be ten minutes of ominous silence followed by ten minutes of shouting and pounding on the desk with both hands. When he had all the objects on the desk dancing up and down in unison he would cry, ''It stinks! It stinks!'' Then he would put his head in his hands and just sit there quietly glaring.[48]

To be fair, Perrin has stated that he never found Mankiewicz drunk or a desk thumper,[49] and there was bad blood between the producer and the Marxes from the beginning. When Perelman and Johnstone arrived in California to script the first picture, Mankiewicz issued a caveat: the Marxes are ''mercurical, devious and ungrateful. I hate to depress you, but you'll rue the day you ever took the assignment. This is an ordeal by fire. Make sure you wear asbestos pants.''[50] It may be that both Groucho and Mankiewicz were right. At any rate, Perelman's reminiscences approximate Groucho's. In ''The Marx Brothers'' he writes about this ''awesome figure'':

Mankiewicz, [a] stormy Teutonic character [with an] immoderate zest for the grape and gambling . . . was a brilliant man, but if he had any loveable qualities, he did his best to conceal them. He had a tongue like a rasp, and his savage wit demolished anyone unlucky enough to incur his displeasure.

On a very hot midday in July . . . Mankiewicz betook himself to a celebrated restaurant in Hollywood . . . where he treated his palate to two whiskey sours and a Gargantuan lunch consisting of lentil soup with frankfurters, rinderbrust with spaetzle, red cabbage and roast potatoes, and noodle pudding, irrigating the mixture with three or four flagons of Pilsener. Then, eyeballs protruding, he lumbered painfully to his car and drove to his office at Paramount. Thrusting aside the handful of messages his secretary extended, he enjoinèd her not to admit any callers . . . and sank into a blissful snooze.

Barely ten minutes later, he was awakened by a timid, repeated knocking at the door. Mankiewicz's face, mottled with perspiration and mounting fury, swelled like a sunfish as he sat up, prepared to decapitate whoever had flouted his express orders.

''Who the hell is it?'' he shouted. ''Come in, damn you!''

Two pale-faced young men, twitching with fright, entered haltingly. They were Arthur Sheekman, and myself. . . .

''I—I'm sorry to intrude,'' I began, ''but the fact is—the truth of the matter—''

''What the devil do you want?'' Mankiewicz barked. ''Get the marbles out of your mouth!''

''Well, it's like this,'' I squeaked, moistening my lips. ''In this sequence we're working on, we're kind of perplexed about the identity of the Marx

Brothers—the psychology of the characters they're supposed to represent, so to speak. I mean, who are they? We—we wondered if you could analyze or define them for us.''

"Oh, you did, did you?" he grated. "O.K., I'll tell you in a word. One of them is a guinea, another a mute who picks up spit, and the third an old Hebe with a cigar. Is that clear, Beaumont and Fletcher?''   (pp. 158–60)

As with *Monkey Business*, the plot is fairly insignificant. Groucho (Professor Quincy Adams Wagstaff) is the new president of Huxley College, where his son (Zeppo) is in attendance. The exposition reveals that Zeppo has been paying too much attention to the college widow Connie Bailey (Todd), the college has not had a winning football team since the 1880's, and the time is Prohibition. Groucho hires Barovelli (Chico), the local ice man/liquor delivery man, and Pinky (Harpo), the dogcatcher, to play football on the basis that, since he finds them in a speakeasy, they must be football players. A gambler who is connected with the widow Bailey hires two thugs to play for the competing college (what else but Darwin?). The second half of the movie is basically action as there are attempts to steal the teams' signals, a kidnaping goes astray, and the football game is played (filmed at Occidental College) with our heroes emerging triumphant in an unconventional way.

The Marx Brothers were never interested in fourth-wall realism, and the only time that Perelman uses the technique is when he wants to establish a mood that he is about to destroy with a satirical attack. Consequently, when the outgoing president of the college delivers his farewell address in a somber attitude before his staid, gowned faculty, it is no surprise when Groucho is discovered shaving on stage while waiting to be introduced and that he leads the faculty in a dance and the students in a song—"Whatever It Is, I'm Against It." Verbal nonsense is immediately introduced when Groucho says to the former president, "Why don't you go home to your wife? I'll tell you what, I'll go home to your wife, and outside of the improvement she'll never notice the difference." Zeppo, who sings "Everyone Says I Love You," a song sung or played by each of the brothers at various times, is castigated by his father for having spent twelve years in one college— Groucho went to three colleges in twelve years and dallied with three widows! Word play is always present, too, of course. Groucho shouts, "I'd horsewhip you, if I had a horse." After asking a young woman in the student body to get off Zeppo's lap so that he "can see the sun rise," he confides, "I married your mother because I wanted children. Imagine my disappointment when you arrived."

The famous password sequence at the speakeasy is almost completely made up of puns. Chico is the doorman who will not let anyone in who does not say the password, swordfish. He gives Groucho a hint that the word is the name of a fish, eliciting the following exchange:

Groucho: Is it Mary?

Chico: Ats'a no fish!

Groucho: She isn't? Well, she drinks like one.

The scene continues with dispositions on haddock (headache, aspirin, chocolate caramel) and sturgeon ("That's a doctor cuts you open whena you sick").

Other examples of the ubiquitous word play and punning, mostly delivered by Groucho, are when he notes that he always likes to date two girls because he hates "to see one walk home alone" and when he is accused of being full of whimsy, to which he retorts, "I always get that way after I eat." He also advises, "You're heading for a breakdown. Why don't you pull yourself to pieces?" The most quoted exchange in the film comes when Groucho's secretary informs him that the dean has been waiting to see him:

Secretary: The dean is furious! He's waxing wroth!

Groucho: Is Wroth out there too? Tell Wroth to wax the dean for a while.

Chico and Harpo are involved, too, though on a more visual level, as in the pick-pig-hog-hug progression during the kidnaping segment. The visual and verbal come together elsewhere, as well. During Groucho's lecture to an anatomy class, Harpo switches charts, pictures of a horse and a calendar pinup girl replacing a representation of the human anatomy. Groucho is unperturbed. "We now find ourselves among the Alps," he continues, "The Alps are a very simple people, living on rice and old shoes." He concludes by offering the advice that "The Lord alps those who alp themselves," a line taken directly from Johnstone's *I'll Say She Is*. Before the scene degenerates in a peashooter fusillade, Groucho warns Harpo that he can not burn a candle at both ends only to see Harpo produce a candle burning at both ends. "Just for that you stay after school," Groucho commands an attractive coed. "But professor, I didn't do anything," she protests. Groucho leers— "I know, but there's no fun keeping him after school." And, when Groucho yells "where's the seal" for stamping a contract, everyone knows that Harpo will produce an animal.

Sight gags abound. When Harpo is asked to cut the cards, he does so, with a hatchet. When he eats lunch, he unzips his banana, and when a policeman writes him a ticket, he writes the cop a ticket. When the officer threatens him saying, "See this badge," Harpo opens his coat to display dozens of badges. Later, when Groucho is paddled around a lake in a canoe by Connie (despite his trepidation after having read Theodore Dreiser's *An American Tragedy*), a tussle occurs that terminates with the widow in the water, calling for a lifesaver. Groucho throws her a piece of candy.

The critics are less lavish with their praise for *Horse Feathers* than they were with the previous film. Groucho feels that the reason for this may be that the audience had become used to the Marx Brothers' brand of humor, and he offers a review by *Variety*'s Abel as evidence, since Abel refers to the scenes with Todd as "getting to be a trade-marked comedy routine."[51] In his *New York Times* review Mourdant Hall speaks of "originality and ready wit," but he does not mention the screenwriters.[52] Zimmerman and Goldblatt call the film a satire on American education. Incidentally, this is a topic that Perelman had dealt with before and felt at home with, and perhaps some of the picture's strength is derived from these facts. Zimmerman and Gold-blatt go on to compare the movie with the first vaudeville act that the Marx Brothers had performed some fifteen years previously, "Fun in Hi-Skule," and they find this project "more sophisticated, elaborate and finely edged" than the earlier routine.[53] They see *Horse Feathers* as a "cinematic advance" for the brothers because of the "more spa-cious" settings and the occasional move out doors, as well as the use of music that "serves as a lyrical leitmotive . . . much in the same fashion as the melodies of the early Rene Clair movies."[54] Recognition that someone was doing something right came in the form of a photograph of the four brothers in the trash can chariot that appeared on the August 15, 1932, cover of *Time* magazine.

Part of the reason that *Horse Feathers* is a better picture than *Mon-*

key Business is that, loose as the plot line is, it is tighter than that of the previous movie. There is more unity of action—"Everyone Says I Love You" works as a unifying device, for example, when there is a segue from Chico playing the piano and singing the song to a shot of Harpo sitting on a curb and whistling the same piece to his horse. There were no transitions like this in the earlier film. The means of accomplishing the cut itself is another example of a more cinematic approach to the material for instead of a jump cut there is a wipe that permits the music to overlap the two scenes. The use of more two shots and close-ups makes the action more immediate, and the fades make transitions less abrupt. Another device employed effectively is an expressed awareness of the audience; several times Groucho turns and addresses the camera directly in an aside. Further, although not as funny as the verbal element, action is utilized to a large degree to carry both plot and humor, which is appropriate since film is a medium of action, not words. Action alone is used in the football game and the farcical comings and goings in the widow's front room are embellished by the dialogue ("This must be the main highway"; "Follow me—I've been doing this all day"; "a hotdog stand would do alright here"), but it is the action that makes the words funny, not the other way around. The Marx Brothers would have made good movies without Perelman's scripts, and Perelman would have been a good writer without the Hollywood experience, but it is clear that both parties benefitted from the partnership.

There is no question that Perelman's connection with the Marx Brothers was significant in his career. There is also no question that the encounter produced one of the more interesting and confusing episodes in the humorist's life, and one that he felt the effects of for some time. As Zimmerman and Goldblatt contend, "if Perelman was more literary than theatrical, his jaundiced attitude toward language flowed easily through Groucho's character. In *Monkey Business* and *Horse Feathers* each one of Perelman's lines is perfectly tailored to Groucho, and Groucho . . . accords each line its proper balance and bite. 'I was doing this kind of comedy long before I met S. J. Perelman,' Groucho once said, describing the ideal situation for a perfect marriage of writer and comic."[55] Moreover, in Zimmerman and Goldblatt's opinion, Perelman's "influence in *Monkey Business* is felt everywhere—in the highly literate script, in the beautifully honed edge on Groucho's puns, in the methodical madness and mordant tone of the film. It is no accident that two films Perelman worked on are the most verbal the brothers made and among the best.''[56] Sadly, one of the results of the Perelman/Marx disengagement was a dramatic lessening of the quality of the author's screenplays. None of the other movies that he scripted rose to equivalent heights. He had earned a large amount of money, and his reputation had been enhanced, but once the break came, presumably because Perelman felt mistreated, he no longer had access to a vehicle so perfectly suited to expressing his thoughts on film. Additionally, in the Marx Brothers movies he was not confined to working within the strict limits of a plot; if something occurred to him that was funny, whether it fit the story line or not, it could be used. When he wrote movie scripts after this period in his life, his talents were confined by how well they fit within a certain plot structure.

Between 1932, when *Horse Feathers* was scripted, and 1956, Perelman wrote or contributed to eleven screenplays. The first was *Sitting Pretty*, a 1933 Paramount comedy. Not to be confused with a superior film released under the same title fifteen years later and starring Clifton Webb, this eighty-five minute opus was directed by Harry Joe Brown and featured Ginger Rogers (Dorothy), Jack Oakie (Chick Parker), Jack Haley (Pete Pendleton), Thelma Todd in one of her last performances (Gloria Du Val), Gregory Ratoff (Tannenbaum), Lew Cody (Jules Clark), Harry Revel (Pianist), Mack Gordon (Song Publisher), Hale Hamilton (Vinton), and Walter Walker. The screenplay was based on a story suggestion by Nina Wilcox Putnam, and Revel and Gordon wrote the music and lyrics.

Having graduated from tin-pan alley as a songwriter and a lyricist, Oakie and Haley hitchhike to Hollywood, where they make it big. In the post-Depression United States, this plot was diverting enough that Mourdant Hall's *New York Times* review praises the film for the ''Genuine humor and catchy music [that] abound'' in it. A ''thoroughly diverting frolic . . . enhanced by the excellent fun'' is Hall's assessment.[57] In another *New York Times* review *Sitting Pretty* is called ''a decided improvement over the majority of musical features. It has a good groundwork of comedy which is never too fractious.''[58] Given the nature of musical comedies, this evaluation is probably accurate, even though the film cannot be considered a major cinematic achievement. It is a workman-like specimen, however. It is diverting. While not something that one would make plans to see, if it appeared on the late night television movie, much of today's audience would stay tuned.

Brown is best known for producing Randolph Scott westerns, so it is not surprising that his tale of the adventures of songwriters Oakie and Haley in Hollywood, where they meet a girl-next-door type, Rogers, and a vamp, Todd, did not leave much of an impression in the history of filmmaking. In "Three Little Photoplays and How They Grew," Perelman provides additional clues as to why the movie is not better than it is. He was teamed with another writer, whom he identifies as Jack McGovern. McGovern considered himself a "plot expert, a master constructionist," who felt at odds with someone whom the producer, called Anatol Crown by Perelman, had enjoined to "pepper the script with plenty of good brittle dialogue . . . as typified in the comedies of Philip Barry and George Kelly" and who was thus to be suspect as "an aesthete, a bookworm, and . . . a pouf."[59] During the summer that they worked on the screenplay, the authors accommodated their differences in personality by reducing contact with each other to a minimum through the marvelous scheme of writing alternate sequences, a plan that Perelman claims "worked out surprisingly well—even if the combined first draft made no sense at times."[60]

Complicating matters, or maybe making things more simple, was the fact that the producer was not paying much attention to the script due to a liaison with a starlet. Finally, though, there was a showdown between the writers and the producer. Crown, it develops, thought that a vital ingredient had been lost, the story's credibility:

"Boys, the central premise in this picture can't miss, and why do I say that? . . . I say that because it's pure gold. Oakie and Haley, two talented hoofers stranded in New York, find jobs in a wholesale meat concern trimming sides of beef, unpacking the frozen turkeys, and grading sow bellies. The boss has a beautiful daughter that they flip over, so to win her hand they organize a musical show to celebrate the old man's birthday which builds up into the biggest hit on Broadway. That to me is a dynamite springboard for laughs and entertainment, but somehow you failed to make it believable." He looked around uncertainly. "Did anyone else have that reaction?"

The gagmen, who through an oversight or because their status was too lowly had not been provided with copies of the script, were handicapped for an answer, but all three felt the story wholly plausible and fraught with paroxysms of mirth. The songsmiths began a long Talmudic analysis of various

Broadway hits to demonstrate that logic would have been an impediment, if not downright fatal, to their success.   (pp. 180–81)

The song-writing team of Gordon and Revel did manage to provide one of the film's better moments, a tune called "Did You Ever See A Dream Walking?" Perelman has proudly announced that he has "miraculously escaped seeing [the movie] to this day."[61] In the final analysis, though, *Sitting Pretty* is a perfectly acceptable example of the Hollywood B film and in fact is better than a majority of its light, easy-going contemporaries.

Next came *Paris Interlude* (Metro-Goldwyn-Mayer, 1934). Based on their play of the previous year, *All Good Americans*, the film was adapted by the Perelmans, directed by Edwin L. Marin, and featured a cast that included Madge Evans (in the role played by Hope Williams on stage, Julie Bell), Otto Kruger (as a new character, Sam Colt), Robert Young (Pat Wells), Una Merkel (Cassie), Ted Healy (Jimmy), Louise Henry (Mary Louise), Edward Brophy (Ham), George Meeker (Rex Fleming), Bert Roach (Noble), and Richard Tucker (Stevens).

As a side note, and to illustrate the public's attitude toward the cinema in general at this time, movies still shared the program on stage with other productions. When *Paris Interlude* was screened at the Capitol, for instance, Vincent Lopez and his Hotel St. Regis Orchestra were also presented in a stage show along with Florence and Alvarez, the Saxon Sisters, the Gaudschmidt Brothers, Frances Hunt, John Morris, and Fred Lowry. As late as 1941 films were still being advertised as "photoplays" in the *New York Times*, and in 1943 some New York City movie theaters charged an admission of only twenty-eight cents until noon. By way of comparison, in 1941 when Lillian Hellman's new play, *Watch on the Rhine*, starring Paul Lukas played at the Martin Beck Theater, seats for the evening performance ranged from $1.10 to $3.30, and matinee seats for Elmer Rice's *Flight to the West* at the Royal Theater ranged from fifty-five cents to $1.10 on Wednesdays, Saturdays, and Sundays.

The *New York Times* film critic sums up the plot as proving that "les Americains in Paris were neither good nor dead, just careless." The reviewer feels that "the film people do seem to have kept the Perelman humor under wraps in the film version," and finds fault with the "adapters," whose opening out of the script is not seen as positive and who have provided the movie with few "really funny moments." In conclusion, the review states, "It is impossible not to like 'Paris Interlude' a little, though the film doesn't really deserve it." [62] Again, the product is a fairly typical B movie both in plot and character development as well as cinematic technique. No reason is given for the title change.

Then came *Florida Special* (Paramount, 1936). Based on a story by Clarence Budington Kelland, "Recreation Car," the script was co-written by the Perelmans, David Boehm, and Marguerite Roberts, and produced by Albert Lewis. Directed by Ralph Murphy, the movie features Jack Oakie (Bangs Carter) and Sally Eilers (Jerry Quinn) in a romantic murder mystery that takes place aboard a southbound train. The rest of the cast includes Kent Taylor (Wally Nelson), Frances Drake (Marina Stafford), J. Farrell MacDonald (Police Captain Tim Harrigan), Sam Hearn (Schlepperman), Dewey Robinson (Skeets), Claude Gillingwater (Simeon Stafford), Clyde Dilson (Louis), Dwight Frye (Jenkins), Sidney Blackmer (Jack MacKlyn), Matthew Bets (Herman), Harry G. Bradley (Conductor), Jean Bary (Violet), and Sam Flint (Doctor). The running time is seventy minutes.

J.T.M., reviewing the film for the *New York Times*, finds the "seriocomic" treatment of a "predatory mob of gem thieves" who are trying to steal avaricious misanthrope Stafford's million dollar fortune in jewels enjoyable. Singled out are the "fast cracks" delivered by Oakie and "the mile-a-minute pace of the picture." [63] The film is certainly a step above *Paris Interlude*, at least in part because of its more solid plotline which combines the mystery and comic elements adroitly. This movie never takes on so serious a tone that it can be perceived as a thriller, yet the humor develops naturally out of the characters' natures and within the context of the situations in which they are found, and thus the comedy maintains a realistic quality and does not degenerate into silliness. Since most of the action takes place on the train, this further contributes to the sense of a well-developed structure and artistic control.

Florida Special was followed by *Sweethearts* (Metro-Goldwyn-Mayer, 1938), directed by W. S. Van Dyke, II, and starring Jeanette MacDonald (Gwen Marlowe) and Nelson Eddy (Ernest Lane), along with Frank Morgan (Felix Lehman), Ray Bolger (Hans), and Mischa Auer (Leo Kronk). Others in the cast included Florence Rice (Kay Jordan), Herman Bing (Oscar Engel), George Barbier (Benjamin Silver), Reginald Gardiner (Norman Trumpett), Fay Holden (Hannah), Allyn Joslyn (Dink), Olin Howland (Appleby), Lucile Watson (Mrs. Marlowe), Gene Lockhart (Augustus), Kathleen Lockhart (Aunt Amelia), Berton Churchill (Sheridan), Raymond Walburn (Orlando), Douglas McPhail (Harvey), Betty Jaynes (Una), and Dallas Frantz (Concert Pianist). Produced by Hunt Stromberg, *Sweethearts'* book and lyrics were written by Fred De Gresac, Harry B. Smith, and Robert B. Smith, with Victor Herbert's music and special lyrics by Bob Wright and Chet Forest. Dance choreographer was Albertina Rasch, and Dorothy Parker and her husband Alan Campbell are billed as the scenarists.

With its Victor Herbert songs this 120-minute color film about two operetta stars who constantly fight when offstage is considered one of MacDonald and Eddy's best. Perelman, in *Westward Ha!*, called *Sweethearts* "a pestilence" and described MacDonald as "The Iron Butterfly" and Eddy as "The Singing Capon." [64] The *New York Times*, in the person of film critic B.R.C., felt otherwise. In a review full of acclaim for this "most sumptuous Christmas package," phrases such as "a superlatively elaborate example of cinematic pastry-cookery" and "a package that you never seem to get through unpacking" are used to express the reviewer's pleasure with the movie. [65] Two days later another *New York Times* critic, Frank S. Nugent, expresses similar sentiments in a very brief review. "A wedding cake in color," Nugent calls the movie, which is acted "with more verve than it merits," and "Almost resentfully, we have to say that we enjoyed it—in spite of everything." [66] It is a wonder that the audience did not come down with food poisoning or a sugar overdose.

The conception of *Sweethearts*, Metro's first color picture in three years, is described in "Three Little Photoplays and How They Grew." Two years after their four-month stint on *Greenwich Village* (see below), Perelman and his wife returned to California from their Pennsylvania farm at the invitation of another MGM producer, Stromberg (of *Firefly*, *Maytime*, and *Rose Marie* fame). Stromberg insisted that he had "brought you folks out here without a definite property in mind" so that they could exercise their creative judgment and choose the material for their next film project. [67] He topped off this amazing offer by admitting that he was looking for a vehicle for William Powell and Luise Rainer. Thrilled at the prospect of being given a free hand, the Perelmans developed a premise based on a recent Alfred Lunt and Lynn Fontanne stage success called *At Mrs. Beam's*.

Thirteen days later Stromberg got around to asking for a reading and quickly dismissed the idea as not having good box-office potential. Instead, he asked, were the Perelmans aware of George Bernard Shaw's play *Arms and the Man* and Oscar Straus's musical version of the play, *The Chocolate Soldier*? Then Stromberg announced that he intended to star MacDonald and Eddy in the movie, which he immediately decided would be based on Herbert's "most emetic operetta" (Perelman's words), *Sweethearts*, which had nothing to do with Shaw's work. The writers felt betrayed by the man for whom they had at first felt a rapport because of his candor. Stromberg's notion of the project was sufficient cause to persuade them that they had been tricked:

"I visualize Nelson in this production as a man's man," it ran in part. "Athletic, a bon vivant, and independently wealthy, he is always to be found where the sporting fancy congregates . . . cheering on the contestants, posting wagers, deeply absorbed in the fray. He knows but little of love and romance, having been raised in Hell's Kitchen where he hewed his way with his fists in sharp contrast to Jeanette's patrician background. She has sprung from an unbroken line stretching back to the *Mayflower*, the creme de la creme bulwarked by money and social position. Dainty, headstrong, impetuous, she is like some gorgeous orchid; she recks not of the morrow, avid to indulge that instant whim which will not be denied. Collide they must, these two strong personalities, producing musical sparks that pour from their throats in Victor Herbert's deathless score."   (p. 185)

The Perelmans wrote a treatment along the lines requested, but before they could turn it into a screenplay, Laura had to be replaced because her pregnancy was coming to term. Astonishingly, Parker and Campbell was imported to take her place.

To make sure that every advantage of the technicolor process was exploited, MGM built sets so elaborate (a Dutch windmill, an Angelus set, the Iridium Room of the St. Regis Hotel) that even international bankers commented on the studio's impressive industry. Perelman's final words on the film are appropriately barbed, even when it is remembered that despite his protestations and disclaimers he accepted the assignment and a salary: "the damage wrought by *Sweethearts* is still being dealt with by therapists, I presume. But they can hardly hold my wife and me responsible. God knows we had little enough to do with it." [68]

Next came credits for *Ambush* (Paramount, 1939), for which, according to Perelman, "Laura and I were supposed to introduce the humorous element." Kurt Newmann directed the production, adapted from a story by Robert Ray. The cast includes Gladys Swarthout (Jane Hartman), Lloyd Nolan (Tony Andrews), William Henry (Charlie Hartmen), William Frawley (Inspector Weber), Ernest Truex (Mr. Gibbs), Broderick Crawford (Randall), Rufe David (Sheriff), Raymond Hatton (Hardware storekeeper), and Hartley Tufts (Sidney).

This "unblushing excursion in the cops-and-robbers vein," as *New York Times* reviewer B. C. labels the movie, has "just enough comic by-play to keep it unmistakenly within the bounds of purest fiction." The "light, amusing stuff" consists of the escapades of a gang of bank robbers who kidnap a secretary during their getaway and use her to commandeer a truck. The rest of the picture is taken up with the inevitable chase that follows. The fact that Miss Swarthout was a former Metropolitan Opera singer leads the film critic to comment on her role in a "sizzling, serio-comic melodrama which reflects an operatic touch only in the liberties it takes with probability."[69]

Boy Trouble (Paramount), written in partnership with Laura, was also released in 1939. The film is no longer available for public viewing and no major critics ever reviewed it so it has effectively disappeared.

The following year, the Perelmans teamed up with Marion Parsonnet to write the screenplay for *The Golden Fleecing* (MGM). Lynn Root, Frank Fenton, and John Fante had supplied the original story, and Root directed the picture. Starring are Lew Ayres (Henry Twinkel), Rita Johnson (Mary Blake), Lloyd Nolan again (Gus Fender), Virginia Grey (Lila Hanley), Leon Errol (Uncle Waldo), Nat Pendleton of *Horse Feathers* (Fatso Werner), George Lessey (Buckley Sloan), Richard Carle (Pattington), Ralph Byrd (Larry Kelly), Marc Lawrence (Happy Dugan), Thurston Hall (Charles Engel), James Burke (Sibley), Spencer Charters (Justice of Peace), and William Demarest (Swallow).

The story revolves around the dilemma of a young insurance salesman who sells a policy to a customer whom he belatedly finds out is a mobster with a price on his head, so the salesman is faced with the problem of keeping his client alive. As *New York Times* reviewer T. S. says, this "is an idea with comic possibilities."[70] But, "The comic muse must have been woolgathering elsewhere during the production," and "M-G-M has set up a comic situation, then tripped over it." The fault, as assessed by the film critic, is that "the mishaps are more

complicated than inventive [and] the scenes . . . monotonously paced"
because the "nimble direction and acting with an edge on it" that are
vital to bringing off comedy are both missing. At least Perelman and
his wife seem to have done their job and they escape castigation. Another in the Perelmans' string of B movies, *The Golden Fleecing* is an
entertaining example of the genre and deserved a friendlier critique.

In 1942 *Larceny, Inc.* (Warner Brothers) was released to a better
reception. Directed by Lloyd Bacon, the picture has an all-star cast
that includes Edward G. Robinson ("Pressure" Maxwell/J. Chalmers
Maxwell), Jane Wyman (Denny Costello), Broderick Crawford (Jug
Martin), Jack Carson (Jeff Randolph), Anthony Quinn (Leo Dexter),
Edward Brophy (Weepy Davis), and Jackie Gleason in a bit part (Ho-
bart). Harry Davenport, John Qualen, Barbara Jo Allen, Grant Mitchell, Andrew Tombes, Joseph Downing, Fortunio Bonanova, Joseph
Crehan, and Jean Ames also appear. Everett Freeman (who later worked
on *The Secret Life of Walter Mitty* and *My Man Godfrey*) and Edwin
Gilbert translated the Perelman's play *The Night Before Christmas* to
the screen. The film version has a ninety-five minute running time.

A well-thought-of-comedy, *Larceny, Inc.* concerns three ex-cons
(Robinson, Crawford, and Brophy) who use a luggage store as a front
for their shady activities when another gangster (Quinn) tries to move
in on them. Bosley Crowther, of the *New York Times*, who considers
the film "amusing," is particularly impressed by the dual roles assigned Robinson. He also enjoys the farcical elements and the upbeat
ending, yet finds that "some of the faults of the original are still apparent." The faults that he lists are that "It is somewhat forced, somewhat obvious and there are repetitious stretches here and there. Also
the dialogue is not quite as brisk and clever as such farce dialogue
should be." But, he continues, "the characters are whimsically assorted."[71] The original version will be dealt with in more detail in
Chapter Three.

While in Hollywood the author and his wife were hired by MGM's
brilliant Irving Thalberg "to work on a loathsome little thing called
'Greenwich Village' because we had once lived on Washington
Square."[72] The movie was an uninspired, eighty-two-minute-long
musical directed by Walter Lang and starring Carmen Miranda (Princess Querida), Don Ameche (Kenneth Harvey), William Bendix (Danny
O'Mara), Vivian Blaine (Bonnie Watson), Felix Bressart (Hofer), Tony
and Sally DeMarco, the Revuers, B. S. Pally (Brophy), Emil Rameau

(Kavosky), Frank Orth (Ordway), and the Step Brothers. When the picture was released in 1944 (produced for Twentieth Century-Fox by William La Baron) the credits read screenplay by Earl Baldwin and Walter Bullock, adapted by Michael Fessier and Ernest S. Pagano from a story by Frederick Hazlitt Brennan. Presumably this is the same *Greenwich Village* mentioned in ''Three Little Photoplays and How They Grew,'' similarly worked on at Thalberg's behest. Aside from the obvious conclusion that Baldwin and Bullock probably rewrote the Perelmans' script, no reason has ever been given to explain the delay between approximately 1935 when the humorist and his wife must have written the original treatment and the screening of the Baldwin/Bullock version nine years later. Naturally, it is also impossible, given these conditions, to discern the amount of the final cut that can be attributed to the Perelmans.

Crowther lambasted the production about a ''hick composer'' who moves to the fabled bohemian world of the Village around 1922 where he works on a concerto and competes with a local nightclub owner for the film's love interest. ''The most meager sort of material, neither bright nor original, is used to fill out the wide-open spaces,'' Crowther complains. If this were not damning enough, he goes on to say that ''Technicolor is the picture's chief asset.'' Mainly the reviewer fixes the blame on poor acting, but a lackluster musical score is also no help. He concludes that ''the whole show gives evidence that no one had very much confidence in it.''[73] Perelman is just as succinct in his condemnation of the film, which he calls ''the most towering pyramid of clichés ever piled up by the human head,'' a condition that arose at least in part because Thalberg never clearly indicated whether he ''wanted *La Vie de Bohème* or another *Rip Tide: The Story of a Woman's Conflicting Emotions* or a singing disaster film like *San Francisco*.''[74] Perhaps it is just as well that Perelman and his wife escaped inclusion in the credits crawl.

In 1948, as mentioned above, Perelman adapted his stageplay *One Touch of Venus* (Universal-International) to the screen. Writing credit for the film rendition is given to Harry Kurnitz. Interestingly, in this version, directed by William A. Seiter and produced by Lester Cowan, the hero falls in love with a store-window statue of Venus that comes to life. Robert Walker plays Eddie Hatch and Ava Gardner is Venus. The rest of the cast includes Dick Haymes (Joe Grant), Eve Arden (Molly Stewart), Olga San Juan (Gloria), Tom Conway (Whitefield

Savory), James Flavin (Corrigan), and Sara Allgood (Landlady). Sharing the stage at the Capitol Theater live were Jean Sablon, Betty Bruce, Dick and Gene Wesson, the Kanazawa Trio, and Ted Straeter and his band.

The plot of the movie's dramatic original is dealt with in the following chapter, so it will not be traced here. However, Crowther finds the film a "cheap, lackluster farce" in comparison with the play. The charm of the stage production "is conspicuously absent. . . . A second-rate brand of slapstick has replaced the musical's gossamer style,"[75] in his opinion. Inexplicably, Crowther finds Mary Martin, the stage Venus, more beautiful and graceful than Gardner, so his normally valid opinion might be questioned in this case.

Perelman also was assigned the task of translating Dale Carnegie's *How to Win Friends and Influence People* into a screenplay as a vehicle for Joan Crawford and Fanny Brice, but the project was "mercifully never completed."[76] Ironically, during his decade in Hollywood, Perelman came to write some of the same kind of movies that he often parodies in his prose.

In 1956 Perelman, along with James Poe and John Farrow, received the New York Film Critics Award and the Academy of Motion Picture Arts and Sciences Oscar awarded for the year's best screenplay for his script for the film version of Jules Verne's novel, *Around the World in Eighty Days* (United Artists). At the ceremony Hermione Gingold accepted the Oscar for him. Perelman's experience with the 70mm giant-screen extravaganza produced by Michael Todd and directed by Michael Anderson was not fondly remembered. In "Disquiet, Please, We're Turning!" from his "Around the Bend in Eighty Days" series, Perelman has the most unflattering designations for Todd, "a cheap chiseler reluctant to disgorge royalties, a carnival grifter with the ethics of a stoat."[77] Nevertheless, the movie, filmed in gorgeous color on locations around the world, filled with stereophonic sound effects, and featuring forty-four international stars in cameo roles, was the winner of the Academy Award for best picture. David Niven starred as Phileas Fogg and Mexican actor Cantinflas played his servant, Passepartout. Together the two set out to win a wager made at the Reform Club in London by circumnavigating the globe in eighty days, a seemingly impossible task in the nineteenth century in which the story is set. In a series of adventures and misadventures reminiscent of Perelman's own travels, and using every conceivable kind of conveyance, the pair finally returns to London—literally in the nick of time, having ridden through India on an elephant, travelled to Shanghai, been exposed to an opium den in Hong Kong through the contrivance of Detective Fix (played by Robert Newton), their comic nemesis who wanted to hold them until a subpoena arrived, raced across the American continent, and taken a voyage to Liverpool. One of the most memorable scenes in the movie is when Fogg and Passepartout are in a hot air balloon that barely clears a mountain peak; they reach down to scoop up an ice bucket full of snow to cool their champagne just as it does so.

Besides the Academy Award for an adaptation, the film also earned best picture, editing (Paul Weatherwax and Gene Ruggiero), cinematography (Lionel Linden), and musical score (by Victor Young) honors. The cameo roles were played by, in alphabetical order, Charles Boyer, Joe E. Brown, Martine Carol, John Carradine, Charles Coburn, Ronald Coleman, Melville Cooper, playwright Noel Coward, Finlay Currie, Reginald Denney, Andy Devine, Marlene Dietrich, the Spanish bullfighter Dominguen, Fernandel, Sir John Gielgud, Hermione Gingold (*see Westward Ha!*), Jose Greco, Sir Cedric Hardwicke, Trevor Howard, Glynis Johns, Buster Keaton, Evelyn Keyes, Beatrice Lillie, Peter Lorre, Edmund Lowe, Shirley MacLaine (Perelman: she "was miscast in that number; she had all the exoticism of a cold waffle"), Victor MacLaglen, Tim McCoy, A. E. Mathews, Mike Mazurki, John Mills, Robert Morley, Alan Mowbray, newscaster Edward R. Murrow, Jack Oakie, George Raft, Gilbert Rowland, Caesar Romero, Basil Sidney, Frank Sinatra, Red Skelton, Ronald Squire, and Harcourt Williams.

About this two-hour-and-fifty-five-minute-long spectacular (not counting the intermission) Crowther remarks, "this . . . is a sprawling conglomeration of refined English comedy, giant-screen travel panaramics and slam-bang Keystone burlesque."[78] The movie opens with Edward R. Murrow introducing a clip from Georges Melies' imaginative masterpiece *A Trip to the Moon*. The camera pulls back from this black-and-white silent film to reveal a rocket rising into a blue sky filling the wide screen. As the sand boils up around the base of the rocket, it seems to swirl out and around the audience while Murrow explains how the ship symbolizes a changing world. For

Crowther this prologue to Verne's nineteenth-century fable established an eccentric pattern in which "The unities of content and method are not detectable."

Two other episodes involving modes of transportation deserve special notice, for they reflect something about Perelman's general approach to writing, whether for films or in prose. He is certainly innovative, as evidenced in the movie's opening sequence, yet he is not shy about borrowing from others in order to advance his plot. The hot air balloon incident, as already noted, is not contained in the novel, but Perelman lifted it from another Verne novel to incorporate it in the film, and it is visually very effective. Likewise, there is a cinematic tradition that can be traced back to films starring Buster Keaton, W. C. Fields, the Marx Brothers, and Wallace Beery in the 1920's and 30's in which a steamboat or a train is torn apart by its passengers who feed the wood stick by stick into the boiler when all other fuel is gone and more steam is needed to win a race or to escape pursuers. *Around the World in 80 Days* includes just such a shipboard scene as the crew crosses the Atlantic Ocean, one of the many movie clichés that Perelman freely appropriated.

Almost from the beginning of filmmaking there has been a theoretical debate about the nature of cinematic adaptations: should they, or can they, be true to the original? When Harold Pinter's adaptation of John Fowles' *The French Lieutenant's Woman* was released in 1981, a quarter of a century after *Around the World in 80 Days*, the novelist and the film's director both commented on the relationship of the film to the book. Fowles cautions that the use of language and the kinds of themes dealt with in a novel are such that "all those aspects of life and modes of feeling . . . can *never* be represented visually." Therefore, screenwriters should not try to "remain faithful to the book" because that approach tends to lead to wordy scripts that lack dramatic dialogue. Director Karel Reisz agrees: "Do you have to be faithful to the novel? . . . no. You don't have to be faithful to anything, you have to make a variation on the theme of the novel which . . . is a film, not a filmed novel. . . . A novel is capable of taking you inside a person; it gives you their speculations, their feelings, their historic associations and so on. That's something that movies can only hint at. But the moment you've accepted that fact, then the whole notion of being faithful becomes meaningless because in cinema you have to substitute something filmic.''[79] Clearly Perelman subscribes to the same theory.

Given that the motion pictures for which Perelman wrote the scripts following *Monkey Business* and *Horse Feathers* are B movies and typical of the genre, there was no need to examine his cinematic techniques in the individual films. It is interesting, however, to note the devices that he relies upon in *Around the World in 80 Days*. To some extent the filmscript reflects Perelman's prose—the opening sequence, for instance, analogous to the *Times* fillers that he sometimes uses as the initiating point for his casuals, and Murrow's moralizing that ''speed is good only when wisdom leads the way'' (i.e., disaster can be offset by hope) provides a thematic setting for the movie, but this is a fairly shallow concept without a great deal of social significance behind it, and the theme is developed only very superficially in the film.

Around the World in 80 Days, however, is superb entertainment, and it is this facet of the novel that Perelman's script emphasizes. Because he is adapting someone else's work, he is not concerned with a plot: that has already been devised by a master of plot construction. In addition, he is dealing with an action/adventure picture—the plot mainly consists of getting from one place to another and the incidents that take place along the way are used to delay the arrival for a given amount of running time or to serve as obstacles that the protagonist must overcome. Essentially, the movie follows the chase format, a cinematic staple from the early films of Edwin S. Porter on. Thus, Perelman focuses on two elements: an exposure to the world intended to offer his audience hope by familiarizing them with foreign cultures by showing that in some ways those cultures are similar to twentieth-century American culture and that even when they are different they are interesting and valuable in their own rights, and the travelogue nature of that exposure, particularly that having to do with movement. The cinematic techniques that he employs are designed to stress these two elements.

In his early movie scenarios, Perelman was content to set up the camera and let it record the action. In *Around the World in 80 Days* the camera is involved in creating the action; the difference is something like that which differentiated the two Marx Brothers films, but in this picture the humorist more imaginatively employs the camera to emphasize his images. There are a great variety of camera angles, from extreme close-up reaction shots to panoramics of landscapes and crowd scenes. Like eighteenth-century landscape paintings, most of this film's landscapes contain human figures. There are innumerable establishing shots in market places and countrysides to give the viewers a taste of whatever nation Fogg is currently passing through, and Perelman exploits the 70mm process to produce a sense of expansiveness, though not the expansiveness of a John Ford western, as the camera does not simply pan across a distant horizon. Instead, a majority of Perelman's shots are tracking shots, taken from a moving train, the back of an elephant, or some other mode of transportation. This expands the shot even further than a pan would, and it also reinforces the sense of movement that he is trying to create. Since the same kind of shot is used as the travellers move from one country to another, the tracking shots also allow Perelman to develop a sense of continuity that grows out of Murrow's opening statement and unifies the film thematically and visually.

In developing a sense of movement, Perelman uses the sensation of being a part of the action accruing from the construction of the screen used to accomodate the 70mm film to his advantage. At the same time, this permits him to involve his audience in a feel for the societies that he is depicting to a greater extent than would be possible in the conventional 35mm format. Each scene is full of authenticating details of time and place—sets, costumes, activities—from the names on storefronts to the baby strollers being used. As each new civilization is introduced to the audience, there is some sort of procession going on, again combining movement and cultural elements in one sweeping visual image. Other devices that Perelman uses to create his illusion include the reflection of the balloon in farm ponds and castle moats as it floats over Europe, and the magnificent tracking shot from behind the counters of food that appear in the foreground while the camera follows the hungry Passepartout through a Japanese market. Movement, cultural differences, and the character's hunger are all brought together masterfully so that Perelman can make his thematic points and move the plot along at the same time.

The cuts and camera movements are more inventive and smooth in this epic than in Perelman's earlier pictures. In that opening sequence, again, he establishes the techniques that he is going to use to blend together theme and content: the picture of the rocket rising shifts to a picture of the Earth taken from the receding rocket—the revolving

Earth then becomes a globe turning beneath Murrow's hand as he states the movie's theme.

Sound is also used effectively throughout. The film's main musical theme flows continually as the tour progresses, but each new country is serenaded with appropriately identifiable music and the noise of native voices. The non-synchronous sound of Big Ben tolling over the establishing shots of 1872 London coalesces with the sound of clock chimes, and the camera moves into focus on Niven checking his pocket watch. In a similar manner voice-overs are utilized in establishing the tone for the Reform Club scenes as bits of conversation and deep, rich, muffled sounds precede Niven's entrance. Sound is used for humorous effects, too, particularly in relationship to Passepartout. When he enters the employment office, the sound of the squeaking gate contrasts with the solemnness of his surroundings and sets him apart from those in the room—those who would not be flexible enough, conveyed by the accompanying visual as the camera tracks along the long line of humorless men who sit silently and stiffly against the wall, to accompany Fogg on the upcoming trip. There is even a light, whimsical Passepartout musical theme that follows the character through the picture and helps set him apart from his staid master. When the Princess is lying on her husband's funeral pyre, the glimpse of Passepartout's shoe on the foot of the corpse becomes comprehensible because of the quick intermingling of the Passepartout theme with the Indian music, alerting the audience to what is about to happen and releasing the tension built from the seeming hopelessness of the situation.

Of course, there are some carryovers from Perelman's previous work. Occasional pieces of dialogue or plot developments have a decidedly B-movie ring to them. At the same time, Perelman was always adept at sight gags, and these appear frequently in *Around the World in 80 Days*. When Detective Fixx spies on Fogg aboard the steamship, for example, the camera also reveals Passepartout observing the detective as the watcher is watched. Slapstick (as in the confrontation with John Carradine in the California election campaign sequence) is constantly present, and comic bits such as the literal cliff hanger when the train crosses the collapsing bridge or the delaying of an identity-establishing angle of piano-playing Frank Sinatra in the saloon, are intercut more efficiently than in some of Perelman's earliest cinematic attempts. The exchange between the Royal Guards on sentry duty ("He's in America!") is an obvious attempt at humor; the use of music and an exterior shot of the castle to imply that Queen Victoria is also informed is more subtle. The cuts from Passepartout at the burning stake intercut with shots of the calvary rushing to the rescue convey a humorous effect that is not spectacular, but the pattern is more adventurous than merely moving the camera to follow the comic antics of Groucho, Harpo, and Chico.

Perelman's love of language is evident as always. The vocabulary—"hectoring," "wenching," "persiflage," "efficacy"—adds the screenwriter's characteristic touch. Occasionally, there are ingredients included that, like the vocabulary, seem to have little to do with the movie itself aside from pleasing Perelman. The flamenco dancing of José Greco and his troupe is an example of a scene that at first glance appears to be superfluous. Actually, though, there is not much contained in the movie that is not directly related to Perelman's purpose. *Around the World in 80 Days* is ultimately an escapist film, and the audience is taken on the grand tour. The flamenco dancing is as much a part of the spectacle and exposure to foreign cultures as any other scene in the film.

Perelman has taken advantage of almost all the visual possibilities of his medium in creating the atmosphere that he wants. Extravagantly expensive, the movie was filmed in Technicolor on 140 full-scale sets on 112 locations by 34 directors and involved 74,685 costumed extras. The grandeur of the undertaking required a wide screen, and Perelman realized the wide screen's potential fully. Perhaps because the plot consists of a series of vignettes held together by a group of central characters, perhaps because he utilized the possibilities of the medium more completely than ever before, perhaps because of a combination of these things, *Around the World in 80 Days* is the writer's most cinematic endeavor. It is also his most successful film, and one that remains indelibly impressed in the minds of a generation of moviegoers.

In spite of Crowther's assessment, the movie was Perelman's most professional and polished looking film, immensely popular, and did what it was intended to do. Whether being true to Verne's original or merely using the novel as a point of departure, *Around the World in 80 Days* provided a full evening of entertainment.

A final screenplay that was never written is the third subject reported on in "Three Little Photoplays and How They Grew." In the late 1950's Perelman's agent informed him that Michael Todd wanted the author to fly out to the Coast to discuss turning Miguel de Cervantes Saavedra's *Don Quixote* into a film. At a press luncheon at Toots Shor's Restaurant held in February 1957, Todd announced plans to film the Cervantes novel. To be in color and filmed in the Todd-AO wide-screen process, the proposed film was described as a "lavish large-scale" production to be made on an "unlimited budget" entirely in Spain, according to a news account.[80] Todd also indicated that a new, special technical device would be utilized in the filming. The film, reuniting Mexican actor Cantinflas and Perelman, was to have a "broad conception" that stressed entertainment.

A visit to the Todd/Elizabeth Taylor desert hideaway (sublet from Marion Davies) during a miserably hot July ends, after Todd has abandoned Perelman for some time, when Perelman admits that he finds Cervantes' novel so boring that he has never been able to read past page six. Todd is not surprised, he says, because during a steam bath earlier in the day he had been warned by Harry Cohn (probably the same man who had been chief of Columbia Pictures for many years) that Perelman had been released by Universal Studios after only two days. "Which shows how life always catches up with you," Perelman concludes in the final line of one of the last essays that he wrote.[81]

As much as Perelman disparaged Hollywood during the "Golden Era," comments made about contemporary filmmaking in 1969 and 1970 indicate that he thought no more highly of the film industry then. He refers to the concept that the 1930's were special by saying, "Purest nonsense. It was assembly-line stuff, just people doing a job."[82] About later periods he is equally unflattering. The youth movement in movies, he states in the MacPherson interview, is amusing: "The 'professionalism' of young movie makers is a source of sardonic pleasure. They're all so much more technical, talk of truck shots and whip shots. Then what turn out are what we called 'chasers'—snow melting, a little Chopin tinkling behind it. They're sort of playing at it and giving themselves enormous seriousness about the whole thing."[83] He also finds the amount of space given to film critics, "the gods and goddesses," undeserved and unneeded. He uses the example of *The New Yorker* editor Harold Ross's attitude toward film criticism to support his point, echoing Thurber's contention in *The Years With Ross* that Ross did not consider film an art form and thought that writing about a pasttime that appeals only to little old ladies a waste of time: if "a review ran over one paragraph he became very restive. I think page on page is extremely boring," Perelman told MacPherson.

A comparison of Perelman's filmscripts and his prose points up some of the differences between visual and verbal humor as well as the difficulties of translating Perelman's language into another medium. It is clear that he excells at the written form where the words create the images rather than reenforce them. In the extended format of the film his mastery of language cannot overcome the impact of a weak structure or unimaginative narrative story line, something that even in his prose is occasionally a detrimental element and may have kept him from becoming even more critically acclaimed. Possibly this is one of the reasons that he wrote so many B-movie scripts—his episodic and essentially traditional plots limited him by not allowing for a broad enough context in which to develop his thoughts. At the same time, these qualities are acceptable in the B-movie genre to the extent that they are almost conventions. Perelman was a superb parodist and these pictures lend themselves to and embody parodies of their own genre. Perelman's B-movie endeavors are among the most successful in the field, and when he was at his free-wheeling best and released from narrative constraints as in the Marx Brothers and Michael Todd experiences, he produced several major feature films.

By way of a general conclusion about Perelman's writing for the cinema, then, it can be said that while none of his filmscripts are great, several are very good, and they are all entertaining. As in his prose writing, Perelman's screenplays demonstrate the author's ready wit, imagination, and ability to devise a plot that holds his audience's attention. Furthermore, the prolonged, if intermittent, thirteen-picture Hollywood episode provided the author with plenty of material to write about. More importantly, writing for the movies strengthened his prose style by expanding his perspective and his approaches to his subjects. A more cinematic eye was incorporated into his prose, and quick-moving images lighten his writing as a result. In a sense, too, the weight of his intellectualism was dispersed to some extent by his visual awareness of the world about him, and although he remained always introspective, he did not do so to the exclusion of the outside world. This undoubtedly helped keep the humorist in touch with the common man's plight throughout his career.

With his professional attitude toward writing as a craft so clearly and frequently articulated, it is not surprising that Perelman found his association with Hollywood difficult. Possibly he did not enjoy more success as a filmwriter because of the attitudes toward writers that he encountered in Hollywood that were irreconcilable with his own. Film, he found, "was a director's medium rather than a writer's. . . . I have always felt that the statement attributed to Irving Thalberg, the patron saint at Metro-Goldwyn-Mayer, beautifully summed up the situation: 'The writer is a necessary evil.' As a sometime employee of his, I consider that a misquotation. I suspect he said 'weevil.' "[84]

NOTES

1. William Zinsser, "That Perelman of Great Price Is Sixty-Five," *New York Times Magazine* (January 26, 1969): 27.

2. She was a French leading lady of American silent films such as *Spanish Love*, *White Gold*, *Forbidden Woman*, and others.

3. Griffith appeared in *Single Wives*, *Modern Madness*, *Syncopating*, etc.; Pringle was in *Three Weeks*, *Wife of a Centaur*, *Adam and Eve*, *Soldiers and Women*, *Jane Eyre*, etc.; Naldi starred in *Dr. Jekyll and Mr. Hyde*, *Blood and Sand*, *The Ten Commandments*, *The Sainted Devil*, etc.

4. Jay Martin, *Nathanael West: The Art of His Life* (New York: Farrar, Straus, and Giroux, 1970), p. 58.

5. Zinsser, p. 72.

6. S. J. Perelman, *The Last Laugh* (New York: Simon and Schuster, 1981), p. 148. In *The Marx Brothers at the Movies* (New York: Signet, 1968), p. 6, Paul D. Zimmerman and Burt Goldblatt repeat Perelman's description of the brothers' act that he saw when they toured Rhode Island in 1916.

7. Perelman, *The Last Laugh*, p. 148.

8. Ibid., p. 149.

9. Hector Arce, *Groucho* (New York: Putnam's Sons, 1979), p. 184.

10. Perelman, *The Last Laugh*, pp. 149–50. In *Groucho and Me* (New York: Manor, 1974), pp. 238–41, Groucho reports that the losses amounted to between $240,000 and $250,000. Note, incidentally, how closely the accounts resemble each other in both details and wording.

11. Perelman, *The Last Laugh*, p. 150.

12. Ibid.

13. Ibid., p. 148.

14. William Cole and George Plimpton, "S. J. Perelman: The Art of Fiction," *Writers at Work: The Paris Review Interviews, Second Series* (New York: Viking, 1965), p. 253.

15. Martin, p. 261.

16. Ibid., p. 345.

17. Quoted in "S. J. Perelman," in *Contemporary Authors*, ed. by Francis Carol Locher (Detroit: Gale, 1978), vols. 73–76, p. 497.

18. Quoted in J. A. Ward, "The Hollywood Metaphor: The Marx Brothers, S. J. Perelman, and Nathanael West," *Southern Review* 12 (July, 1976): 663.

19. Ibid.

20. Zinsser, pp. 72–74.

21. Arce, pp. 188–90.

22. Zimmerman and Goldblatt, pp. 43–45.

23. S. J. Perelman, "The Winsome Foursome," *Show* (November, 1961), pp. 34–38. Perelman's interview by Mel Calman ("Perelman in Cloudsville," *Sight and Sound*, 47 [Autumn 1978]: 248–49) repeats some of these points. Significantly, it may be that the event became more terrifying in Perelman's mind over a period of time; in the earliest published account of the incident, it is reported that after Groucho opined that "It stinks," he went on to say, "we'll get to work on it in the morning." See Theodore A. Goldsmith's "Probing Perelman," *New York Times*, March 26, 1944, sect. 2, p. 1.

24. Perelman, *The Last Laugh*, pp. 154–57. This version is almost exactly the same as the one that appeared in *Show*, as is Perelman's "Going Hollywood with the Marx Brothers," which was published in *Esquire* (September 1981, pp. 60–64, 66).

25. Arce, p. 189.

26. Groucho Marx and Richard J. Anobile, *The Marx Bros. Scrapbook* (New York: Darien House, 1973), p. 213.

27. Andrew Sarris, *The American Cinema, Directors and Directions*, (New York: Dutton, 1968), p. 247.

28. Cole and Plimpton, p. 251.

29. Perelman, *The Last Laugh*, p. 158.

30. Ibid.

31. Ibid. As a interesting aside, one of Groucho's interviewers thinks that the break between the two grew out of a minor flirtatious incident involving Sheekman's wife and Perelman at a dinner at Groucho's.

32. Groucho, Marx, *The Groucho Phile* (Indianapolis: Bobbs-Merrill, 1976), p. 290.

33. Marx, *Groucho and Me*, p. 336.

34. Marx and Anobile, p. 155.

35. Ibid., p. 213.

36. Arce, p. 190.

37. Perelman, *The Last Laugh*, p. 150.

38. Ibid., p. 151.

39. Ibid., pp. 151, 152.

40. Marx, *Groucho and Me*, pp. 238–41.

41. Zimmerman and Goldblatt, pp. 46–47.

42. Quoted in Marx and Anobile, p. [96].

43. See Arce, p. 190.

44. Mourdant Hall, "The Screen: Groucho and His Brethren," *New York Times*, October 8, 1931, p. 22.

45. Quoted in Marx, *The Groucho Phile*, p. 183.

46. S. J. Perelman, W. B. Johnstone, B. Kalmar, and H. Ruby, *The Four Marx Brothers in Monkey Business and Duck Soup* (New York: Simon and Schuster, 1973), p. 4.

47. Marx, *The Groucho Phile*, p. 88; *The Marx Bros. Scrapbook*, pp. 147–48, 173.

48. Marx, *Groucho and Me*, p. 240.

49. Marx and Anobile, p. 214.

50. Arce, p. 188.

51. Marx, *The Groucho Phile*, p. [97].

52. Mourdant Hall, "The Screen: Groucho Marx and His Brothers in a New Film Filled with Their Characteristic Clowning," *New York Times*, August 11, 1932, p. 12.

53. Zimmerman and Goldblatt, p. 63.

54. Ibid., p.65.

55. Ibid., pp. 45–66.

56. Ibid., p. 43.

57. Mourdant Hall, "The Screen: Jack Oakie, Jack Haley and Ginger Rogers in a Screen Musical Comedy Dealing with a Song-Writing Team," *New York Times*, December 2, 1933, sect. L, p. 9.

58. Mourdant Hall, "Two Jacks and a Queen," *New York Times*, December 10, 1933, sect. 10, p. 7.

59. Perelman, *The Last Laugh*, p. 178.

60. Ibid., p. 179.

61. Ibid., p. 172. Amusingly, Perelman also insisted that the song title is "Jevva See a Dream Walking?" and called the movie *Sittin' Pretty* (p. 177).

62. A.D.S., "The Screen," *New York Times*, July 28, 1934, p. 16.

63. J.T.M., "The Screen in Review: At the Rialto," *New York Times*, May 29, 1936, p. 15.

64. Perelman, *The Most of S. J. Perelman* (New York: Simon and Schuster, 1958), p. 342.

65. B.R.C., "At the Capitol." *New York Times*, December 23, 1938, sect. L, p. 16.

66. Frank S. Nugent, "Chips Off the Yule Log," *New York Times*, December 25, 1938, sect. 9, p. 7.

67. Perelman, *The Last Laugh*, p. 183.

68. Ibid., p. 187.

69. B.C., "At the Criterion," *New York Times*, February 9, 1939, p. 17.

70. T.S., "At Loew's Criterion," *New York Times*, November 7, 1940, p. 33.

71. Bosley Crowther, "The Screen," *New York Times*, April 25, 1942, p. 9.

72. Perelman, quoted in Zinsser, p. 74.

73. Crowther, "The Screen: 'Greenwich Village,' with Carmen Miranda, Comes to Roxy—film from Paris at the 55th St.," *New York Times*, September 28, 1944, sect. 2, p. 1.

74. Perelman, *The Last Laugh*, p. 182.

75. Crowther, "Ava Gardner and Robert Walker in 'One Touch of Venus,' Feature at Capitol," *New York Times*, October 29, 1948, p. 29.

76. Perelman, quoted in Zinsser, p. 74.

77. Perelman, *Vinegar Puss*, p. 33.

78. Crowther, "Screen: Mammoth Show," *New York Times*, October 18, 1956, p. 37. In some cuts, now available on videotape, the Melies' clip has been deleted.

79. John Fowles, Foreword to *The French Lieutenant's Woman: A Screenplay*, by Harold Pinter (Boston: Little, Brown, 1981), pp. ix,ff.

80. Anonymous, "Of Local Origin," *New York Times* (February 20, 1957), sect. L, p. 36.

81. Perelman, *The Last Laugh*, p. 192.

82. Zinsser, p. 74.

83. Myra MacPherson, "Perelman's Rasping Wit Becomes an Anglo-File," *Washington Post*, October 18, 1970, sect. E, p. 4.

84. Cole and Plimpton, p. 253.

3

Plays

Perelman dabbled occasionally in writing for the legitimate theater, though with only a modicum of popular success. In part his failures occurred simply because of bad luck—his *The Beauty Part* experience recounted below is a prime example of this. It might be expected that his humor would be especially well suited for the stage, since it relies so heavily on verbal gymnastics, but this is its weakness, too. As with his films, Perelman is unable to sustain his kind of humor for any great length of time (which is why he is so successful using the short story format), but his stage plays are more wooden than his screenplays are because, unlike film, drama is not designed to bridge the gaps between the bursts of verbal humor, since it does not have the sense of movement afforded by a camera.

Perelman's first attempts at dramatic writing were contributions to the revue *The Third Little Show* ("His Wedding Night," featuring Ernest Truex), produced in New York in 1931, another revue, *Sherry Flip* in 1932, mentioned above, and an "unsuccessful piece called *The Ladders*."[1] Perelman claims that *Sherry Flip* "set the American theatre back a hundred years."

Walk a Little Faster, a series of sketches written with Robert MacGunigle, opened at the St. James' Theater in New York on December 7, 1932. Beatrice Lillie played in the starring role, but apparently her talents clashed with Perelman's material, at least in the opinion of the *New York Times* theater critic Brooks Atkinson. "The truth of the matter is that *Walk a Little Faster* does not put [Lillie] through her funniest paces," wrote Atkinson, because "the sketches are mostly silly."[2] Other critics singled out Perelman's "Scamp of the Campus" sketch for special praise, though, and the revue did run for 119 performances, a respectable number compared with other works such as Arthur Miller's first Broadway success, *All My Sons*, which ran for 328 performances. Any run over one hundred performances is considered "long" in Broadway history prior to 1940.

The following year Perelman and his wife wrote *All Good Americans*, a comedy about Americans living in Paris in which a chic fashion designer has to decide between marrying a struggling writer or a succesful business man. The play, which opened at the Henry Miller Theatre on December 5, 1933, and ran for thirty-nine performances, was directed by Arthur Sircom. Courtney Burr produced the comedy, Mordecai Gorelik was the set designer, and the cast included Hope Williams, Fred Keating, Eric Dressler, Mary Philips, and James Stewart.

Atkinson enjoyed the play's jokes, but he still felt that "Mr. and Mrs. Perelman have written a second-rate Barry comedy with a trying scene of whimsical pantomime toward the end."[3] He goes on to quote some of the lines ("In school we used to have just the best coffee," simpers one character; "Where did you go to school," retorts the heroine, "Maxwell House?") and then determines that "Neither the director nor the authors have succeeded in whipping 'All Good Americans' into a fluent performance. When the joke factory is not turning out one laugh to the minute, the comedy looks indolent."

The *Theatre Arts* reviewer is even more critical than Atkinson, railing that "For the thousandth time *All Good Americans* tells the thin story of American expatriates in Paris. . . . Neither the story, dialogue, nor acting can pull the play into the line of the moderately worthwhile."[4]

Immediately after the premier performance of the play, a reporter interviewed the dramatists. The producer, who seems to have had a sense of the absurd akin to his writers', pointed out the Perelmans: "She's Laura to us and to Sid, and she wouldn't give you so much as a drachma for a Lucy Stoner. Sid's the phobe and Laura's the phile of the merger. They're both out of debt. Sid once did a handstand on the stairs leading up to the Trocadero."[5] The couple then explained what the drama is about and how they came to write it:

"It's about our expatriates in Paris," said the male Perelman. "You know! All tangled up with love, liquor and loneliness, excursions to Malmaison and Chantilly, forgetting all about it at the Rotonde, and figuring out the rate of exchange. Sometimes I think it's like 'Oedipus Rex,' and sometimes I think it's like early O'Neill, and once I thought it was like Jimmy Gleason."

"What was like early O'Neill?" interrupted Laura.

" 'Beyond the Horizon'," said Mr. Perelman.

"A friend of ours was vacationing in Pernambuco [said Laura]. He sent us a postal card and instead of showing the beach on Sunday it showed a Brazilian coffee plantation. Now you go on from there."

"One look at the card and something started to surge within me," said Mr. Perelman. "The connotations of coffee. That was it. French coffee lays our countrymen low. You are my countrymen, aren't you? There was the plot. Now for the dialogue. For a minute I got to thinking about the postcards that the man sells outside the Café de la Paix, but I mastered my baser emotions and decided that it must be a clean play. . . . It's all about Americans in Paris. Americans who roll in from the Dome at dawn to find their franc notes have turned to confetti. Hope Williams is trying to decide between her job and Fred Keating. [Burr] is miffed because we won't put a French sailor in the barroom scene for sentimental reasons. . . . We had a scene at the tomb of Napoleon, but Arthur Sircom talked us out of it. Said he had a dash of Russian in him and that it always reminded him of Austerlitz."

To some extent the play was based on the authors' wedding trip to Paris in 1929 and someone must have felt that it was entertaining since the next year MGM released the film version, *Paris Interlude*, discussed in the preceding chapter.

During the summer of 1934, while Perelman and West were both at the Pennsylvania farm, they decided to collaborate on a comedy. Perelman had already had considerable experience in collaborating with other authors (*Parlor, Bedlam and Bath*, the various movies and dramatic works noted above) and, as Martin says, "West and he were sympathetic in their tastes" and West "was especially enthusiastic about Perelman's work."[6]

The two in-laws believed that "it would be possible for an audience to absorb a play on a very high level," and they spent the summer trying to put together a first-rate play that would be ready for a fall mounting. The result was *Even Stephen* (originally titled *Guardian Angel: A Three Act Comedy*). Martin has provided a summary of the play:

The heroine of the play is Diana Breed Latimer, a female novelist, author of *Stone Walls Do Not*, the forthcoming *Orchids of Evil*, and other similarly sensational novels. She quotes her own works continually, having absurdly confused her fiction with real life. As the play opens, she arrives at Briscoe, a girls' college in New England, to complete her current book, an exposé of flaming youth in college. Looking for publicity material, her publisher, Marcel Schwartz, follows her there. Obviously, both West and Perelman had in mind the sensation caused at Brown by the publication of Percy Marks's *The Plastic Age*, regarded by the public as a college exposé. Diana Breed Latimer—a triple-named woman author like those mocked in *Miss Lonelyhearts*—is a female, calculating version of their Brown instructor. "Vice exists everywhere," she announced, "but in the hothouse atmosphere of a woman's college . . . it becomes intensified. It thrives, it spreads like a giant creeper twisting and torturing the loves of its unfortunate victims. . . . [The girls] are helpless victims of the hypocrisy that hems them in with iron-bound rules—chains their amorous little bodies so that they writhe with repressed desires." Distorting and inaccurately piecing together scraps of information, she and Schwartz release a story of midnight orgies to the press, which leads to several complications.   (pp. 250–55)

According to Martin, West and Perelman's broad comedy expands along several lines as well, including some of Perelman's perennial subjects. Publishing and publicity practices are satirized in the play ("Diana Breed Latimer Week! Why, for Christ's sake, I'll get your picture on a postage stamp!"), as are "sensational novels of exposure and sex, college professors and their wives, newspapermen, romantic young poets, and mad scientists." The inspiration for the play, as Martin implies, can certainly be traced back to Perelman and West's college days at Brown. Faculty member Marks's sensationalized novel about college life in the Jazz Age was satirized in *The Plastered Duchess*, the senior class play presented on St. Patrick's Day in 1924. The three-act musical farce was written by West and his classmates Frank O. Hough and John West. It is likely that Quentin Reynolds contributed to the writing too. Perelman, still an aspiring cartoonist, painted a surrealistic backdrop for the bawdy production. The actors (Reynolds played a duchess and Philip Lukin was a slave girl) and audience were drunk throughout the performance (West passed out during the second act) and things got so out of hand that several cast members feared that they would be expelled from the college. The play must have been considered a success, though, for Perelman's scenery was cut up for souvenirs.

The first draft of *Even Stephen* was finished in September and Perelman and West submitted it to Max Gordon and other producers, but it was rejected. For some time the authors felt that they could find a backer through their neighbor Kaufman or acquaintances in the theater such as Alexander Woollcott and Marc Connelly; they were never successful. West referred to the collaboration for some time afterward, though finally, in 1939, he wrote to Perelman that he was writing a screenplay at Universal Studios called *The Victoria Docks at Eight* and that he had used "a few jokes from our script 'Even Stephen,' which I take to be a completely dead noodle so far as both of us are concerned." He even promised "that the contribution is under twenty-five per cent, so you won't have to take screen credit,"[7] but ironically neither writer had to worry about such a situation, because the film was abandoned later that year and neither film nor play ever got any closer to being produced.

Six years later Perelman made a minimal contribution of some sketches to another revue, *Two Weeks with Pay* (1940), which was taken on tour. The revue contained nothing very exciting and even the reviewers paid it little heed.

In 1941 the *New York Times* critic, Atkinson, again was disappointed in the lack of plot in a Perelman play. *The Night Before Christmas: A Comedy in Three Acts*, written in collaboration with Laura, contained hilarious segments, but the play as a whole was unsuccessful. Burr, the producer of *All Good Americans*, produced *The Night Before Christmas* too. Directed by Romney Brent, the play opened at the McCarter Theater in Princeton, New Jersey, on March 29, 1941, for its pre-Broadway run and then moved into New York's Morosco Theater on April 10, 1941, where it ran for only twenty-two performances. The set director was Boris Aronson and the players were George Mathews (Ruby), Ruth Weston (Madame Rochelle), Forrest Orr (Otio J. Faunce), Phyllis Brooks (Denny Costello), Harry Bratsburg (Leo), Louis Sorin (Sam Bachrach), Shelley Winters in her Broadway debut (Flora), and a supporting cast of nineteen.

This farce is about two safe-crackers who buy a run-down luggage shop next door to an old-fashioned bank on Sixth Avenue. While they drill through the cellar wall toward the bank's vault they become involved with customers and "professional associates from institutions of correction all over the country." "For a play that never seemed to get started I thought it would never end," reports the *Journal-Ameri-*

can reviewer.[8] Atkinson's opinion is that the playwrights "have stuffed a number of funny ideas into 'The Night Before Christmas' . . . but they have drawn an incomplete comedy out of it."[9] He goes on to conjecture that "Since Mr. Perelman is one of the most insane wags of his time, and his wife must be slightly mad at least by association, it would be a service to humanity to find out why their Sixth Avenue scuffle is not one of the most hilarious escapades of the season. Perhaps the narrative is too episodic and truncated. Perhaps some of the casting is wrong or Romney Brent's direction lacks momentum." Humanity is not blessed with Atkinson's corrective services, though, for he decides not to go any further in his analysis. Instead, he comments that "all this skulduggery is stirred up with some of the most flamboyant jargon ever written by mischief scribblers." Atkinson continues, saying that "foolish playgoers are likely to laugh their silly heads off at isolated sequences of conversation and incidents in the story," yet he concludes that the play "never accumulates a story that develops out of normal life into comic fantastification" because "even lunatic comedies have to proceed with a certain logic." Still, reviewers in the *New York Journal*, *New York Herald-Tribune*, *New York Sun*, *New York Post*, and *New York Mirror* praised the play, and it was transferred to the screen in the guise of *Larceny, Inc.* within a year.

An interesting sidelight is that almost simultaneously with the New York premiere of *The Night Before Christmas* Perelman wrote an article that appeared in the *New York Times* in which he talked about writing the play. In "From This You Make a Living" he states that there was a good reason for collaborating with his wife on this project: "The guiding principle invoked for this union of talents was the same supple maxim which animates such distinguished couples as Dorothy Parker and Alan Campbell, . . . namely, keep the money in the family."[10] In order to write this "modest little comedy," the couple "retired in mid-July of last year to Boiling Diapers, our charming leasehold in Eastern Pennsylvania." When it proved to be too hot on the farm, they wound up staying in a "Forty-seventh Street fleabag." Other than this information, the article is not enlightening, revealing nothing about the composition process itself.

Of the eleven plays and parts of plays that Perelman wrote either by himself or in collaboration with others, *One Touch of Venus* proved to be the most popular, running for 567 performances. The source for the musical was *The Tinted Venus*, a story written by F. Anstey, the editor of the British humor magazine *Punch* in the 1890's and a comic novelist whom Perelman admired. Perelman's collaborators on this play, Ogden Nash, whom Perelman had met in Hollywood, and Kurt Weill, who wrote the score, were already well established as writers, Nash primarily as a writer of humorous verse (in *The New Yorker* from 1930 on, the same period as Perelman; *Hard Lines*, 1931; *The Bad Parents' Garden of Verse*, 1936) and Weill, a German who moved to America in 1935 as a collaborator with Bertolt Brecht on *The Three-Penny Opera* and on *Mahagonny*. The play opened at the Imperial Theater in New York on October 7, 1943, starring Kenny Baker as Rodney Hatch with Mary Martin (whom Perelman calls "the most agreeable and disciplined performer I've ever known" in the Zinsser interview[11]) in the role of Venus. The supporting cast included sixteen members. The musical comedy was staged by Elia Kazan, with choreography by Agnes de Mille, musical direction by Maurice Abravanel, set design by Howard Bay, and costuming by Paul du Pont and Mainbocher. Cheryl Crawford produced the show. In 1948 the movie version based on Perelman's screenplay was released, as discussed in Chapter Two.

The two-act play is divided into twelve scenes and set in New York City, primarily at the Whitelaw Savory Foundation of Modern Art. The play opens with a chorus singing a comic song that is used to set the tone, in the same way that "Air #1" does in John Gay's *The Beggar's Opera*. Savory (John Boles) has purchased a three-thousand-year-old statue of Venus of Anatolia in Istanbul, and today it is delivered—amidst a series of allusions to Gimbels, Oxford University, Don Ameche, "Truth or Consequences," Coca-Cola, the Axis, *Readers Digest*, the *Police Gazette*, Fifth Avenue, Algeciras, Hohokus, Chevrolets, Blondie and Dagwood, Dick Tracy, baseball great Bill Dickey, Dr. Crippen, Dante, Madam du Barry, Huckleberry Finn, Shangri-La, Menuhin, "Rhapsody in Blue," Don Quixote, Fu Manchu, Rubens, Goya, Velazques, El Greco, Giotto, Watteau, Renoir, Matisse, Cezanne, Modigliani, Rivera, Orozco, Tchelitcheff, Gropper, Gauguin, Van Dyck, Watkins, Romney, Gainsborough, Rembrandt, Gilbert Stuart, Titian, Greuze, Maillais, Shahn, Rouault, Gross, Bellows, Chirico, Sheeler, and Picasso—an eclectic list that seems to go on endlessly and is overpowering. It is interesting that Perelman uses the same stylistic devices (such as allusions and catalogues) in his plays as in his prose and also that he seldom repeats himself in these lists.

The plot is simple. Rodney Hatch (Baker, who "exuded boyish

charm'' [12]) is a barber who happens to be in the studio when the statue is delivered. He puts his girlfriend's engagement ring on the statue's finger and the figure suddenly comes to life—the goddess of love in search of love, especially sensuous love. After some complications and coincidences including the "murder" of Rodney's girlfriend and the appearance of an Anatolian religious fanatic trying to recover his goddess, Rodney falls in love with Venus, who has been pursuing him avidly. His perception of married life is too prosaic for her, though, and in spite of her protestations of undying love, Venus cannot stand the punctuality and humdrum events promised as part of her life in the suburbs of Ozone Heights, and she returns to an inanimate state. While Rodney stands in the museum gallery looking at the resurrected statue and mourning the loss of his love, a simple girl from Ozone Heights who looks amazingly like Venus wanders in, and the two go off to live happily ever after.

The comedy is Perelman's best-known stageplay; while a plot summary makes it sound as though it verges on the sophomoric, on stage it is very effective. Altogether there are fourteen songs, the most famous of which is "Speak Low," and two ballets in the play. While there are comedic failures (such as the premise behind the title of the song "Way Out West in Jersey"), *One Touch of Venus* has its share of funny lines that are typically Perelmanesque and seem to echo earlier lines, especially from the Marx Brothers filmscripts. "Tony's in bed with Sciatica," one character reports to another. "Why tell me? Tell Mr. Sciatica," the second answers. Later Venus is offered an invitation: "Why don't we slip into something comfortable . . . like my den?" Another exchange between Rodney and Venus sounds as though it could have come from Thorne Smith's *The Night Life of the Gods* (which has plot similarities with *One Touch of Venus*):

Rodney: You can't lead me around by the nose!

Venus: A man's nose is his castle.

Rodney: I'll show you who's going to wear the pants in this family!

Venus: With a figure like hers, I hope it's you. [13]

Sounding like Marion in Smith's *Topper*, Venus goes on, "speaking purely as your future roommate." Another conversation reveals Perelman's sense of the literal:

She seems a faithful little thing.
Oh, I'd put my arm in the fire up to there for Mr. Savory.
That's rather specialized work, isn't it?   (pp. 49–50)

Individual lines include, "A girl on the couch is worth two on the mind" and "That's a very interesting fixation you have my boy. I'd like to meet your mother." Even the song lyrics are playful:

> Since Sally ran off with her obstetrician,
> Her hair's turned red and she looks like a Titian;
> Of course, I'd hate to swear in court
> What kind of Titian: Beaut—or mort—.   (p. 78)

Besides Perelman's affinity for puns, the dialogue also demonstrates his love of the sound of words:

> Your Bemis valve is clogged, brother.
>   The frogging is scored on your
>   lynch-pin and that bandles the bushing!
> Hey, are you a plumber?
> Been working with drips all my life!   (p. 58)

One Touch of Venus is theatrical, yet it does not exploit the medium in ways that make it any more effective than Perelman's essays. It is typical popular Broadway fare, providing an entertaining evening but lacking any enduring significance.

Lewis Nichols wrote two reviews of the play for the *New York Times*, one that appeared the morning after the premiere and one that was published nine days later. In the first review he raved that "the theatre season finally reached Broadway."[14] "Freshness, an adult manner and lavishness of display" contribute to making the play the "first fully professional musical show in some time" to appear on the Great White Way, in his opinion. Nichols generally finds the writing creditable: "Mr. Perelman and Mr. Nash are in there with a book which, while not perfect throughout, is better than those of most musicals." (Presumably this is meant as praise, though given the nature of most musicals it may not be overwhelming.) The critic does complain that the pace of the early part of the show is slow, "the fault there likely lay in the slow-starting book," but "Taken together, 'One Touch of Venus' provides one of the better evenings in the theatre."

In his second review Nichols expands on these remarks somewhat. The shows presented on Broadway during the 1943 season had so far been an uninspiring lot, and Nichols finds life a "bit more cheerful now" that this "one new hit" is sufficient in itself to permit him to label the season "great."[15] He also provides an interesting piece of information about the play's pre-Broadway tryout. Normally, a new show opens in New Haven, Connecticut, and then, depending on how successful it is, travels to Boston and then to Philadelphia before being taken to Broadway. Nichols reports that "Down from Boston during the depths of the late unpleasantness came a report that the Kurt Weill—S. J. Perelman—Odgen Nash musical was, as the trade puts it, lousy." The theater-going public ignored the rumors, and enough tickets were sold before the play even arrived in New York that it was proclaimed a box office hit.

Nichols, now having had some time to reflect on the play, still finds the writing praiseworthy, with a minor exception: " 'One Touch of Venus' is not another 'Oklahoma!' although it well may be the best new musical show to have opened since that time. Its earlier sections are not so funny as most of the remarks normally chattering off the Perelman-Nash typewriters, some of the show is neither fast nor brilliant and a few of the players are much better than the material with which they are forced to work. But on the whole it is a very good show." Perhaps Nichols felt that *One Touch of Venus*, like many shows that amuse on initial viewing, was a little thin when recollected in tranquility. For the American stage this is not atypical, or even undesirable, since the primary functions of a Broadway show are to make money and to provide an enjoyable, entertaining evening, which *One Touch of Venus* does. The allusion to *Oklahoma!* has an unintended ironic overtone attached to it; the Richard Rogers-Oscar Hammerstein play had opened just the previous season, a mere seven months earlier, and thus the claim that nothing so good had appeared in the intervening time is not very impressive.

In 1946 Perelman was again writing for the theater, but this time with less success. Along with Nash, Al Hirschfeld, and musician Vernon Duke, he scripted *Sweet Bye and Bye* in a room at New York's Warwick Hotel (see *Westward, Ha!*). The play was produced in New Haven, but it never got as far as the Broadway stage. Apparently this failure affected Perelman (as critic Atkinson has said, he never forgot that *Sweet Bye and Bye* did not make it past Philadelphia), and he abandoned playwriting for sixteen years. He also took a vacation from screenwriting at about this same time and concentrated on his prose writing.

The most unfortunate incident in Perelman's theatrical career occurred in connection with his next play, *The Beauty Part*, when a New York City newspaper strike had a profound effect on its potential reception. On December 26, 1962, this comedy was mounted at the Music Box Theater on Broadway. With Bert Lahr in five characterizations, the comedy lampooned the "cultural explosion" that seemed to make it "incumbent on everyone to express themselves in words or paint" or "to leap around in homemade jerseys," as Perelman explained in a pre-production interview.[16] Reactions to the play were promising, with laudatory reviews by critics such as Howard Taubman of the *New York Times*, but the newspaper strike precluded the normal reviews and publicity, and as a result the play closed only two and a half months later, after a run of eighty-five performances. Ironically, favorable reviews such as Taubman's, cited below, were available to people outside New York City, where the strike was not in effect.

In addition to Lahr in the roles of Milo Leotard Allardyce Duplessis Weatherwax, Hyacinth Beddoes Laffoon, Harry Hubris, Nelson Smedley, and Judge Herman J. Rinderbrust, several other players appeared in multiple parts: Alice Ghostley (Octavia Weatherwax, Kitty Entrail, and Grace Fingerhead), David Doyle (Mike Mulroy, Bunce, Maurice Blount, Curtis Fingerhead, Wagnerian, and Hanratty), Gil Gardner (Van Lennep, Fish-Market Boy, Elmo, and Policeman), Bernie West (Sam Fussfeld, Seymour Krumgold, Wormser, and Poteat), William Le Massena (Hagedorn, Boris Pickwick, Emmett Stagg, Hennepin, and Bailiff), Arnold Soboloff (Vishnu, Vernon Equinox, Rukeyser, and Joe Gourielli), Charlotte Rae (Gloria Krumgold, Mrs. Younghusband, Rowena Inchcape, and Mrs. Lafcadio Mifflin), and Fiddle Ciracola (Chenille Schreiber and Sherry Quicklime). Apparently some humor was expected from seeing the same actor in several roles, creating a pleasurable shock of recognition effect combined with amused confusion over who was who when. Also in the comedy were Larry Hagman and Patricia Englund and three others in supporting roles. The play was directed by Noel Willman and produced by Michael Ellis and Edmund Anderson. William Pitkin was the set designer, Alvin Colt the costumer, and Don Walker composed the incidental music.

The two-act (eleven scenes) play is set in New York and California. It opens in the luxurious Weatherwax triplex on Park Avenue where we are introduced to multimillionaire Weatherwax, his wife, and their Yalie son Lance. Upon finding out that the family fortune (which is so great that "There's loose rubies all over the foyer"[17]) is based on the Weatherwax All-Weather Garbage Disposal Plan, the embarrassed Lance declares that he is separating from the family and will pursue two goals, his love, April Monkhood, and a life as a creative artist. The rest of the play concerns Lance's efforts to realize these goals and the many interrelated characters and themes that weave in and out of the plot line.

Money is a major concern. April abandons Lance when he reveals that he has renounced his family ties to the Weatherwax fortune, and various other characters (notably Harry Hubris) become interested in Lance only after they learn about his financial connections. Hyacinth Beddoes Laffoon's interest in Lance as a member of her editorial staff is formed on this basis and extends only to the point where she learns that the Weatherwax Trust and Loan Company will not give her a loan.

Unable to get help from either April or Mrs. Laffoon to become a writer, Lance turns to the renowned painter Goddard Quagmeyer for whom he is to serve as an apprentice, but he is disillusioned when Quagmeyer sells out his artistic sensibilities and principles for the money offered by Hollywood producer Hubris. Act One ends with Hubris proclaiming that Lance will become a movie director—"To show my faith in you, I'm going to let your folks put up the money for an independent production!"[18]

In Act Two, Lance and Hubris, disguised as a Chinese houseboy and his father, are in Santa Barbara trying to steal the manuscript of a Civil War novel ("Nobody before ever looked at the Confederacy through the eyes of a Creole callgirl. . . . ") that they intend to adapt to the screen. Everything becomes farcically confused when the author's jealous husband tries to pass off his wife's work for his own so that he can sell it to a pornographic book publisher. Next, Lance becomes involved in an outrageous television project in Pasadena. The "Communist Plot" and problems with unions and blue collar workers are subjects included in a series of adventures that conclude with April (*"an attractive girl in her early twenties given to self-dramatization and endowed with magnificent secondary sexual characteristics and practically no sense of humor*"[19]) being hauled into court by the vice squad for popping out of a fake pie "clad in the world's scantiest bikini."[20] The court is presided over by Judge Herman J. Rinderbrust, who uses the televised proceedings to advertise products (such as a cemetery) in which he has a financial interest. Justice is allocated according to how the judge's economics might be affected, and April's case is dismissed when Lance produces some "relevant and germane" evidence, a check in the judge's name in the amount of $500,000.[21] The play ends with the traditional fertility ceremony celebration of comedy—April and Lance are married—and Milo Weatherwax showers everyone, including the audience, with a "little bundle of happiness . . . everybody's joy"[22]—greenbacks.

Perelman's points are evident. Money controls everything, even creativity. False culture takes its lumps, too. "Every housewife in the country's got a novel under her apron," laments Quagmeyer before his defection to the service of Mamon, "And the dentists are even worse. Do you realize that there are twice as many dentists painting in their spare time as there are painters practicing dentistry?"[23] When Mrs. Krumgold is asked what the subject should be of a painting that she has commissioned, she replies, "Oh, who cares? So long as it doesn't clash with the drapes. They're silver blue."[24] The superficiality of modern American culture is summed up in an exchange between Lance and Hubris about the actor hired to play the title role in a picture about the life of John Singer Sargent:

HUBRIS: Mentality's one problem you won't have with Rob Roy Fruitwell. Strictly a matzo ball.

LANCE: But John Singer Sargent was a genius.

HUBRIS: (*Triumphantly*): That's the beauty part. This cluck is a sensitized sponge that he'll soak up the info you give him and project it.   (p. 62)

The use of the phrase "the beauty part" in this context is a clear statement of the point that Perelman is making throughout the play— we are a nation with little or no cultural depth inherent or evident in the common person on the street.

Humor results from premises such as Milo Weatherwax's interest in money overcoming everything else (several times when his wife mentions their son Lance, he asks, "What Lance is that?"[25]), puns ("Who are all these people? My dear, it's the copulation explosion!''[26]), and other kinds of wordplay (one character is described as having been on the dean's list at UCLA, but since this distinction is modified with the phrase "morning, noon, and night," it is clear that academic achievement is not what was recognized[27]). These devices seem less prevalent than in Perelman's prose; the plays are more diffuse because they rely almost solely on dialogue, so the omniscient narrator's commentary is missing (again, this suggests why the scenario format is not always successful for the author).

In a pre-opening talk with Paul Gardner, who calls the play "an irreverent glance at the current itch for creativity," Perelman speaks about his conception of *The Beauty Part*. "It seems to be incumbent on everyone to express themselves in words and paint. I'm sure someone somewhere is painting with feathers. Self-improvement is fine. It's all right for people to leap around in homemade jerseys, but that isn't self-expression," the dramatist explains.[28] It was during this era that prizes in art shows were being awarded for paintings done by chimpanzees (J. Fred Muggs distinguished himself in this field), an elephant (the brush was tied to her tail), a man who painted by dipping handfuls of worms into paint and then allowing them to wriggle across the canvas, a Japanese gentleman who painted the top of his bald head and rubbed it on the canvas, another painter who hung balloons filled with paint over a canvas and popped the balloons with darts, and a man who painted nudes (literally—he doused naked women with paint and then had them roll around on the canvas). As Ring Lardner might say, you could look it up! And, since Perelman is never shy about exposing arrogance, pretentiousness, or foolishness for what it is when he finds it exhibited by the public, the cultural movement was a natural target for his satirical jibes.

Reviewers find *The Beauty Part* a little marred, yet they also find it successful. One summary calls the play a series of "loosely connected satirical sketches . . . [about] a Candide-like youth . . . [a] disjointed but often excruciatingly funny lampoon of twentieth-century cultural affections" that did not reach the audience that it "merited" because of the newspaper strike.[29]

Among the other comedies running on Broadway during this season were Burt Shevelove and Stephen Sondheim's *A Funny Thing Happened on the Way to the Forum* (featuring Zero Mostel and Jack Gilford), Herb Gardner's *A Thousand Clowns* (starring Jason Robards),

Abe Burrows' *How to Succeed in Business Without Really Trying* (a perfect vehicle for Robert Morse and Rudy Vallee), Sumner Arthur Long's *Never Too Late* (a Paul Ford triumph), Neil Simon's *Little Me* (with Sid Caesar), and Alan Bennett's British import *Beyond the Fringe* (which brought Peter Cook and Dudley Moore to America). Parenthetically, the cost of admission had jumped to a range of $2.90 for matinees to $9.90 for orchestra divans at evening performances, a sizeable increase over the 1943 ticket prices quoted earlier. Considering this competition, Taubman's assessment of *The Beauty Part* is impressive. The play, says Taubman, permits "an awesome discovery—S. J. Perelman and Bert Lahr were meant for each other. . . . [They] make happy music together." The reviewer is ecstatic about Lahr's performance, but he is laudatory about the scripting as well, understanding how well Perelman has provided a framework in which Lahr's talents can be showcased. He finds that "In 'The Beauty Part,' as in his pieces for 'The New Yorker', Mr. Perelman's muse exfoliates like a mad, lush tropical plant. Just when you think that its satirical shoots have got out of hand, they may turn on you unexpectedly and sting." As Lahr relies on Perelman's script, so too does the script depend upon Lahr's abilities: "this prose is not really designed for the theatre. There are times when the ear cannot absorb its extended cadences. On some of its most abandoned flights Mr. Perelman's writing drifts serenely off the stage. . . . But depend on Mr. Lahr to fetch it back." Elsewhere the critic proclaims that "Mr. Perelman's lampoon of dilettantism is so broad at times that it loses its edge—but when Mr. Lahr takes over, all is well."[30] Since the ultimate criterion for determining a drama's success is based on its performance, it is fair to state that the play is successful, even if it requires an actor of Lahr's stature to make it so. There is no doubt that Lahr does not prevail in spite of the script, and the fact that a master actor is required for the work's potential to be fulfilled certainly does not diminish the quality of the play.

Even the typical charge levelled against Perelman's playwriting, plotlessness, is not really a valid complaint in connection with *The Beauty Part* because it is not a play in the formal sense of the word; it hearkens back to the revues that the dramatist contributed to early in his career, and it attempts to achieve its goals in a more innovative way than, say, *How to Succeed in Business Without Really Trying* does. Both plays were on the boards at the same time, and much of their satire was directed at similar objects, but Burrows elected to fashion a conventional story line while Perelman chose to approach his subject matter through a sequence of blackout-like scenes held together by common characters and themes. Too, there is enough plot structure present to supply a framework, despite Taubman's admonition, "Don't try to make sense of the plot of 'The Beauty Part.' Don't even dignify it by calling it a plot. In substance . . . it is a series of exuberantly free fantasies on [a] theme."

In retrospect, while *The Beauty Part* is entertaining, some of the enthusiasm it generated is probably partially due to the reviewers' shared bemusement with the current artistic excesses that Perelman satirizes. Robert Brustein and Richard Gilman both label *The Beauty Part* a cartoon in their reviews (Brustein calls it an "animated cartoon"[31] while Gilman refers to the play as a "cartoon comedy"[32]). Brustein finds Perelman's "picaresque adventures" demonstrating that "culture is the biggest sell of all" appealing. "It lacks form, focus, or consistent intention," he grumbles, "but it is immensely amusing, and there are enough teeth left in its mouth, after the inevitable out-of-town extractions, to provide some bite as well." The reviewer is ambiguous about Perelman's writing, however. He speaks of Perelman's "jaundiced look" and decides that "the author's personal bassinet [a reference to the play's ending] would have grown fuller had he chosen a less naked approach to his subject." The dramatist's approach to his material, his flaunted awareness of his audience, catches Brustein's attention: "Perelman's cynicism . . . is a wholesome antidote to the usual theatrical hypocrisy; and 'The Beauty Part', like Felicien Marceau's 'The Egg' (which it resembles in many ways), manages to give us a refreshing glimpse into the hidden motives behind our canting ideals. . . . Most of these characters and situations are burlesque standards—some even appeared recently in that more compromised work, 'Little Me.' . . . What Perelman adds to the familiar brew is his linguistic flair . . . generous topical references and sardonic comment. It is the sharpness of the satirical tone which seems new."[33] A problem that Brustein sees, though, is that "the author is recruiting his audience from the very community he would excoriate." Thus, "his moral position is indecisive, vacillating between ridicule and celebration of the audience's assumed values." Brustein concludes with a recommendation: "Perelman has the capacity to become a very good stage satirist, but like so many writers in his dilemma, he must first be willing to accept an embattled role." It is doubtful that such a stance would have suited Perelman or accomplished what he intended as well as the style that he uses; such an antagonistic approach would destroy the comedy's humor and thereby negate the very function of comedy of educating the audience by getting it to laugh at social foibles.

Gilman finds little that he approves of in *The Beauty Part*: "its satiric velocity is curtailed and its virtues of personal statement and unbeholden spirit are considerably weakened by professional hi-jinks and a broadness of platform."[34] Contradictorily, he calls the play "authentic, vivifying and, for the most part and within its limitations, secure." What are the play's limitations? "Largely those of its creator . . . who is a superior cartoonist, but not a dramatist and especially not a visual one. . . . he sketches, intensifies and leaves out . . . but his strength is verbal . . . holding up to us the broad mirror of . . . our comic quest for seriousness. He has done little that has been effective in the theatre." This "loosely strung-together series of skits" Gilman designates "radio humor," and he believes that "we aren't likely to be more than momentarily amused by a fable of our national hunger for self-expression, a parody of both fake High—and genuine—Middle Culture."

Gilman's opinion notwithstanding, Perelman's comedy was generally well received by playgoers, it is not nearly as badly written as the critic indicates, and it shows improvement over his previous dramatic efforts. The first act of *The Beauty Part* is dramatically superior to *One Touch of Venus*, for example. It is more solidly written, comparably almost Shavian in quality and tone, and it is funnier than its predecessor; it is a comedy of character and situation, not just jokes strung together, and there is some social commentary, delivered humorously, but with a touch of seriousness. Sadly, the second act falls apart and becomes empty farce that is more concerned with diverting than with being unified, though it is funny on stage.

Although there is nothing in the list of *dramatic personae* or in any of the stage directions specifying the assignment of multiple parts, this is one aspect of *The Beauty Part* that does demonstrate an exploitation of the dramatic medium. As noted above, it would be obvious to the audience that different characters were being played by the same actors, knowledge that would be a cause for some amusement, but more importantly would also reinforce Perelman's theses, for it would be an explicit exhibition that the attitudes being brought to our attention are ubiquitous, knowing no class, educational, professional, or geographical bounds. The abrupt shifts in location are easily accommodated in drama, too, and dialogue functions as a transitional device. Moreover, dialogue is an excellent mode through which Perelman's love of words can be expressed, and it is probable that his recognition of the format's possibilities for extending the manipulation of language in a natural-seeming way lay behind his frequent adoption of the scenario in his essays.

One of the artistic decisions made regarding the staging of the play illustrates Perelman's recognition of how language works on stage. In this play language is the "rococo element," so the sets are restrained rather than elaborate. The dramatist acknowledges that "The obvious impulse is to match comic words with a comic set, but that results in a confusion of elements." [35] This decision is exactly right; in architectural terms, flamboyant scenery would detract from the words and would create a tumultuous, "busy" atmosphere. This is especially true in a play that contains as many characters as *The Beauty Part* does. The words make a much better impression against a less colorful, more subdued backdrop. The costumes are fancy enough to make the characters stand out when they are speaking, and the audience focuses on each speaker as though he or she is framed in a pin-point spot light.

An intriguing aspect of *The Beauty Part* has to do with its composition. It has been mentioned that Perelman borrowed from himself on occasion. In this play a number of specific lines of dialogue, indeed whole scenes, many of them among the best in the play, were taken verbatim or nearly so from Perelman's prose pieces from as long ago as nineteen years earlier. He borrowed most freely from "Farewell My Lovely Appetizer," "How Sharper than a Serpent's Tooth," "The Hand that Cradles the Rock," "De Gustibus Ain't What Dey Used to Be," and "Who Stole My Golden Metaphor?" These pieces are discussed in Chapter One, but the stories themselves are not essential— the words liberated are more important than the context from which they are taken.

The first borrowing in *The Beauty Part* occurs in Act I, scene 1, during a conversation between Octavia Weatherwax and the private detective, Mike Mulroy. Mulroy calls Mrs. Weatherwax by her first name, leading to the following exchange:

MULROY: Octavia—

OCTAVIA (Recoils from him): You knew my first name all along.

MULROY (Sheepishly): Maybe I overstepped.

OCTAVIA: You have. I'm one of the richest women in America, Mulroy. A mere nod from me creates a convulsion in Wall Street. My son, Lance, is Skull and Bones at Yale. It's time for you to leave the room.

MULROY: Yes, Ma'am. *(Retrieves hat, points to vase on stand)* My, that's lovely. Genuine Sevres, isn't it?

OCTAVIA: Yes. How did you know?

MULROY: Oh, I dabble in porcelain a bit.

OCTAVIA: Isn't that strange? I rather sensed you had a flair.

MULROY: I haven't been a private snoop twelve years for nothing.

OCTAVIA: It was nine last time.

MULROY (kneels impetuously at her feet): It seemed like twelve till you came along.   (pp. 22–23)

The original for these lines is Perelman's *The New Yorker*, December 16, 1944, spoof of hardboiled detective stories, "Farewell My Lovely Appetizer," reprinted in *Keep It Crisp* and other volumes, in which the narrator, private eye Mike Noonan, confronts a client:

"I go for girls named Sigrid with opal eyes," I said.
"Where'd you learn my name?"
"I haven't been a private snoop twelve years for nothing, sister."
"It was nine last time."
"It seemed like twelve till you came along." [36]

Even the detectives' first names are the same.

In the scenario, "How Sharper than a Serpent's Tooth," also reprinted in *Keep It Crisp*, there is an exchange between Milo and his wife. A similar conversation appears in *The Beauty Part*. The extent of Perelman's self-borrowing is obvious here. [37] Except for changing the son's name from Rapier to Lance (not too big a change at that), making some minor alterations to bring up to date or to reduce the amount of slang, thus making the dialogue sound more realistic on stage, and adding a few details to accommodate the play's plot, the segment that was printed originally in *The New Yorker* on January 5, 1946, reappears almost intact in the dramatic version some seventeen years later.

Another scenario of his own from which the author borrowed heavily is "The Hand That Cradles the Rock" (*The New Yorker*, July 1, 1950, reprinted in *The Ill-Tempered Clavicord*). The short story is set in a woman publisher's office where she confers with her editorial staff. In the play the setting and most of the characters and lines are the same, but Lance is introduced as a job seeker. A few lines are rearranged, the language is a bit more modern (the word "whip" is substituted for "knout"), or rougher ("I won't stand for any softsoap or hogwash" becomes "no ass-kissing!"), and there is recognition of the performance dimension when some lines attributed to "OMNES" are parcelled out to individual characters (providing more sense of movement and immediacy on stage), yet there can be no doubt that most of Act I, scene 3 originated with the prose piece.[38]

"De Gustibus Ain't What Dey Used To Be" (*The Road to Miltown*) is another scenario from which Perelman appropriated a sizeable chunk to insert into *The Beauty Part*. The selection that first appeared in *The New Yorker* on April 18, 1953, created the character of Lance's beloved, April Monkhood. The hero's name (Cyprian) and Fussfeld's occupation are different, but essentially the scene in *The Beauty Part* is a repetition.[39]

The character of Vernon Equinox and Perelman's commentary on art, the public's taste, and the duplicity of other artists orginates in "Who Stole My Golden Metaphor?," a short story that was first published in *The Road to Miltown*. When Equinox surfaces again, in *The Beauty Part*, he brings with him many of the same concepts that had been expressed in his earlier incarnation.

The ethics of incorporating parts of long-ago-published short prose works in a full-length dramatic form do not seem to have concerned Perelman. In the writer's defense it should be pointed out that the passages are his own, that retrieving bits and pieces of material and combining them in longer works is a time-honored custom (how many scholars publish a number of essays on a subject and then collect them as a book? Some of the most respected academics make a habit of this practice), Perelman revises the work somewhat, and frequently the transfer to drama produces a more effective presentation than was possible in prose.

Waste not, want not.

On November 4, 1974, *The Beauty Part* was revived at the American Place Theater under the direction of James Hammerstein. The set was by Fred Voelpel and costumes were designed by Pearl Somner. Armand Assante, Joseph Bova, Ron Faber, Cynthia Harris, Mitchell Jason, Peter Kingsley, Bobo Lewis, Susan Sullivan, and Jarrold Ziman composed the cast. When the revival opened it was scheduled to run only through November 22. From the reactions of a new generation of critics, it is probably just as well that a longer run was not scheduled.

Perelman's concept of the play remained constant over the years following its first production. In a pre-opening interview he describes the play in terms very similar to those that he used twelve years before:

"The Beauty Part" is about the widespread yearning for creativity," he said. "The itch for self-expression. The passage of time hasn't really changed my point. If anything, the lust for self-expression has become even more intensified since the work was first produced."[40]

Perelman also indicates that there is no reason to update the play because the circumstances that stimulated its creation in 1962 are still in force. And, as he had in the pre-production interview then, he comments on contemporary playwriting:

"Broadway has been reduced in quality and importance," he maintained. The theaters—and the theater sections of newspapers—have been taken over by rock stars and blue movies. He hastened to add that he had no bias against pornography. Indeed, he recalled a time when he would escape the iron lung of MGM's writers' building to motor through downtown Los Angeles in search of a film entitled "The Sex Maniac," but that was a different epoch, he said, a time when art and pornography were miles apart—literally. Now they were cheek by jowl—literally. As for the serious theater, "too much of it is four people being rude in a room."

Writing about several plays running concurrently on Broadway, Walter Kerr includes a few comments about *The Beauty Part* revival because of its farcical elements, which he finds unsuccessful without Bert Lahr's presence.[41] Clive Barnes is even more critical in his review, appropriately titled, "Perelman's 'The Beauty Part' Turns Up Again, Alas."

Although he did not see the original production, Barnes finds "This mixture of philistinism, cynicism and vulgar name-dropping, . . . old and tired," at least in part because Bova lacks Lahr's comic power.[42] Of all of the actors, only Susan Sullivan as April is found "vital." Primarily, though, Barnes places the blame squarely on the author: "Mr. Perelman possibly imagined that he was fearlessly viscerating false gods, and demonically destroying the phony world of art, books, movies and television. He wasn't. He was just being silly." For Barnes, *The Beauty Part* mistakes "deadpan facetiousness for wit and gallery-playing yahooism for satire." Presumably the same could be said about a revival of almost any of the comedies that were running on Broadway when *The Beauty Part* first appeared. Comedy that is not based on character too frequently becomes dated because it is topical or because it is written in the style of a period. The latter failing seems to be functioning in the case of *The Beauty Part*.

In *The Last Laugh* Perelman mentioned in passing that the "only thespian flight" that he had ever indulged in "had been a minor role in a high school pageant based on Pocahontas."[43] Nevertheless, the author was attracted to the stage very early in his career, and he wrote for the theater for a number of years. He came very close to producing major Broadway hits, but he never quite made it.

The fact that his writing was not of a serious nature may well have kept him from becoming an important dramatist, but that has nothing to do with the popular theater anyway. However, there may be some legitmate reasons for Perelman's never having achieved a facility in his dramatic writing equal to that in his prose work. His bad luck certainly was one cause, for he was thereby denied the opportunity to expand his talents. This compounded his lack of experience in the genre, since further chances to add to the experience were severely limited. Because of the enormous cost of mounting a theatrical production, it is impractical to expect an author to evolve as quickly as a dramatist as it is possible to do in the shorter prose forms that Perelman espoused. Those took much less time to complete and cost only the price of a few sheets of paper, and they could appear in any of several magazines within a short period of time.

Groucho had complained, in connection with the author's screenwriting, that one of Perelman's shortcomings was that he "wasn't a constructionist for the stage."[44] Whereas the short prose pieces that he wrote were sufficient to develop his salient points, and his humor works well on the printed page because of the reasons already delineated in relation to his screenwriting (the development of ideas, no need to fill the spaces between the lines, and so forth), when it comes to film and dramatic writing, the necessity arises to devise a plot that will carry his material for an hour and a half to two hours. This is not one of Perelman's strong suits, and his plots tend to be either merely a collection of loosely connected episodes/sketches or unimaginative and conventional.

Still, the plays are entertaining, and they contain numerous good jokes and bits of scintillating dialogue. Too, Perelman's use of language in the plays frequently is comparable to that in his prose works.

Finally, one method for determining Perelman's success as a playwright is to compare his own work against the benchmark he establishes in evaluating the writing of other dramatists. In his conversation with Gardner regarding *The Beauty Part*, Perelman commented on contemporary dramatists: "The trouble with the theatre today is that it's like lukewarm oatmeal. It's all formula writing that could be done on an I.B.M. machine. . . . Our young playwrights take themselves too seriously. They need to read more. They need a point of view. . . . Years ago, the putting of words on paper was important. With the emergence of radio and television, the writers who had something funny to say were content to submerge themselves as gag writers for comics."[45] He makes similar statements about prose writers and screenwriters throughout his career, and in each case it is clear that Perelman applies these standards to himself when he engages in writing. As a dramatist, he has a sound background based on his extensive reading, he is willing to employ unusual approaches in some instances, he has a definite and clearly expressed point of view, and while he does not take himself seriously, he does think that his craft is important. None of this in itself makes Perelman a good dramatist, but it does reflect an attitude toward dramaturgy that leads to a sound product.

It is a shame that Perelman did not have more opportunity to develop his dramatic skills, for he showed a good potential that remained unrealized. As a playwright, he certainly will never be ranked with Eugene O'Neill, Arthur Miller, or Tennessee Williams, but the American theater is richer for his contributions.

NOTES

1. See "The Marx Brothers" (S. J. Perelman, *The Last Laugh*, New York: Simon and Schuster, 1981, pp. 147–60), for instance, regarding *Sherry Flip*. *The Ladders* is referred to by Norris W. Yates in his *The American Humorist: Conscience of the Twentieth Century* (Ames, Iowa: Iowa State University Press, 1964), p. 333; the play apparently was never presented on Broadway.

2. Quoted in Michael T. Leech, "Perelman, S(idney) J(oseph)," in *Contemporary Dramatists*, ed. by James Vinson (London: St. James Press, 1977), p. 624.

3. Brooks Atkinson, "The Play: Paris Where 'All Good Americans' Go— Hope Williams and Fred Keating," *New York Times*, December 6, 1933, p. 29.

4. Quoted in Edwin Bronner, *The Encyclopedia of the American Theatre 1900–1975* (San Diego: A. S. Barnes, 1980), p. 21.

5. Anon., "Who Are The Perelmans?" *New York Times*, December 10, 1933, sect. 10, p. 2.

6. Jay Martin, *Nathanael West: The Art of His Life* (New York: Farrar, Straus and Giroux, 1970), p. 250.

7. Ibid., p. 364.

8. Quoted in Bronner, p. 334.

9. Atkinson, "The Play: On the 'The Night before Christmas' the Perelmans Crack Safes and Jokes in Sixth Avenue," *New York Times*, April 11, 1941, p. 25.

10. Perelman, "From This You Make a Living," *New York Times*, April 13, 1941, sect. 10, P. 3.

11. William Zinsser, "That Perelman of Great Price is Sixty-Five," *New York Times Magazine* (January 26, 1969): 27.

12. Zinsser, p. 27.

13. S. J. Perelman and Ogden Nash, *One Touch of Venus* (Boston: Little, Brown, 1944), p. 44.

14. Lewis Nichols, "The Play: 'One Touch of Venus', which Makes the Whole World Kin, Opens at the Imperial," *New York Times*, October 8, 1943, sect. 6, p. 14.

15. Nichols, "One Touch of Venus," *New York Times*, October 17, 1943, sect. 2, p. 1.

16. Quoted in Paul Gardner, "S. J. Perelman Will Attack 'Cultural Explosion,' " *New York Times*, October 9, 1962, sect. L, p. 47.

17. S. J. Perelman, *The Beauty Part* (New York: Simon and Schuster, 1963), p. 24.

18. Ibid., p. 79.

19. Ibid., p. 31.

20. Ibid., p. 126.

21. Ibid., p. 136.

22. Ibid., pp. 141–42.

23. Ibid., p. 52.

24. Ibid., p. 56.

25. Ibid., pp. 24, 29.

26. Ibid., p. 84.

27. Ibid., p. 72.

28. Gardner, p. 47.

29. Bronner, p. 45.

30. Howard Taubman, "Theatre: 'Beauty Part,' " *New York Times*, Western Edition, December 28, 1962, p. 5.

31. Robert Brustein, "Candide among the Culture-Vultures," in *Seasons of Discontent: Dramatic Opinions, 1959–1965* (New York: Simon and Schuster, 1965), p. 149.

32. Richard Gilman, "Bert Lahr: The Cavalry Arrives," *Common and Uncommon Masks* (New York: Random House, 1971), p. 213.

33. Brustein, pp. 150–51.

34. Gilman, pp. 213–14.

35. Gardner, p. 47.

36. S. J. Perelman, *The Most of S. J. Perelman* (New York: Simon and Schuster, 1958), pp. 193, 194.

37. Compare:

OCTAVIA:. . . . this is the handwriting on the wall. Our marriage is washed up—napoo—*ausgespielt.*

MILO: Maybe you're right. I've felt for some time that things haven't been the same between us.

OCTAVIA: Oh, well, the fat's in the fire. How are we to break the news to Rapier?

MILO: Rapier? What Rapier is that?

OCTAVIA: Why, our nineteen-year-old son, which he's home from Yale on his midyears and don't suspicion that his folks are rifting.

MILO: Oh, yes. Where is our cub at the present writing?

OCTAVIA: In the tack room furbishing up the accouterments of his polo ponies.

OCTAVIA:. . . . Milo, this is the handwriting on the wall. Our marriage is washed up—napoo—*ausgespielt.*

MILO: You're trying to tell me something. . . . Maybe you're right. I'll admit I've been chafing at the bit a bit.

OCTAVIA: Ah, well, the fat's in the fire. How are we to break the news to Lance?

MILO: What Lance is that?

OCTAVIA: Why, our twenty-year-old son, which he's home from Yale on his midyears and don't suspicion his folks are rifting.

MILO: Of course, of course. . . . Where is our cub at the present writing?

OCTAVIA: In the tack room furbishing

MILO *(acidly):* Far better off to be
furbishing up on his Euclid, lest he
drag the name of Weatherwax
through the scholastic mire.

OCTAVIA: Shhh, here he comes now.

MILO: My boy, the Weatherwax union
has blown a gasket. Our frail
matrimonial bark, buffeted by the
winds of temperament, has foundered
on the shoals of incompatibility.

RAPIER: Get in the groove, fatso. I
don't latch onto that long-hair
schmaltz.

MILO: To employ the vulgate, your
mother and I have pphhht.

RAPIER *(with quick sympathy):* That's
rum, chum.

MILO: Yes, it's hard on us oldsters,
but it isn't going to be easy for you,
either.

RAPIER *(frightened):* You mean I've
got to go to work?

MILO: Certainly not. As long as
there's a penny of your mother's
money left, we'll make out
somehow.

RAPIER: Look, guv'nor, I . . . that is,
me . . . aw, cripes, can I ask you
something man to man?

MILO *(aside):* I was afraid of this.

RAPIER: Well, I've been running with
a pretty serious crowd up at New
Haven—lots of bull sessions about
swing and stuff—and I've been
wondering. Where does our money
come from?

MILO *(evasively):* Why—er—uh—the
doctor brings it. In a little black bag.

RAPIER: Aw, gee, Dad, I'm old
enough to know. *Please.*

. . . .

MILO: We-e-ell, all right, but my,
you children grow up quick
nowadays. Have you ever heard of
the Weatherwax All-Weather
Garbage Disposal Plan?

up the accoutrements of his polo
ponies.

MILO *(Acidly):* Far better to be
furbishing up on his Euclid, lest he
drag the name of Weatherwax
through the scholastic mire.

LANCE *(Exuberantly, offstage):* Dads!
Mums!

OCTAVIA: Shush! Here he comes now.

. . . .

MILO: My boy, the Weatherwax
union has blown a gasket.

LANCE: You've lost me, Dads.

MILO: To employ the vulgate, your
mother and I have split out.

LANCE *(Sobered):* Rum go, Dads.

MILO: Yes, it's hard on us oldsters,
but it isn't going to be easy for you
either.

LANCE *(Frightened):* You mean I've
got to go to work?

MILO: Don't be asinine! Not as long as
there's a penny of your mother's
money left.

LANCE: Look, Pater, I . . . that *is,*
me . . . aw, jeepers, can I ask you
something man to man?

MILO: Lance, a chap with a
sympathetic sire don't have to beat
about the bush.

LANCE: Thanks, Pop. Well, I've been
running with a pretty serious crowd
up at New Haven—lots of bull
sessions about *Lolita* and Oscar
Wilde. . . . And I've been
wondering more and more of late.
Where does our money come from?

MILO *(Evasively):* Why—er—the
doctor brings it. In a little black bag.

LANCE: Aw, gee, Dad, I'm old
enough to know. Please.

MILO: My, you children grow up
quick nowadays. *(Fatalistically)*
Very well. Have you ever heard of
the Weatherwax All-Weather
Garbage Disposal Plan?

RAPIER: You—you mean whereby garbage is disposed of in all weathers by having neatly uniformed attendants call for and remove it?

MILO: Yes. That is the genesis of our scratch.

RAPIER (burying his face in his hands): Oh, Daddy, I want to die!

MILO: Steady on, lad. After all, think of the millions which their flats would be a welter of chicken bones, fruit peels, and old teabags were it not for our kindly ministrations.

RAPIER (sobbing): I'll never be able to hold up my head in Bulldog circles again.

MILO: Nonsense. Why, you wear the keenest threads on the campus and are persona grata to myriad Eli frats.

RAPIER (his face drawn and a new maturity in his voice): No, Father, this is the end of halcyon days in the groves of Academe. I'm going away.

MILO: Where?

RAPIER: Somewhere beyond the horizon—to fabled Cathay or Samarkand and Ind, if need be. Anywhere I can find other values than the tinkle of money and the clang of refuse cans.

MILO (his eyes shining): There speaks a Weatherwax, my boy. Here, I want you to have this little keepsake.

RAPIER: What is it?

MILO: A letter of credit for seven hundred grand. It won't buy much except dreams, but it belonged to your mother.

RAPIER: Thank you, sir. (He starts out.)

MILO: Wait a minute, I can't let you go like this. You'll need money, introductions, shelter—

RAPIER: I'll patch up that old private railroad car of mine—the one underneath the Waldorf-Astoria.

LANCE: You—you mean whereby garbage is disposed of in all weathers by having *neatly uniformed attendants* call for and remove it?

MILO: Yes. That is the genesis of our scratch.

LANCE (As the realization sinks home): Oh, sir, I want to die!

MILO: Steady on, lad. After all, think of the millions which, were it not for our kindly ministrations, their homes would be a welter of chicken bones, fruit peels, and rancid yoghurt.

LANCE: I'll never be able to hold up my head in Bulldog circles again.

MILO: Nonsense, lad. Why, you wear the keenest threads on the campus and you're persona grata to myriad Eli frats.

LANCE: No. Father, this is the end of halcyon days in the groves of Academe. I'm going away.

. . . .

MILO (Shrugs, extracts envelope): Very well, then. Before you start, I want you to have this keepsake.

LANCE: Gee, Dads.

MILO: It won't buy much except dreams, but it's been in the family for generations.

LANCE: What is it?

MILO: A letter of credit.

LANCE: I can't take it, sir. To me it's like tainted.

MILO: Great Scott, lad, you can't walk out of here empty-handed. You'll need money, introductions, shelter—

LANCE: No, Dad.

MILO: But I won't let you sleep in the street! There's our old railroad car underneath the Waldorf-Astoria. Take it—it's only using up steam.

LANCE (Simply): I'm sorry, Dad. From now on, I walk alone. (HE exits. OCTAVIA enters, looks nonplused after him)

MILO: Take ours, too. It's only using up steam.

RAPIER (simply): I'm sorry, Dad. From now on I walk alone. Goodbye. (*He exits, colliding with his mother. . . . Octavia looks back at him, puzzled.*)

OCTAVIA: Why, goodness, what ails the child?

(*The Most of S. J. Perelman*, pp. 211–13)

38. Again compare:

HYACINTH (looking up abstractedly): What's that chattering sound?

BUNCE (eagerly): It's Hagedorn's teeth, Mrs. Laffoon. I've been meaning to squeal on him the first opening I got. Gosh, you ought to hear the noise he makes over the partition! A man can hardly concentrate—

HYACINTH: Oh, you have trouble concentrating, do you?

BUNCE: No, no, no—it'd take a lot more than that to upset *me*! Why, I could work in a boiler factory!

HYACINTH: You may yet, the way you've been delivering around here. Meanwhile, Hagedorn, let's have those choppers out before the next conference. That is, if you last that long.

HAGEDORN (quietly): They'll be out right after lunch hour, Chief. You won't have to mention it again.

HYACINTH: Splendid. Now, then, I've had my ear to the ground recently and I get the impression some of you disagree with my policy on *Shroud*.

VAN LENNEP: Hell's bells, Hyacinth! Where'd you ever pick up that idea?

HYACINTH: From the dictaphone I had installed in the water cooler.

(*reading from a typed report*) "Just give the old windbag enough rope.

OCTAVIA: Why, goodness, whatever ails the child?

(*The Beauty Part*, pp. 24–29)

HYACINTH:. . . . What's that chattering sound?

BUNCE (Eagerly): It's Hagedorn's teeth, Mrs. Laffoon. I've been meaning to squeal on him. Gosh, you ought to hear the noise he makes over the partition! A man can hardly concentrate.

HYACINTH: Oh, you have trouble concentrating, do you?

BUNCE: No, no—it'd take a lot more than that to upset *me*! I could work in a boiler factory!

HYACINTH: You may yet. Meanwhile, Hagedorn, let's those choppers out before our next conference.

HAGEDORN: I'll see my extractionist in the lunch hour, Chief.

HYACINTH: Well, see that you do! Now, then, I've had my ear to the ground lately and I get a very . . . strange . . . impression. Some of you disagree with the policy of my new magazine, *Shroud*.

VAN LENNEP: Hell's bells, Hyacinth! Where'd you ever pick up that crazy idea?

HYACINTH: From the dictaphone I had installed in the water cooler. Does this sound familiar, Van Lennep? (*Reads from flimsy*) "Just give the old windbag enough rope. You'll see, the public'll pin her ears back."

You wait, the public'll pin back her ears.'' Does that sound familiar, Van Lennep?

VAN LENNEP (squirming): I—I was talking about Miss Lovibond, who solicits those ads for bust developers and lost manhood. You said yourself we needed more tone.

HYACINTH: Well, all right, you twisted out of that one, but watch your step. I'm sentimental enough to think this organization can't function without one-hundred-per-cent loyalty.

VISHNU: And you've got it, Mrs. Laffoon. We worship the ground—

HYACINTH: At the same time, I won't stand for any soft soap or hogwash when I come up with a notion. The fact that Mr. Laffoon has ninety-three million dollars and owns all the real estate on Wacker Drive is beside the point. I want honest, sturdy, independent reactions—is that clear?

OMNES: Like crystal. . . . Gee, I wish I could express myself so forcefully! . . . Boy, what an editor! . . . etc.

HYACINTH: O.K. Well, I've just had a couple of hunches for brightening up *Shroud* that I'd like to try out on you. (*Quickly*) Oh, I know what you're going to say, that they *might* be feasible or that they *could* work—

HAGEDORN: No sirree, I can tell already they're world-beaters! A kind of a glow shines out of your face whenever you're on the beam.

HYACINTH: First, these covers we've been running. They're namby-pamby, no more punch than in a textbook. Look at this one—a naked girl tied to a bedpost and a chimpanzee brandishing a knout.

BUNCE: I see the structural weakness. It demands too much of the reader.

HYACINTH: Correct. We've got to

VAN LENNEP (squirming): I—I was referring to Miss Lovibond, who solicits those adds for lost manhood. You said yourself the magazine needed more chic.

HYACINTH: Well, you squirmed out of that one all right, but watch your step. I'm sentimental enough to think this organization can't function without one-hundred-percent loyalty.

VISHNU: And you've got it, Mrs. Laffoon.

BUNCE: Why, we venerate the ground you walk on!

VAN LENNEP: Right down the line.

HAGEDORN: I'll say, Chief.

HYACINTH: At the same time, no ass-kissing! I want honest sturdy, independent reactions—is that clear!

BUNCE: Like crystal!

HAGEDORN: Boy, I wish I could express myself so forcefully!

VAN LENNEP: She really cuts it, doesn't she?

HYACINTH: O.K. Well, I've just had a couple of skull-busters that I'd like to try out on you. First, these covers we've been running. Look at this one—who's responsible for this? A naked girl tied to a bedpost and a chimpanzee brandishing a whip. No more punch than a seed catalogue!

VAN LENNEP: I see the structural weakness.

BUNCE: Demands too much of the reader.

HYACINTH: Correct. We've got to drill him right between the eyes. Now, I visualize a cover with a real revolver barrel pointing at you.

OMNES: Hey . . . Hey . . . Hey . . . Hey . . . Hey . . .

HYACINTH: And a wisp of smoke curling out. The smoke would be engendered in a mechanism hinged to the back cover.

drill him right between the eyes.
Now, I visualize a cover with an
aperture and a real revolver barrel
protruding from it. With an acrid
wisp of smoke curling out. Imagine
that confronting you on a newsstand!

VISHNU: Where would the smoke be
engendered?

HYACINTH: In a mechanism hinged to
the back cover. To be sure, it's a
trifle bulky and we might fall afoul
of the smog ordinance in some
areas—

VAN LENNEP (ecstatically): Nah, that
can all be worked out! Baby, what a
brain wave. It'll knock Publishers'
Row right back on its heels!

HYACINTH: You think it's got
undertow?

VAN LENNEP: Ho-ho, I can almost
hear those dimes and nickels
showering down!

HYACINTH: You bet you can; it's the
cashier counting your severance pay.
So long, Van Lennep, it's been nice
knowing you. (*sadly, as he leaves*)
He just wouldn't learn. There's no
room at Laffoon for a toady.

VISHNU: I knew it was a come-on
from the start, Hyacinth. Did you
notice how I gave a negative little
shrug?

BUNCE: Me, too. I had difficulty in
repressing a smile.

HAGEDORN: Smoke boxes on the
back cover! Man, that was rich!

HYACINTH: Well, let's see how the
next one appeals to you. . . .

BUNCE: Mmm, that's a provocative
slant. Trouble is it stirs me and yet it
kind of leaves me cold. Thermally,
it's ambivalent.

VISHNU: Ditto. I want to throw my
arms around it but something
indefinable holds me back.

HYACINTH: You, Hagedorn?

OMNES: Hey! Hey! Hey! Hey! Hey!
Hey! Hey! Hey!

LANCE: But Mrs. Laffoon, wouldn't it
be kind of bulky?

HYACINTH: Yes, and we *could* run
afoul of the Sullivan Law.

VAN LENNEP: Nah, that can all be
worked out!

HAGEDORN: Baby, what an
inspiration!

VISHNU: It'll knock Publisher's Row
right back on their heels!

BUNCE: Hyacinth, I don't say these
things lightly. This idea's got
undertow!

VAN LENNEP: I can almost hear those
dimes and nickles showering down!

HYACINTH: You bet you can. It's the
cashier counting your severance pay.
So long, Van Lennep. *Saranoya!* (*As
HE exits chopfallen*) There's no
room at the top for a yes-man. . . .
Now let's see how my next idea
appeals. . . .

BUNCE: It stirs me and yet it leaves
me cold.

HAGEDORN: I want to throw my arms
around it, but something holds me
back.

VISHNU: It's as broad as it is long.

BUNCE: How do you—

VISHNU: —feel about it—

HAGEDORN: —yourself?

HYACINTH (simpers): It's my idea.

VISHNU: And you can afford to crow.
I know I'd be proud of it!

HYACINTH: Well, I'm not. It's a
bomb.

(*The Beauty Part*, pp. 43–46)

HAGEDORN: Straight from the
shoulder, Mrs. Laffoon, it's as broad
as it is long. How—How do you feel
about it yourself?
HYACINTH: Well, naturally, it's my
own idea—
VISHNU: Yes, and you can afford to
crow. I know I'd be proud of it.
HYACINTH: I suspected you would.
Personally, I think it's all wet.
(*The Most of S. J. Perelman*, pp. 441–
43)

   39. Compare:

SCENE: *A one-room apartment in
Manhattan occupied by April
Monkhood, a young career woman.
At some time prior to rise, April and
her four walls have tired of each
other, and she has called in
Fussfeld, a neighborhood decorator,
to give the premises the twenty-five
transfusions recommended above.
Fussfeld, a lineal descendant of
Brigadier General Sir Harvey
Fussfeld-Gorgas, the genius who
pacified the Sudan, has attacked the
assignment with the same zeal that
characterized his famous relative. He
has placed at stage center a
magnificent specimen of Bechtel's
flowering crab, the boughs of which
are so massive that it has been
necessary to stay them with cables
and turnbuckles. This has perforce
complicated the problem of the fishnet partitions on their ceiling tracks,
but, fortunately, most of these have
ripped off and now depend from the
branches, supplying a romantic effect
akin to that of Spanish moss. What
with the hodge-podge of damask,
yard goods, fake leopard skin, floral
wallpaper, silk fringe, and notary
seals, it is difficult at first to*

SCENE: *APRIL MONKHOOD'S
apartment. A standard Village locale
such as is occupied by any young
career woman, but recently
redecorated to express the
personality of the occupant. Fishnet
looped around walls, interspersed
with glass spheres. Two or three
score notary seals, both gold and
red, pasted indiscriminately on
window shades, drapes and sofa. A
profusion of fake leopard-skin
upholstery, fake Negro sculpture and
corresponding claptrap of the sort
found along East 8th Street.*
TIME: *Two days later.*
AT RISE: APRIL MONKHOOD, *an
attractive girl in her early twenties
given to self dramatization and
endowed with magnificent secondary
sexual characteristics and practically
no sense of humor. . . .
FUSSFELD, a telephone repairman,
stands nearby at an end table. . . .*
FUSSFELD: I'd sprinkle a couple of
magazines around, or maybe a dish
of cashews. They're tasty and they
help soak up the humidity.

   . . . . .

LANCE: Oh, great. I mean, it like
hits you right in the eye.

distinguish any animate object.
Finally, though, the eye picks out a
rather scrawny kitten, licking its lips
by an overturned goldfish bowl. A
moment later, April Monkhood enters
from the kitchenette, practically on
all fours. She is a vivacious
brownette in knee-hugging poltroons,
with a retrousse nose which she
wears in a horsetail. Behind her
comes Fussfeld, a small, haggard
gentleman with a monocle he affects
for chic. However, since he is
constantly losing it in the decor and
scrabbling about for it, he fails to
achieve any impressive degree of
sang-froid.

. . . . .

FUSSFELD: I'd sprinkle around a
few periodicals, or a can of salted
peanuts or so. Anyway, a place gets
more homey after your friends drop
around.

. . . . .

APRIL: You don't think it's
overdone, do you?
CYPRIAN: Overdone? Why, it's stark!
You couldn't omit one detail without
damaging the whole composition.
APRIL (*hugging him*): You old
sorcerer. You know just the words to
thaw a woman's heart. Now, I've an
inspiration. Instead of going out for
dinner, let's have powdered snails
and a bottle of Old Rabbinical under
the crab.
CYPRIAN (*Fingering his collar*): Er—
to tell you the truth, I—I find it a
little close in here. You see, I fell
into a grain elevator one time when I
was small.
APRIL: Nonsense, it'll be heaps of
fun. I loath those big, expensive
restaurants. Sit ye doon while I mix
us an aperitif. (*She thrusts him*
backward onto the studio couch,

APRIL: Does it say anything to you?
You don't feel it's overdone?
LANCE: Overdone? It's underdone!
You couldn't omit one detail without
damaging the—the entire concept.
APRIL (*hugs him*): You old sorcerer.
You know just the words to thaw a
woman's heart. (*she kisses him*)
Let's have a drink to celebrate. Sit
ye doon (*Lance sits on couch*)—and
I'll open a bottle of Old Rabbinical.
(*Pushes him backward on studio*
couch and whisks bottle from
cabinet, from which she proceeds to
fill two glasses. The phone rings; she
answers hurriedly) Yes? . . . Who?
. . . Oh, hi! . . . No, I Can't. I
have people here . . . What? No, I
have to wash my hair . . . Yes, silly
. . . Why don't you do that? I'm
always here . . . 'Bye. (*Hangs up*)
Really, some men are just
impossible. They think all they have
to do is whistle.
LANCE: Who was that?
APRIL: My ex-fiancé, of all people.
LANCE: Hanh? You never told me
you'd been engaged.
APRIL: Oh, Sensualdo and I haven't
seen each other in ages.He's a
monster—an absolute fiend.
LANCE: Sensualdo? His name sounds
Mexican.
APRIL: Uh-uh—Peruvian. One of
those insanely jealous types. Tried to
stab a man I was having a Coke
with. That's what broke up our
engagement.
LANCE: Is he—er—back there now?
APRIL: In Peruvia? Well, he shuttles
between there and Staten Island.
Something to do with vicunas or
emeralds—I really don't know.
(*The Beauty Part*, pp. [31]–34)

almost decapitating him with a guy
wire, then whisks a bottle from a
cabinet.) Who do you suppose called
me today? My husband, of all
people.
CYPRIAN: Hanh? You never told me
you were married.
APRIL: Oh, Sensualdo and I've been
separated for years. He's a
monster—an absolute fiend.
CYPRIAN: Is he a Mexican?
APRIL: Uh-uh—Peruvian. One of
those insanely jealous types, always
opening your mail and accusing you
of carrying on with his friends. He
tried to stab a man I was having a
Coke with. That's what broke up our
marriage.
CYPRIAN: W-where is he now?
APRIL: Right here in New York. His
lawyers are trumping up evidence for
a divorce—What's the matter?
(*The Road to Miltown*, pp. 38–42)

40. Stefan Kanfer, "Perels of Wisdom before an Opening," *New York Times*, November 3, 1974, sect. 2, p. 5.

41. Walter Kerr, "If It Isn't Funny, It Must Be Farce," *New York Times*, November 10, 1974, sect. 5, p. 1.

42. Clive Barnes, "Perelman's 'The Beauty Part' Turns Up Again, Alas." *New York Times*, November 5, 1974, p. 28.

43. Perelman, *The Last Laugh*, p. 156.

44. Quoted in Paul D. Zimmerman and Burt Goldblatt, *The Mark Brothers at the Movies* (New York: New American Library, 1968), p.[45].

45. Gardner, p. 47.

4

Themes and Techniques

Take one part American humor tradition, sprinkle in elements from the Yiddish theater, and blend these ingredients thoroughly in a piping hot comic genuis' mind, and the result is S. J. Perelman's style. Not surprisingly, that style is unique and recognizable. As Ogden Nash, one of Perelman's collaborators, says in a review of *Chicken Inspector No. 23*, "Perelman's style is so uniquely his own that his readers in *The New Yorker*, which long ago established the peekaboo custom of printing the contributor's name at the tail of the article . . . need only glance at the first paragraph to identify its author." [1]

What are the components of this style that combine to make the product so easily identifiable? Rather than devoting a long chapter to an examination of Perelman's style, I have chosen throughout this study to deal with various stylistic components as they occur in his individual pieces. (See for example, *Dawn Ginsbergh's Revenge* and "The Idol's Eye.") In part this is because, as often as not, how this writer says something is both more interesting and more important than what he is saying. In part, too, because these stylistic elements are so integral to his work, they make much more sense when examined within that context, as opposed to dealing with them in categories. However, a brief review of the elements of his style is valuable as a means of providing a unifying overview of Perelman's canon because that stylistic sum is greater than the technical parts, because his style is in itself interesting to analyze, and because for most scholars that style is the *sine qua non* for studying his work in the first place.

The attention concentrated on Perelman's use of language is in no way meant to belittle humorous writing or the social functions of his humor; his work is read for enjoyment and to commiserate with a kindred spirit in a vindictive world. Nevertheless, while his work may not be read for its philosophy or grand thoughts, among the numerous elements that contribute to and are characteristic of Perelman's writing, it is useful to start a study of his style with a look at his subject matter. The thematic content of his prose is important, of course, because to a large degree this determines his style and his audience (which in turn influence the author's style).

Ironically, as might be expected with a writer of comedy, Perelman was not studied by scholars during his lifetime, nor is he remembered now for any special or significant thematic hobyhorse, as Louis Hasley points out in "The Kangaroo Mind of S. J. Perelman."[2] Though the writer does occasionally imply dissatisfaction with certain governments, agencies, and so forth, with the exception of his "Cloudland Revisited" series, Hasley's assessment is essentially correct. There are certain topics and themes that recur regularly in Perelman's work, yet they are seldom developed to any great extent, and they tend to be less significant than the questions about life, death, and the nature of reality that are usually expected to be addressed in great literature. Perelman observes and comments on the surfaces of life. Even on those occasions when he is concerned with cosmic questions, he does not choose to delve very deeply. One consequence of this is that life seems to catch up with art, as Perelman admits in several interviews. To Cole and Plimpton he states that, "The effort of writing seems more arduous all the time. Unlike technicians who are supposed to become more proficient with practice, I find I've grown considerably less articulate. . . . Also the variety of subjects is restricted the longer I stay at this dodge."[3] Although he attributes this latter point to "ennui," he claims in his interview with MacPherson that it has become increasingly difficult to be absurd in a world that itself has become so absurd that his wildest compositions are tame in comparison.[4]

Columnist Hal Boyle describes Perelman as "a man who looks with skepticism on everything in life except the messages he finds in Chinese cookies." "These," Perelman tells Boyle, "I accept literally," and he goes on to deny being a cynic, though he admits the possibility that he is an idealist.[5] At the base of his writing is a sense of perspective, an ability to see ridiculous or amusing aspects in *quotidian* experiences through his wire-rimmed glasses. This is coupled with a talent for communicating his discoveries to his audience so that they can share in the laughter. Catastrophe (the Depression, the Coconut Grove fire, politics, World War II, Korea, Viet Nam) is avoided—it is catastrophe enough to be trapped in a restaurant by a former flame who has been caught in compromising situations by a progression of husbands in spite of being "a giantess in an emerald-green frock, trimmed with salmon beads, a veritable grenadier of a woman. . . . Askew on her head . . . a fawn-colored duvetyn turban whose aigrette was secured by the Hope diamond or its rhinestone equivalent . . . [with] the odor of malt pervading her embrace," as the humorist relates in "Call and I Follow, I Follow!" [6]

As an author, Perelman is a society writer rather than a writer about social concerns. His topics are not politics but everyday subjects—films, books, travel, appliances, advertisements—topical but timeless only in the strictest sense of the word in that they represent annoyances of the kind that will always plague mankind, not because they address the largest questions about the nature of existence. "Humor is purely a point of view, and only the pedants try to classify it," he told Zinsser.[7] "For me its chief merit is the use of the unexpected, the glancing allusion, the deflation of pomposity, and the constant repetition of one's helplessness in a majority of situations. One doesn't consciously start out wanting to be a social satirist. You find something absurd enough to make you want to push a couple of antipersonnel bombs under it. If it seems to have another element of meaning, that's lagniappe. But the main obligation is to amuse yourself." About style, the author's final words are "The only thing that matters is the end product, which must have brio . . . vivacity." [8]

If the critics are right, Perelman's goal in using humor has been met. Ogden Nash writes that Perelman "exposes the fool in his folly not through reduction, but through magnification to the absurd, so that the subject stands larger than life and twice as ludicrous, foot in mouth and egg on his chin, hoist by his own assininity" so that "the rest of us" have "a happy chance to laugh at some of the perfect asses in this imperfect world."[9] In Sanford Pinsker's opinion this translates into Perelman's adopting the guise of "an irritated innocent, a man of rarified taste and extravagant metaphor who sets his particular 'No!' in thunder against our culture's expectations and its junk."[10]

Norris Yates, Walter Blair, and Hamlin Hill place Perelman in that current of the mainstream of American humor typified by the writers for *The New Yorker*, particularly those of the 1930's and 1940's such as Thurber and Benchley, who created a composite Little Man figure, even if each author's creation was slightly different. What the Little Man characters share is an unsuccessful rebellion against "ancient standards."[11] They are average men, victims of an illogical outside world epitomized by that frightful generic monster, woman. Perelman's art and contribution to the Little Man genre is to use that persona as a vehicle for expressing his essential attitude toward modern life, an attitude at once jaundiced and hopeful, expecting the unexpected as well as the expected, and encyclopedic while self-centered. Sex frequently appears in Perelman's writing, but almost always it is alluded to suggestively, not blatantly. It is mentioned, but not seen or realized. It is in the background, but only wistfully. Often the Perelman persona or protagonist observes a woman lasciviously, seemingly like a male chauvinist, yet it is the naive, and certainly ineffectual, lasciviousness of a schoolboy that controls the observation. The longing is not dirty—it is sometimes slightly amazed, and it is doomed to remain unfulfilled. Like comedian Rodney Dangerfield, Perelman's Little Man character "don't get no respect" from the opposite sex. Thus, some of the humor in the stories comes from seeing how the hero will bungle a budding relationship through his lack of experience and misunderstanding of how to behave suavely. The very things that he does and says to impress the woman are better designed to make him appear foolish to her than as an object of sexual desire. One of the ironies that the Perelman persona/protagonist ultimately must face, though, is that even if he does everything exactly right, as unlikely as that would be, the woman probably will not find him attractive anyway. Why this is so varies and may not even be known. He may be too plain, or not dashing enough; in other words, he may be too normal. She may be too stuck up or unperceptive to appreciate him. She may be too bright or too dumb. Whatever the reason, he does not evoke erotic fantasies—and probably he has known all along that this would be so. In any case, Perelman maintains an uneasy kind of stage-struck wonder in his confrontation with women, almost as though he is unable to shed the sense of appreciation of movie-star goddesses that carries over from his youthful film viewing days and which somehow attaches itself like an aura to all women.

The ways in which the Little Man fails in his romantic quest are humorous in themselves, and the expectation of failure permits the distancing that allows both Perelman's persona or protagonist and the reader to laugh at the humor in the situation.

The Perelman persona is interesting in other situations, too. He/she exists in a world tinged with fantasy. The world is near enough to normal to be familiar, but the persona—self-described as broad shouldered, with rugged good looks or the feminine equivalent and possessing special abilities—introduces an unreal quality. The character is what one would wish to be, not what one is. Yet the character cannot be blamed entirely for succumbing to delusion because Hollywood, advertisers, and magazines like *Harper's Bazaar* not only incite such delusions, they actively foster them. Hence, Perelman is provided with a brace of targets; the sources of delusion and those gullible folks who allow themselves to be ensnared by the illusions—himself and his readers included. For Yates the result is Perelman's "sane psychoses." For Blair and Hill, the bumbling through a universe conspiring against him relates Perelman to Benchley and "earlier comics, such as Artemus Ward, Charles Heber Clark, Georgè Horatio Derby and others. (The performance of the typical American humorist, Harry Levin claimed in 1972, 'is that of an eiron . . . like Socrates . . . Will Rogers . . . or like the accident-prone anecdotists of *The New Yorker*')."[12] Alone, and slightly insane in a mad, mad world, the protagonist is subdued and humiliated as well. Given the modern world surrounding them, Perelman's readers can identify with his personae easily. Blair and Hill chastise Perelman for not extending himself into the arena of satire, thus permitting his audience to escape "any message" by virtue of being overcome by "waves of banter, frivolity, and whimsy."[13] These scholars miss an important point, though. Perelman's persona is beaten, but he is not vanquished. Humor offers hope, ultimately, and Perelman's Little Man wanders away from the scene of the accident dazed, but not defeated. He will rise again, grin slightly crooked but in place, to face whatever dragons or windmills await him tomorrow. And, as he waddles Chaplinesquely out of sight, the Perelman protagonist may be a little dusty, but there is a jauntiness to his step as he rounds the corner and disappears into the sunset. At bottom, a sense of humor and, finally, a refusal to take himself seriously become survival traits.

It may be, then, that the writer's choice of topics (travel, appliances with minds of their own, movies, pompous clerks, and so forth) brings him face to face with the human condition in such a way that the condition cannot exert enough force on his psyche to overpower him. There is a significant episode in Perelman's life that lends credence to this thought. One night in March, 1929, Perelman stopped at the Kenmore Hall Hotel to invite Nathanael West to dinner at Siegel's, their favorite restaurant in Greenwich Village. An acquaintance of Perelman's who wrote an advice column for the *Brooklyn Eagle* under the pen name Susan Chester had promised to show him some of the letters that she had received with the idea that the humorist might be able to "put such material to comic use." [14] Chester regarded the column as a joke, and offered letters like the following as evidence:

Dear Susan:
I have always enjoyed reading your column, and have benefited by your expert advice. Now I must ask you for advice myself. I have been married for twenty years. I have a girl 19 and a boy of 17. From the very beginning I realized that I had made a mistake in marrying my husband. But the children came soon after, and I was obliged for their dear sakes to stand through thick and thin, bitter and sweet. And also for decency sake. . . . [15]

The letter was signed "Broad Shoulders" and had the added note, "Susan don't think I am broad shouldered. But that is just the way I feel about life and me."

The pathos of these pleas for help overwhelmed Perelman, and he declared himself unable to take advantage of Chester's notion. West used the experience as the basis for his most famous novel, *Miss Lonelyhearts*.

If Perelman's themes do not excite scholars, his mastery of the English language and his manipulation of prose for comic effect have continually drawn praise, and his ability was such that he could apply his style to practically any topic and produce humor. E. B. White, a contemporary, admirer, and friend of Perelman's, tells a story about Perelman's preoccupation with words that sums up both the man and his work: "Sid commands a vocabulary that is the despair (and joy) of every writing man. He is like a Roxy organ that has three decks, 50 stops, and a pride of pedals under the bench. When he wants a word it's there. He and Laura showed up at our house in Sarasota a couple of winters ago. They had been in an automobile accident—a bad one, the car a complete wreck. Laura came out of it with some

bruises. Sid with a new word. The car, he learned, had been 'totaled.'
I could see that the addition of this word to his already enormous store
meant a lot to him. His ears are as busy as an ant's feelers. No word
ever gets by him." [16]

Most critics concentrate on Perelman's marvelous command of his
raw material, words. His sure, deft manipulation of the English language is especially appreciated by the British. Novelist and poet John
Wain declares in an *Observer* article that "most poets will confess a
weakness for Perelman," a fact that he attributes to the author's "in-
timate acquaintance with those 'serious' writers whose handling of
language is most obsessively precise." [17] As an example, Wain cites
a passage from the scene in James Joyce's *Ulysses* where Bloom pre-
pares breakfast:

—Milk for the pussens, he said.
—Mrkgnao! the cat cried.

He goes on to quote Perelman to establish a linkage: "I let go the
turkey wing; with a loud 'Mrkgnao' she obviously had learned from
reading *Ulysses*, the cat straightway pounced on it." John Hollander,
another poet-critic, also notes a connection with Perelman's esteem for
Joyce: "I think that his metamorphic vision, that is his ability to take
some idiotic phrase, some idiotic situation and suddenly let it happen
in the full garishness of its ramification, does all come in one sense
from the 'Circe' episode of *Ulysses*. I think that this is a very important text for him, and that one of the things he did was to make the
element of instant externalization, instant metamorphosis, available to
a great deal of post-World War Two American fiction." [18] Wain dis-
agrees with his American counterparts who claim that the humorist is
all form and no content, but like them he finds Perelman's style more
appealing than what it contains:

The effects that a great satiric clown like Groucho Marx produces with his
voice and appearance, Perelman produces in cold print with the pyrotechnics
of his prose. Since language is the richer medium of the two, he is, ultimately,
the more interesting. His technical resources are endless, and they have to be,
for the one invariable quality of all his work is its fertility in surprises. As a
parodist, for instance, he is excellent, but he never parodies one style for long
enough to allow the reader to get used to it. Sometimes he will bounce into

pastiche and out again within one sentence. His other favourite devices are the ricochet of ambiguity (So-and-so was "a lovable old white-haired character who had fought with Meade at Shiloh—he and Meade just never got along"), and the collapsing vocabulary ("He sprang at me, but with a blow I sent him grovelling. In ten minutes he was back with a basket of fresh-picked grovels".)[19]

Among his countrymen Perelman's use of language is accorded like respect. Brooks Atkinson identifies the writer's function as improving "on something that is intrinsically ridiculous," and continues, "Mr. P. is never guilty of literary impropriety. The words he uses are orderly and respectable. But he creates hilarious disorder out of them."[20] All of this is done, Atkinson concedes, "with the care and erudition of an English essayist of the old school, rubbing elbows with Arthur Machen and George Gissing." Douglas Fowler points out that Perelman's use of his initials on the printed page is an "Anglophile affection,"[21] so it would seem that the author shares Atkinson's association of himself and the British belles lettres tradition. Or, there may be no connection at all, which would not be surprising either—Perelman told MacPherson that he "hated" his first name and simply retired it to anonymity.[22]

Other critics who comment on Perelman's language include Wilfrid Sheed and Russell Davies. Sheed writes of the author's "tackling language itself, experimenting with it and snarling at it, and using it to flay the barbarian enemy" and later developing a style that "becomes denser, like the later Henry James, and more turned in on itself."[23] Davies remarks that Perelman is "too wordy for some tastes" and warns that "the sheer variety of references and momentarily-assumed tones [might] batter the reader into exhaustion."[24] Summing up Perelman's collected works, Davies observes:

There's a complete social commentary on the United States embedded in it: More securely embedded, indeed, than ever it was in works of conscious compilation like Mencken's Americana. Because Perelman's prose must surely be the richest treasury of available levels of discourse, what analysts of style like to call 'registers', that has yet been assembled. And his greatest achievement in organizing it, I rather think, was in resisting the very natural tendency (still displayed by American Jewish humorists two or three generations away from the immigration) to puncture every single pretension, to reveal a grubby stain under every picture on the wall. Perelman never pretended to be the common man. The central thread of his style was smoothly learned, frankly literary.

Hollander credits Perelman with making him "aware that there was such a thing as linguistic sensibility, that there was such a thing as a sense of style . . . a sense of elegance."[25] Yates has catalogued many of the individual techniques that are incorporated in Perelman's style. He lists an ironic tone, use of first person narration, a constant sense of values ("integrity, sincerity, skepticism, taste, a respect for competence, a striving after the golden mean, and a longing for better communication and understanding among men"), dramatic frameworks, parody and monologue, "controlled wildness of incident and metaphor," dialect humor, narrators who fight for good causes but are neurotic, an average-man persona that caricatures the author as a wise fool, a range of foes from the mass media, incongruous juxtaposition, a mixture of literal-and-figurative usage, and a combining of two or more fragments by superimposing one upon the other so that the highlights of each and all stand out (a technique the critic dubs "Perelmontage" because of its affinity with the cinematic technique of montage).[26] Referring to Perelman's syntax, Melville Maddocks writes that "The Perelman style—its eminent reasonableness, its barely-mock dignity, its subtly staged collisions between gentility and slang—allows him to keep cover until the last possible moment."[27] Incidentally, it is interesting that Perelman's style is such that Wain calls him the "characteristic American intellectual," Blair and Hill see his persona as a variation on the Little Man, and Yates labels him a representative of the average man.[28] The truth is, Perelman adopts all of these roles at various times, sometimes, indeed, within the same article.

These and numerous other stylistic components have been dealt with in the preceding chapters, but it is useful to look quickly at four elements again because they are so intrinsically a part of Perelman's style. Any analysis of the humorist's work must begin with an acknowledgement of his use of clichés—some of which appear straightforwardly in his prose (that is, they are used as though they are literally true), some of which are used figuratively, and some of which combine the literal and the figurative, starting in one mode and finishing in the other. Next is the wide range of allusions that flow through his writing like a vein of rich ore. Tracking down all of these allusions would provide a scholar with a life's work. The possibility that the "arcane knowledge" involved in Perelman's myriad references to "cultural figures and styles long past, obsolete words, [and] architectural oddities" might limit his audience is answered by the writer's contention that "I write pretty much for myself. If, at the close of business each evening, I myself can understand what I've written, I feel the day hasn't been totally wasted."[29] A more valid answer might be that while the allusions are an important and omnipresent element of Perelman's style, the success or failure of a piece does not depend entirely on the recognition of all of the allusions incorporated in the piece. Allusion is only one element, one that adds to the knowledgeable readers' enjoyment, to be sure, but the less well-informed reader will still find plenty to be amused by even without this added fillip. Thus, although allusions are an elitist element, they do not prevent Perelman from being a popular writer.

Related to clichés and allusions are the constant puns, and Perelman's felicity with puns is enhanced by his immense vocabulary and extensive storehouse of cultural tidbits. Many of his puns evolve out of clichés or allusions. Even the very titles of the humorist's articles and book-length collections serve to exemplify this aspect of his style. While many are puns (*A Child's Garden of Curses*, not verses), almost all of his titles rely on the reader's exposure to a wide range of sources to be able to identify the allusion, some of the sources being fairly esoteric (*The Ill-Tempered Clavichord*, taken from Johann Sebastian Bach's *The Well-Tempered Clavier*). At the same time, the titles provide evidence of the author's awareness of current customs and events in modern society (*Listen to the Mocking Bird* and *Baby, It's Cold Inside* are based on contemporary song titles).

Finally, there is another foundation upon which Perelman's humor and style rest that usually appears in unobtrusive ways but which serves as a solid underpinning and is always there. This is the Yiddish background, partially derived from American-Jewish culture as a whole and partly from the Yiddish theater specifically, that provides the device of the *shlemiel* and the stratagem of the *shpritz* (a "kind of freeform eruption of fantasy, nonsense, and satire, at least theoretically spontaneous and gathering momentum as it goes" that is "the basic form of American Jewish dialogue" according to Fowler) that is mentioned by Yates, alluded to by Ward, and discussed in some detail by Fowler.[30] Israel Shenker goes so far as to state that one of the sources of the humorist's comic style "goes back to biblical culture because a great deal of his wit is the wit that you can find emitted in the Bible,"[31] yet the occasional insertion of Yiddish phrases is one of the few clues evident in Perelman's work that connects him to this tradition. Actually, it should be noted that there is a distinction between literary and American colloquial Yiddish. Perelman relies on Yiddish phrases for effect rather than as an integral component of characterization. His own explanation for using Yiddish words is, "I like them for their invective content. There are nineteen words in Yiddish that convey gradations of disparagement from a mild, fluttery helplessness to a state of downright, irreconcilable brutishness. All of them can be usefully employed to pin-point the kind of individuals I write about."[32]

As was the case with the Yiddish tradition, there are some tangential associations between Perelman's writing and another sub-genre, the American frontier humor tradition. He was well aware of the major authors and works in this tradition, having read many of them during his youth. Most obvious of the connections between his writing and that of his predecessors in the tradition is his fondness for the most outrageous hyperbole delivered in a perfectly straight-faced manner. His attention to the details of life around him might lead to his being classified a local colorist, even though his wide-ranging eye did not confine him to some readily identifiable location such as the "down East" of Seba Smith but rather made him a local colorist for a nation because he concentrated on those elements that transcend county lines and are national in character—films, advertising, and the like. Ultimately, then, the stylistic similarities are interesting because they are similarities and may represent some minimal influences, not because they are indicators of any conscious or well-defined embracing of the tradition. Perelman, and the humorists whom he emulated, can write their kind of humor because the tradition exists, but this does not make them part of the tradition. Particularly in his early pieces at Brown, for instance, Perelman's style was derivative, echoing the humorous journalistic style of the time, and throughout his career he incorporated into his writing those elements that he enjoyed and could use effectively. But, like other major authors, he converted those elements into something identifiably his own, and he rose above the traditions from which he borrowed.

As a journalist, he was also well within the boundaries established by Mark Twain, Artemus Ward, Henry Wheeler Shaw, Finley Peter

Dunne, H. L. Mencken, Ring Lardner, and countless others. There is a convergence between why and where Perelman writes and the American humor tradition. About the impetus behind his writing, he says, "Chiefly, it's commercial, to be very frank about it. And secondly it's the desire to get one's own back. George Orwell listed four principle reasons why people write, the fourth of which was 'revenge.' "[33] Perelman also says, "I regard myself as a species of journalist." The length of his essays, then, is imposed on his writing to some extent by their place of publication. Because of this there are clearly some affinities with journalist-humorists such as Twain and Dunne purely based on what can best be said and how it can be said in the space available. In fact, some of his protagonists display traits similar to those exhibited by various Twain personae or Mr. Dooley. Thus, two elements of Perelman's style coincide. His writing contains the exuberance and the deadpan exaggeration that are common elements in traditional American humor; it has an American tone to it. There is simultaneously a bite in what he writes. "Generally speaking," he claims, "I don't believe in kindly humor." At the same time, journals are his element and Edgar Allan Poe's strictures about the short story are applicable (especially since the short stories referred to appeared in journals). This means that the quick effect is sought. Perelman's recognition of the nature of this type of journalistic writing reflects itself in two areas, technique and compensation. First, "in the technical sense, the comic writer is a cat on a hot tin roof. His invitation to perform is liable to wear out at any moment; he must quickly and constantly amuse in a short span."[34] Perelman, recollecting that Benchley "did a column three times a week . . . and ran into deep trouble,"[35] postulates that "The fiction writer, in contrast, has much more latitude."[36] Whereas the novelist can "side-slip into exposition, [and] wander off into interminable byways and browse round endlessly in his characters' heads," "The development of a comic idea has to be swift and economical." Second, an obvious outcome of writing humor is that "the pieces are shorter than conventional fiction and fetch a much smaller stipend."

"His pieces usually had a lead sentence, or lead paragraph, that was as hair-raising as the first big dip on a roller coaster," reflects E. B. White.[37] Coincidentally, White, another acknowledged master stylist, provides an interesting contrast with Perelman. While White's work is quietly polished, Perelman's is full of exuberance and dazzle and is more animated. Critics occasionally refer to Perelman's refinement, perhaps because of the pseudo-British pose adopted by some of his personae and his own bearing, yet in his best work the characteristic that White identifies is frequently an essential element and reflects a journalistic approach that requires an immediate grabbing of the reader's attention and intense packing of a great deal of material into a relatively small space. This pulling the reader by the lapels through the iron gates of life is characteristically Perelmanesque too; the author moves the reader so quickly and with such verve that his piercing social insights have been inserted into the mind with a piccador's precision almost before the reader is aware that instruction has begun. Ironically, the need to be concise led to a use of language that has a British feel to it. Puns and other forms of word play, *non sequiturs*, clichés (both phrases and situations—which are sometimes taken literally when they are meant figuratively), and literary allusions, all of which have been noted above, Perelman utilized with the sure hand of a superb craftsman. Indeed, it is his knowledge of these tools that makes him such a capable parodist, and it was the necessity of fitting into a journalistic format that caused him to hone them to perfection.

Whether he writes from the point of view of the common man or not, Perelman aptly records the reactions of an American everyman to the world that surrounds him. This is brought out in another link with the American humor tradition, the attitude that he expresses about the rest of the world during his many travels. Almost unceasingly Perelman compares wherever he is at the moment with somewhere in the United States, and the comparison is seldom favorable for the foreign locale. His attitude carries over from physical geography to local custom and inhabitants, too. If he were a little more assertive, he might seem an Ugly American, though it is not in his character to be jingoistic. But, too many things conspire to trip him up or allow him to be taken advantage of, so instead of blatantly parading his disdain for things not American, he spends most of his time ducking. This happens to him at home, too, of course, but at home he understands some of the motives that lie behind whatever is assaulting him, whereas when he is abroad things simply seem to be in the nature of the place and as an outsider he is destined never to comprehend that nature, just to suffer degradation at its hands. There is definitely a kinship between Perelman's travel volumes and Twain's *Innocents Abroad*.

Perelman recognizes that his roots are in America and that not merely is his strength here but that he depends upon America for his very essence as a writer. Before leaving the United States in 1970, Perelman claimed that "It doesn't take guts [to leave]. The dubious privilege of a freelance writer is he's given the freedom to starve anywhere."[38] The time away from home persuaded him otherwise. In an interview after having returned for his sojourn in the United Kingdom, Perelman says that he will never become an expatriate because "A writer needs the constant conflict, the rush of ideas that happens only in his native country."[39]

The use of one final device should be addressed, that of including real or imaginary excerpts from magazine or newspaper stories as a means of initiating a short story ("Nesselrode to Jeopardy," which utilizes a quotation from *Time*, is one of the dozens of pieces in which this stratagem is employed). As indicated in Chapter One, some critics bewail the frequency with which Perelman turns to this device, and they find it heavy-handed besides. However, such a practice is one of the humorist's trademarks, and it became one because it is effective. Beginning a piece in this manner introduces the subject matter, elicits a sense of authority, sets the scene, implies the author's attitude toward his topic, and generally saves time by letting him avoid the otherwise necessary background explanations.

Of those who comment on Perelman's style, one who speaks with uncommon authority is Caskie Stinnett, a former editor of *Holiday*, a magazine in which a number of the humorist's pieces first appeared. She concludes that "There is a certain uniformity in the Perelman pieces—in the craftsmanship, in the construction. They invariably start off with a highly challenging introduction, a ludicrous statement or something that is made in the very first sentence, that so intrigues the reader that you have to follow through to find out just how this nonsense could possibly end up. It's my conviction that Perelman must labour very hard on his introductions because they must be difficult to do, but they're superb and in many cases flawless. I really don't believe that an editor could improve in any way on a Perelman introduction."[40]

Perelman's polishing of his "lapidary prose" is often mentioned by students of his work. He has said himself that "easy writing makes hard reading."[41] How hard he works at polishing is demonstrated in a story that he tells in his interview with MacPherson. As do many professional writers, Perelman kept files of items and ideas that he might be able to utilize as a stimulant for his imagination. Asked by Cole and Plimpton how often Ross or *The New Yorker* suggested ideas for his writing, Perelman replies, "Not too often. Most of the suggestions I get originate in mysterious quarters. [Some] drift in from kindly readers. . . . I'm continually heartened by the fact that people take the time to forward a clipping or a circular they feel might inspire me."[42] To MacPherson Perelman recounted a tale of how one idea struggled on to paper:

> "In 1953 I went to East Africa and I had with me a floppy Panama hat. It was a little large. In the East Africa Standard I read about a Norfolk jacket woven in the Scottish highlands, worn by a man his entire life and passed off to a son. I folded it up and used it to tighten the band."
> Dissolve: Perelman is back in the United States, takes the hat to be blocked, picks up the hat weeks later, finds the article, retires to a bar, reads it there, then weaves a story about his own Norfolk jacket that was borrowed by the late John O'Hara.
> ("The Rape of the Drape").
> Total time: 15 years.
> "That's the longest I've held a piece. The whole point of comic writers is no matter how hard you work, you must give a sense of vivacity, lightness and speed."   (p. E-4)

That Perelman could keep an element of a possible story alive in his mind over this extended period of time and finally bring it to fruition is an indication of several things. It illustrates the strength and breadth of his intellect (first, keeping one element in mind, and then seeing how it relates to another item), it demonstrates his attention to detail, and it shows his patience and willingness to keep after something until he is satisfied that the result meets his high standard. This incident reveals something of the nature of the man behind the humorist and helps explain why his work surpassed that of other authors and why he was so successful for so long.

NOTES

1. Ogden Nash, "A Precious String of Perelman Pearls," *Life* (September 23, 1966): 11.

2. Louis Hasley, "The Kangaroo Mind of S. J. Perelman," *South Atlantic Quarterly* 72 (Winter, 1973): 115–21.

3. William Cole and George Plimpton, "The Art of Fiction: S. J. Perelman,"*Writers at Work: The Paris Review Interviews, Second Series* (New York: Viking, 1963), p. 245.

4. Myra MacPherson, "Perelman's Rasping Wit Becomes an Anglo-file," *Washington Post*, October 18, 1970, sect. E, p. 4.

5. Quoted in Hasley, p. 118.

6. S. J. Perelman, *The Rising Gorge* (New York: Simon and Schuster, 1961), p. 13.

7. William Zinsser, "That Perelman of Great Price Is Sixty-Five," *New York Times Magazine* (July 22, 1966): 76.

8. Cole and Plimpton, p. 249.

9. Nash, p. 11.

10. Sanford Pinsker, "Jumping on Hollywood's Bones, or How S. J. Perelman and Woody Allen Found It at the Movies," *The Midwest Quarterly* 21, no. 3 (Spring, 1980): 374.

11. Norris Yates, *The American Humorist: Conscience of the Twentieth Century* (Ames, Iowa: Iowa State University Press, 1964), pp. 335 ff.; Walter Blair and Hamlin Hill, *America's Humor: From Poor Richard to Doonesbury* (New York: Oxford University Press, 1978), pp. 420 ff.

12. Blair and Hill, p. 436.

13. Ibid.

14. Jay Martin, *Nathanael West: The Art of His Life* (New York: Farrar, Straus, and Giroux, 1970), p. 109.

15. Ibid., p. 110.

16. Quoted in Zinsser, p. 76.

17. John Wain, "S. J. Perelman," in *Essays on Literature and Ideas* (Westport, Connecticut: Greenwood Press, 1978), p. 166.

18. John Hollander, quoted in Philip French, "Perelman's Revenge or the Gift of Providence, Rhode Island," *The Listener* (November 15, 1978): 669. MacPherson reports that Perelman had eleven copies of *Ulysses* when he held the auction at his farm in 1970, and that he could not bear to part with a single one (sect. E, p. 4).

19. Wain, p. 167.

20. Brooks Atkinson, "S. J. Perelman," in *Tuesdays and Fridays* (New York: Random House, 1963), p. 225.

21. Douglas Fowler, *S. J. Perelman* (Boston: Twayne, 1983), p. 108.

22. MacPherson, sect. E, p. 4.

23. Wilfrid Sheed, "The Flinty Eye Behind the Humor," *Life* (September 18, 1970): 12.

24. Russell Davies, "S. J. Perelman 1904–1979," *New Statesman* (October 26, 1979): 646.

25. Hollander, quoted in French, p. 667.

26. Yates, pp. 335 ff.

27. Melville Maddocks, *The Christian Science Monitor* (September 1, 1966): 13.

28. Wain, p. 167; Blair and Hill throughout; Yates, p. 340.

29. Cole and Plimpton, p. 249.

30. Yates, pp. 335, ff.; Ward, p. 661; Fowler, pp. 164–66.

31. Quoted in French, p. 668.

32. Cole and Plimpton, p. 250.

33. Perelman quoted in French, p. 667.

34. Cole and Plimpton, p. 246.

35. Ibid., p. 245.

36. Ibid., p. 247.

37. Quoted in Zinsser, p. 76.

38. Quoted in MacPherson, sect. E, p. 4.

39. Stefan Kanfer, "Perels of Wisdom before an Opening," *New York Times*, November 3, 1974, sect. 2, p. 1.

40. Quoted in French, p. 668.

41. Quoted in Cole and Plimpton, p. 250.

42. Cole and Plimpton, p. 255.

5

A Summing Up

There is, as far as I know, no concise and felicitous word in our language for the sportive essay. The English, who developed such masters of the form as Beerbohm and E. M. Forster, refer to it as a "middle," a vague and deprecatory term that implies it is used to interlard material of real substance. In this country, we are more forthright and less exact; we tend to classify writers like Ade, Lardner, and Benchley as humorists, conjuring up neuralgic images of a jackanapes with upturned hatbrim chewing his cigar and relentlessly spouting yocks. *The New Yorker*, in whose pages most of the following items appeared, calls them casuals, which is obviously a convenient solecism to describe a particular brand of merchandise in its shop. Unsurprisingly, the French come closest to it. If I were to apply for a library card in Paris, I would subscribe myself as a feuilletoniste, that is to say, a writer of little leaves. I may be in error, but the word seems to me to carry a hint of endearment rather than patronage.

In whatever case, and despite my conviction that the pasquinade will soon be as extinct in America as the naphtha launch and the diavolo, I should like to affirm my loyalty to it as a medium. The handful of chumps who still practice it are as lonely as the survivors of Fort Zinderneuf; a few more assaults by television and picture journalism and we might as well post their bodies on the ramparts, pray for togetherness, and kneel for the final annihilation. Until then, so long and don't take any wooden rhetoric.[1]

S. J. Perelman is one of the most popular writers of humor in the history of American literature, and the disparate writers who claim to be "quite an admirer" of Perelman (in contemporary British dramatist Harold Pinter's words), range from Dorothy Parker to Pinter, from Robert Benchley to Sommerset Maugham, from Ogden Nash to T. S. Eliot, from E. B. White to Eudora Welty, from Peter Sellers to Spike Milligan, and from John Updike to Kurt Vonnegut. Benchley once noted that "It was just a matter of time before Perelman took over the dementia praecox field and drove us all to writing articles on economics," and White stated that "Sid's stuff influenced me in the early days . . . he has, from the beginning, bowed to no one." John Hollander, in a commemorative interview appearing in the BBC's *The Listener* magazine, states that Perelman "and Henry Miller were both tremendously important influences on all kinds of novelists, not only karmic ones but, of course on comic ones as well."[2] In the same article Woody Allen recalls, "I discovered [Perelman] when I was in high school. I came across certain pieces that he had written and I immediately was stunned by them. I thought they were just the best and the funniest things that I had ever read, and not at all heavy-handed, which most humour writers are. . . . Perelman . . . is just as light as a souffle. What happens to you when you read Perelman and you're a young writer is fatal because his style seeps into you. He's got such a pronounced overwhelming comic style that it's very hard not to be influenced by him."[3] Sellers and Milligan, originally from British television's *The Goon Show*, claim Perelman as their mentor. Yet, in spite of his popularity and immense artistic output (hundreds of individual pieces, over twenty books, thirteen filmscripts, work in television, and ten stage plays, done over a period of fifty years with no great diminishment in quality), and in spite of his acknowledged influence on other twentieth-century authors, there has been almost no scholarly attention paid to Perelman's writing. Other than Douglas Fowler's introductory monograph, a doctoral dissertation in progress in France, and several interviews, only half a dozen articles in scholarly journals and books on American humorists compose the critical commentary on his canon.

As Norris Yates points out, 1929 saw the publication of Ernest Hemingway's *A Farewell to Arms*, Thomas Wolfe's *Look Homeward, Angel*, Faulkner's *The Sound and the Fury*, Sinclair Lewis's *Dodsworth*, Thurber and White's *Is Sex Necessary?*, Will Cuppy's *How to*

Be a Hermit, and Perelman's *Dawn Ginsbergh's Revenge*.[4] That is pretty heady company, but it may also provide a clue to the minimal scholarly attention that Perelman's work has attracted; Leslie Fiedler's notion of the distinction between high art and low art may be functioning. According to Fiedler, high art is serious in intent and presentation and thus is seen as meriting critical acclaim when it is successful (and even when it fails, high art may be appreciated for its "attempt"). Low art is that which is directed at a popular audience, primarily for the purpose of making money for the author. Though no one denies that Hemingway, Wolfe, Faulkner, and Lewis wrote for money or suggests that they refused their royalty checks, writers who write primarily for journalistic outlets do not seem to be able to overcome the bias among scholars that would result in the reverse being admitted, the possibility that authors who earn a daily wage by their writing for non-hardback publication can produce work worthy of scholarly attention.

Perelman did not go off to glorious adventures, as Hemingway did. He was a hometown boy who went to the local university, and he was never really at ease very far away. He was born, he lived, and he died in metropolitan New York. About as far away as he could comfortably travel was Rhode Island or Pennsylvania. His writing reflects the interests of this kind of man. As a result, his work is not difficult to comprehend. Unlike a Faulkner, or a Pinter, whose writing gains some of its appeal because it provides an intellectual puzzle, Perelman was never accused of being obscure. Some scholars apparently feel that because there is little to explicate there is a corresponding lack of elucidation in his art. Perelman wrote about the plight of an almost just person in an unjust society (his personae were slightly greedy, slightly lascivious, slightly naive, rather Pollyannaish, mostly honest, ethical, sincere—in short, representative of the good, solid, middle-class American that Perelman felt was beleaguered by the insensitive, hucksterish, not quite moral segment of the population). Not all of his writing was as funny as Thurber's "The Night the Bed Fell" (in *My Life and Hard Times*), but then neither was Thurber's.

As a matter of fact, Thurber's comments about writing humor provide some access to Perelman's writing:

A writer verging into the middle years lives in dread of losing his way to the publishing house and wandering down to the Bowery or the Battery, there to disappear like Ambrose Bierce. He has sometimes also the kindred dread of turning a sudden corner and meeting himself sauntering along in the opposite direction. I have known writers at this dangerous and tricky age to phone their homes from their office or their office from their homes, ask for themselves in a low tone, and then, having fortunately discovered that they were "out," to collapse in hard-breathing relief. This is particularly true of writers of light pieces running from a thousand to two thousand words.

The notion that such persons are gay of heart and carefree is curiously untrue. They lead, as a matter of fact, an existence of jumpiness and apprehension. They sit on the edge of the chair of Literature. In the house of Life they have the feeling that they have never taken off their overcoats. Afraid of losing themselves in the larger flight of the two-volume novel, or even the one-volume novel, they stick to short accounts of their misadventures because they never get so deep into them but that they feel they can get out. This type of writing is not a joyous form of self-expression but the manifestation of a twitchiness at once cosmic and mundane.[5]

Thus, Thurber's description of himself as a professional writer and his work in *My Life and Hard Times* seems to correspond to Perelman's nearly contemporaneous situation nicely:

Perelman never took himself too seriously, but he did consider himself a professional, and a craftsman. It may be in connection with this attitude that he was the manager of the radio program "Author, Author," and that he was a member of the Century Association, the Dramatists Guild, the Screen Writers Guild, and the National Institute of Arts and Letters.[6]

Thurber also said, in a rephrasing of Wordsworth, that "Humor is emotional chaos remembered in tranquility."[7] Perelman would have felt at home with this definition as applied to his own work. Another, and maybe even more accurate explanation of Perelman and his works may be contained in a thought that parallels the humorist's attitude toward life that is expressed in the lyrics of a song sung in the late 1970's by country-western performer Waylon Jennings. Perelman certainly would have understood the sentiment contained in the line, "I've always been crazy, but it's kept me from going insane."

Perhaps Perelman's case is one of those where the public is more accurate in their assessment than scholars have been; it is likely that academics will eventually catch up, though, as they overcome the sense that Perelman's work is too pleasurable to be significant. Perelman is a special piece of Americana, but in the final analysis he represents much more than just a reflector and a composer of light-hearted, ephemeral bits and pieces of humor. Ultimately he will be studied as an equal to Lardner, Benchley, and Thurber.

One key to evaluating a writer's career is seeing how well his popularity holds up over time. In human terms Perelman's work must be considered successful, since his books were popular over the entire span that he wrote. In November, 1979 it was announced he would receive posthumously the "Mayor's Award of Honor for Arts and Culture" from New York City, a measure of the author's popularity.[8] For some readers the fact that a writer is alive somehow diminishes his stature. For others, myself included, being able to read a new book by a favorite author, looking forward to seeing what he has done now, brings a very special thrill. Now that Perelman is dead a new dimension has been introduced, but it is obviously too soon to be able to determine how well his writing will endure over an extended period of time. The affection of his readers, described above, offers a hint, though. On a personal basis I can attest that I looked forward to reading *The Last Laugh* as eagerly as I had anticipated the pleasure of reading all of his earlier publications. Yet, there was a difference. Thinking that this would be the last book of his that I could ever read for the first time, I delayed reading it, almost as though it were a special dessert, for I wanted to savor every page, every pun. I was not disappointed; the humor in Perelman's last book was as salutary and agreeable as that in his other books. Unlike most authors, who write themselves out early in their careers, Perelman's talent was sustained throughout his professional life. Even after all of those years of writing, when he died Perelman was still working, and his final articles were in no way inferior to those that he had written during any of those previous years.

Perhaps Perelman's insistence on labeling himself a journalist and writer of short humorous pieces carries its own challenge. As he remarks, "No other kind of writer risks his work so visibly or so often on the high wire of public approval. It is the thinnest wire in all literature, and the writer lives with the certain knowledge that he will frequently fall off."[9] Perelman produced humorous essays as well or better than any other author ever has, and he did it consistently over a period of five decades. The personal, self-deprecating persona, wistfully pursuing ever-fleeing women, the Little Man as victim, the instances of logic carried to such an extreme that it becomes illogical, the absurd juxtapositions—these have become a part of American literature to a large degree because of Perelman's writing and his influence on others.

The final story in the last collection published in Perelman's lifetime, in which he supposedly winds up marrying Gabrielle de Casabas, the paragon of womanhood who wants only him, fittingly ends with a line that summarizes his life and his writing: "Oh, well, kid, I decided, drink up—you win a little, you lose a little. Isn't that what it's all about?" [10] Indeed, Perelman may have found life a little naughty at times, but he always enjoyed being involved in its celebration and he happily shared this with all of us.

NOTES

1. S. J. Perelman, *The Most of S. J. Perelman* (New York: Simon and Schuster, 1958), pp. 431–32.

2. Quoted in Philip French, "Perelman's Revenge of the Gift of Providence, Rhode Island," *The Listener* 102, no. 2637 (November 15, 1979): 669.

3. Ibid., p. 669.

4. Norris Yates, *The American Humorist: Conscience of the Twentieth Century*, (Ames, Iowa: Iowa State University, 1964), pp. 331–32.

5. James Thurber, *My Life and Hard Times* (New York: Perennial Library, 1973), p. 10.

6. "S. J. Perelman," *Contemporary Authors*, ed. by Frances Carol Locher (Detroit: Gale, 1978), vols. 73–76, p. 496.

7. Quoted by John K. Hutchens in his "Introduction" to Thurber's *My Life and Hard Times* (New York: Perennial Library, 1973), p. 5.

8. Anon., "Mayor's Arts Awards to be Presented Nov. 5," *New York Times* (October 27, 1979), p. 12.

9. William Zinsser, "That Perelman of Great Price Is Sixty-Five," *New York Times Magazine* (July 22, 1966): 26.

10. S. J. Perelman, *Eastward Ha!* (New York: Simon and Schuster), p. 126.

Appendix

List of Awards Received by Perelman

New York Film Critics Award for *Around the World in Eighty Days* (1956)

Academy of Motion Pictures Arts and Sciences "Oscar" for Best Screenplay, for *Around the World in Eighty Days* (1956)

Elected to National Institute of Letters (1958)

Honorary Litt. D. awarded by Brown University (1965)

Special National Book Award for contribution to American Letters (1978)

New York City "Mayor's Award of Honor for Arts and Culture" (1979)

Bibliographic Essay

Given the publication of my 1,139-entry *S. J. Perelman: An Annotated Bibliography* by Garland Press in 1985, inclusion of a bibliography in *S. J. Perelman: A Critical Study* would be needless duplication. *S. J. Perelman: An Annotated Bibliography* lists approximately 625 items published by Perelman from his over 560 "casuals" (listed individually with information on the original publication and on reprints) to his collections, plays, film and television work, letters, and even recordings. The bibliography also contains about 515 secondary-source materials, most of which are annotated. This represents a majority of the pieces written by and about the humorist through 1984.

Ironically, I have to say a majority of the pieces because no one knows for sure how much he wrote or where it was all published (and I had to be selective in the reviews that I included). Apparently no one—not Perelman, his family, or his agent—bothered to keep track (which may partly explain why several articles were reprinted with little or no change except for their titles). Indeed, in collecting materials for the bibliography, I discovered a number of pieces that seem to have been forgotten. Most of these were in obscure or unlikely publications, though this certainly was not always the case.

I did encounter a few interesting problems in collecting these materials. For example, several items that appear in the collected volumes are cited as having originally appeared somewhere else, but when I checked the source cited, the item was not included ("And Did You Once See Irving Plain?" is listed in *The Most of S. J. Perelman* as having been published in *Holiday* between 1950 and 1958, for instance, but I was unable to find the piece anywhere in the journal).

One reason that this kind of problem may have occurred has to do with publishing history. *Holiday* was acquired by *Travel Magazine* in 1977, and either there was never an inhouse index or the records were not transferred.

Furthermore, during the early 1940's the *Saturday Evening Post* underwent some editorial changes, and it is possible that some of the pieces bought for the magazine prior to the changes were never published, even though subsequent collections of Perelman's work (particularly *Perelman's Home Companion*) state that certain pieces had "appeared" in the journal. In some cases items have more than one title. The "Swiss Family Perelman" series was published in *Holiday* under that general title. However, some of the episodes were further identified by subtitles (e.g., "Low Bridge, Everybody Down"). Various indexes include these episodes under the subtitles (frequently pieces were reprinted under the subtitle, with no reference to the original series). To make matters even more confusing, there are occasional segments of series that are not subtitled, even when other installments of the same series are. "Sampling Some of the Gripes of a Wayfarer's Wrath in the Not-So-Smiling Islands of Indonesia" in the "Swiss Family Perelman" series is an example of this perplexing practice. The confusion is compounded, though, when the essay is reprinted in the hardback version of *The Swiss Family Perelman* under the title "Fifteen Dutch on a Red Man's Chest"! Another interesting development that I encountered is that there are multiple versions of at least one of the anthologies, a case that is discussed in the Chapter One examination of *Crazy Like a Fox.*

Amusingly, even Simon and Schuster, who published Perelman's last twelve books during his lifetime, were unsure as to whether they could claim Perelman as one of their authors. I called the publicity office at Simon and Schuster one day in order to check some information that I had collected. The situation was certainly one that Perelman himself would have appreciated—I hope. The man who answered the telephone had not heard of Perelman and doubted that Simon and Schuster had published any of his volumes. When I assured him that they had, he did some checking and was able to corroborate my assertion, but indicated that it had been several years since Perelman's last volume had appeared under their imprint, and he insisted that they did not keep information on their authors that long so he could not help me. This was in 1981, two years after Perelman's death and the same year that Simon and Schuster was to publish *The Last Laugh*! On the other hand, however, the archive departments of several journals have an accurate record of what has appeared in their magazines, and their help in finding or confirming countless items was invaluable. The editorial office of *The New Yorker* kindly supplied me with bibliographical information on the over two hundred pieces that Perelman published in that journal. The *Travel and Leisure* editorial offices also willingly helped me check on bibliographical information for both the "Eastward Ha!" and "Nostasia in Asia" series. The *Saturday Evening Post* Archives Department, *TV Guide*'s Reader's Service Department, *McCall*'s Reader Service, and *Redbook* similarly provided assistance that was literally crucial.

It is interesting, and probably a reflection on scholarly attitudes toward both comic writing and living authors, that during his lifetime most of the criticism written about Perelman fell into the category of reviews—of his books, primarily, but of his films and plays too. Indeed, the earliest scholarly publications related to his writing did not appear until after he had already enjoyed a career that extended over more years than the average writer achieves *in toto*. The first published scholarship, other than some fairly literate reviews and several valuable interviews, ranged from mere references to chapters and parts of chapters in books on American humor. While a number of these scholarly commentaries are interesting and insightful, still, none of them was devoted to Perelman as its sole subject matter. I am pleased to say that my bibliography of his publications over the twenty-year span from 1940 to 1960 that was published in the *Bulletin of Bibliography* in January, 1972, was the first scholarly publication solely on Perelman.

Between 1972 and 1979 the amount of scholarly interest in Perelman increased (I was contacted by a doctoral student in France, for instance, who asked for more information on Perelman to be included in her dissertation), though there still was not a great deal on him that found its way into print.

With Perelman's death in 1979, however, the author became a legitimate topic for academic study; he was no longer to be dismissed as merely the innovator of attention-getting titles. More articles appeared. I was invited to write a major author entry on him for the *Dictionary of Literary Biography*. Douglas Fowler read a paper on Perelman's techniques at the Seventh Annual Conference on Literature and Film in Tallahassee, Florida, in January, 1982, and a year later he published the first book-length study of Perelman. In 1983 a dissertation on Perelman was completed, a biography of the author appeared in 1986, and a volume of his letters is being prepared.

And, interest continues to grow, as demonstrated both by the increasing number of articles written in the past several years that are cited in *S. J. Perelman: An Annotated Bibliography* and by the very publication of this study itself. In fact, besides the two posthumous collections of his writing that have been published, Viking/Penguin plans to reprint three of the humorist's anthologies in 1987 (*The Rising Gorge, Baby, It's Cold Inside*, and *The Swiss Family Perelman*) to coincide with the publication of the volume of his letters (in 1984 a call to Viking resulted in a response similar to that from Simon and Schuster, in spite of the fact that Abby Perelman and the estate's literary agent had informed me that these publications were forthcoming and this information had been verified by other hard evidence). Too, the tone of the newly manifested interest in Perelman is changing. Early pieces tended to be of the "beauties" school of criticism, written by people who were admitted fans of the writer and who wrote simply to proclaim their admiration. Now attention is being paid to his style and techniques and to his themes. In fact, scholars are beginning to compare his work favorably with that of other major American comic writers of the twentieth century and earlier; Perelman's name is gradually appearing in discussions that compare him favorably with Ring Lardner, Robert Benchley, and even James Thurber.

Finally, the fact that I was invited to write a proposal for an introduction to a section on Perelman for inclusion in a new anthology of American literature (a Feminist Press project edited by Paul Lauter) is an additional indication of Perelman's rise in stature in American literary history and of the expanding audience that wants to learn more about the man and his writing.

For those interested in examining sources beyond this volume, the following will serve as an introduction to materials available. First, though, a comment on *S. J. Perelman: An Annotated Bibliography*. There are several things that distress a bibliographer, typographical errors and finding items after it is too late to include them being paramount. As an example of the first, *Even Stephen* is printed *Even Stephan* and the subtitle to *Westward Ha!* (*Around the World in Eighty Clichés*) appears as *Around the World in Eighty Days* in the *Bibliography*. Similarly, the date of publication of "Scenario" (February, 1932) was inadvertently omitted. Frustratingly, examples of finding items too late for inclusion involve several potential entries that I had been trying to track down to confirm for months but information on which arrived a few days after printing of the bibliography had started. These include both primary and secondary materials. Thus, the following items may be considered an addendum to *S. J. Perelman: An Annotated Bibliography*.

PRIMARY SOURCES

Perelman, S. J. "The Big Wheel." *Omnibus*, January 27, 1957. Television script; program starring Bert Lahr.

————. "A Farewell to Bucks." *New York Times*, December 3, 1970, p. 47.

————. "Pickings from a New Perch." *New York Times*, December 6, 1970, section 1A, pp. 8, 12.

————. "The Chocolate Cake Kid: A Drama." *New York Times*, December 20, 1976, sect. 3, pp. 11, 16.

————. and Kurt Weill. *One Touch of Venus*. New York: Chappell, 1943. This edition contains the musical score.

Doubly frustrating was my having seen years ago a Perelman title that began "All Good Aerialists," but never again have I been able to locate it or even another reference to the piece.

SECONDARY SOURCES

Anon. " 'Appalled' Perelman Going Eastward Ha!" *New York Times*. September 18, 1970, p. 45.

Report on Perelman's impending move to London.

Anon. "Perelman, Gone 80 Days, A Foggy Memory at Club." *New York Times*, May 25, 1971, p. 5.

Notice regarding Perelman's completion of a trip around the world with his secretary, Dianne Baker, taken "to emulate the trip . . . by Phileas Fogg."

Atkinson, Brooks. "Critic at Large: S. J. Perelman Does His Bit to Prevent Humor From Disappearing in America." *New York Times*, March 4, 1962, p. 30.

Commentary on Perelman's writing prior to the opening of *The Beauty Part*.

Barnes, Clive. " 'Eastward Ho,' Eh Perelman? Ha!" *New York Times*, October 11, 1970, section 8, pp. 1–2.

Commentary on why Perelman might not find his intended move to London as satisfactory as staying in America.

Blyde, Ann. "Medical Care for Visitors," *New York Times*, January 7, 1971, p. 34.

A letter to the editor about Perelman's plans to reside in London.

Faulkner, Alex. "Are Cities Fit Places for Humans?" *New York Times*, October 7, 1970, p. 46.

Letter to the editor responding to Richard W. Wallach's letter regarding Perelman's comments prior to his move to London.

Ford, Cory. *The Time of Laughter*. Boston: Little, Brown, 1967. Pp. 8, 131.

Goldsmith, Theodore A. "Probing Perelman." *New York Times*, March 26, 1944, sect. 2, p. 1.

An overview of Perelman's work in the theatre: "Being a Survey of Some Ups and Downs in the S. J. Perelman Theatre Saga."

Herbst, Josephine. "Nathanael West." *Kenyon Review*, 23 (Autumn 1961): 611–30.

Hewitt, Alan. "G.S.K.: Profit with Honor." *New York Times*, February 16, 1969, section 6, p. 123.

Letter to the editor in response to William Zinsser's "That Perelman of Great Price Is 65." Hewitt feels that George S. Kaufman's contributions to American humor should have been noted.

Hyman, Stanley Edgar. *Nathanael West*. Minneapolis: University of Minnesota Press, 1962. University of Minnesota pamphlets on American Writers Series, No. 21. Pp. 7, 8.

Kesterson, David B. "*The New Yorker*'s First Quarter Century." *Studies in American Humor*, Special Issue, ed. David Kesterson, vol. 3 (New Series), no. 1 (Spring, 1984): 7–10.

Brief introduction to this special issue that includes a summary of Sanford Pinsker's "S. J. Perelman: A Portrait of the Artist as an Aging *New Yorker* Humorist" (p. 8).

Lewis, Anthony. "Perelman Plans Trip, Verne-Style, Around the World in 80 Days." *New York Times*, January 7, 1971, sect. 2, p. 4.

Regarding Perelman's plans, as a member of the Reform Club, to trace the route taken by Phileas Fogg in the Jules Verne novel.

Light, James F. *Nathanael West: An Interpretive Study*. Evanston, Il: Northwestern University Press, 1971. Second ed. Pp. xxiii, 20, 26, 32, 71, 116, 128–29, 141, 198, 203.

Maddocks, Melvin. "The Cream Pie of the Jest." *Christian Science Monitor*, Vol. 58, issue 235 (September 1, 1966): 11.

Book review of *Chicken Inspector No. 23*.

Magill, Frank N., ed. *Magill's Survey of Cinema: English Language Films*. Englewood Cliffs, N.J.: Salem Press, 1980. First Series.

Includes entries by Blake Lucas on *Monkey Business* (Vol. 3, pp. 1144–46) and Leslie Taubman on *Around the World in Eighty Days* (Vol. 1, pp. 101–04). Entries list date of release, color or black and white, running time, cast, director, producer, screenwriter, cinematographer, and editor, and include an abstract and note reviews.

————. *Magill's Survey of Cinema: English Language Films*. Englewood Cliffs, N.J.: Salem Press, 1981. Second Series.

Includes entries by Ralph Angel on *Horse Feathers* (Vol. 3, pp. 1051–53) and Rob Edelman on *Larceny, Inc.*. (Vol. 3, pp. 1304–06).

Mitgang, Herbert. "Books of the Times." *New York Times*, October 14, 1958, p. 35.

Admiring book review of *The Most of S. J. Perelman*.

Mitgang, Herbert. "Book Prize for Perelman, Because. . . . " *New York Times*, April 10, 1978, sect. C, p. 22.

Notice regarding the humorist's receiving a National Book Award special achievement medal.

Pinsker, Sanford. "S. J. Perelman: A Portrait of the Artist as an Aging *New Yorker* Humorist." *Studies in American Humor*, Special Issue, ed. David Kesterson, vol. 3 (New Series), no. 1 (Spring, 1984): 47–55.

Perelman's writing is better suited to *The New Yorker* than is that of other humorists. Pinsker concludes that the author's *persona* remains essentially the same throughout his career.

Schumach, Murray. "Perelman Tries Series for TV." *New York Times*, March 1, 1962, p. 27.

Perelman talks about efforts to turn *Acres and Pains* into a television series.

Slater, Eric. *Don't Mention the Marx Bros*. Salem, New Hampshire: Merrimack, 1986.

An account of Slater's experience with Perelman is included.

Toombs, Sarah. "S. J. Perelman: A Bibliography of Short Essays, 1932–

1979." *Studies in American Humor*, Special issue, ed. David Kesterson, vol. 3 (New Series), no. 1 (Spring, 1984): 47–55.

A chronological listing of selected short pieces, as well as theater, television, and film scripts.

Tyler, Ralph. "Literary Figures Offer Plots and Quips." *New York Times*, August 1, 1976, sect. 2, pp. 1, 13.

Comments from a number of authors about how they would write a proposed sequel to *Gone with the Wind*, including a humorous proposal by Perelman.

Wallach, Richard W. "Perelman's Flight." *New York Times*, September 29, 1970, p. 42.

Letter to the editor which notes that a quote used by Perelman in discussing his move to London has been incorrectly attributed to Jonathan Swift rather than to Thomas Hobbes.

Widmer, Kingsley. *Nathanael West*. Boston: Twayne, 1982. Pp. 7, 8, 9, 124.

SELECTED FILM REVIEWS

Around the World in Eighty Days

> *Newsweek*, October 29, 1956, p. 98.
>
> *Time*, October 29, 1956, p. 72.
>
> *Variety*, October 24, 1956, p. 6.

Larceny, Inc.

> *Variety*, March 4, 1942, p. 8.

In addition to the titles published during Perelman's lifetime and the two anthologies that appeared posthumously, a collection of the author's correspondence, *The Letters of S. J. Perelman*, has been edited by Prudence Crowther (New York: Viking/Penguin). As is often the case in publishing, the volume of letters was delayed and instead of appearing in 1985, as originally planned, it has been rescheduled for publication in 1987.

Dorothy Herrmann's *S. J. Perelman: A Biography*, which also had been scheduled for publication in 1985, similarly was delayed and added to Putnam's (New York) 1986 list with a new title, *S. J. Perelman: A Life*, though Abby Perelman has stated that the biography is not authorized. Biographical information on the humorist can also be found in *Contemporary Authors*, *Contemporary Literary Criticism*, *Current Biography*, *Twentieth Century Authors*, and several encyclopedias and who's whos of various kinds.

A number of interviews with Perelman have been conducted. Many are relatively insignificant, short pieces published in connection with the opening of a play or the publication of a prose anthology. Several deserve to be singled out, however, for the historical details that they provide and for Perelman's comments. The first serious interview was conducted by William Cole and George Plimpton for the *Paris Review* (Fall, 1963, pp. 73–85) relatively late in the author's life. "The Art of Fiction: S. J. Perelman" was considered important enough to be reprinted in Plimpton's *Writers at Work: The Paris Review Interviews, Second Series* (New York: Viking, 1963, pp. 241–56). The interview contains interesting information about Perelman's views on his own writing and his theories regarding the nature of humor. William Zinsser's "That Perelman of Great Price Is Sixty-Five" appeared in the *New York Times Magazine* six years after the Cole-Plimpton interview (January 26, 1969, pp. 26, 72, 74, 76). This is an especially valuable interview, full of facts about Perelman's early activities and the literary figures whom he felt most influenced him. It also includes the most complete biographical information published about the author during his lifetime. Myra MacPherson's "Perelman's Rasping Wit Becomes an Anglo-File" (*Washington Post*, October 18, 1970, sect. E, pp. 1, 4) is a combination article/interview that reveals Perelman's personality. Other interviews include: several short interviews with Israel Shenker, collected in *Words and Their Masters* (New York: Doubleday, 1974); an interview conducted by Roy Newquist and published in his *Conversations* (New York: Rand, McNally, 1976) in which Perelman stresses his sense of tradition and the literary figures whose work influenced his writing; and M. Calman's *Sight and Sound* piece, "Perelman in Cloudsville" (August 4, 1978, pp. 248–49), in which *Monkey Business* and *Horsefeathers* are discussed.

Douglas Fowler's *S. J. Perelman*, a volume in Twayne's American Authors Series (Boston), was published in 1983. The first full-length examination of Perelman's work, this study presents an interesting overview of the writer's life and representative works. Fowler pays special attention to Perelman's place in both American and literary Yiddish comic traditions. Perelman is seen as a caricaturist by Fowler, who discusses the elements of his style in light of this definition. Full of factual details and insights into Perelman's canon, the book is particularly valuable as an informative introduction.

Some years ago, as alluded to above, a dissertation on Perelman was begun at a French university, but I have been unable to determine whether it was ever finished. The first dissertation completed in the United States that deals exclusively with Perelman's work was "Esthetic Transformation: Visual, Syntactic and Rhetorical Features in the Writing Process of S. J. Perelman" (New York University, 1983) by Richard Michael Cassell. This examination of the author's stylistics develops a model to show how rhetorical devices interact in his writing. Cassell focuses on *Westward Ha!*

A number of volumes on American humor and humorists contain sections on Perelman. In his early and influential *Horse Sense in American Humor, from Benjamin Franklin to Ogden Nash* (Chicago: University of Chicago, 1942), for instance, Walter Blair places Perelman in the context of the American humor tradition, and in *The Rise and Fall of American Humor* (New York: Holt, Rinehart & Winston, 1968) Jesse Bier comments on the author's style. Bier, who finds Perelman the most "resilient" humorist of his generation, comments on the author's comic surrealism that derives from his technique of "building" and his combining "comic inanity and scathing satire" (pp. 230, 237, 270). A first-rate analysis of Perelman's use of fantasy in contrast to Benchley and others appears in *America's Humor from Poor Richard to Doonesbury* (New York: Oxford, 1978), co-edited by Blair and Hamlin Hill. The chapter on "The Sane Psychoses of S. J. Perelman" in Norris W. Yates' *The American Humorist: Conscience of the Twentieth Century* (Ames, Iowa: Iowa State University, 1964) relates Perelman's place in the American literary tradition to his contribution to the development of the Little Man character type, mixed with a psychoanalytical approach and some commentary on the impact of Perelman's Jewish heritage on his writing.

My "S. J. Perelman," an entry in *American Humorists, 1800–1950*, volume 11 of the *Dictionary of Literary Biography* (ed. Stanley Trachtenberg, Detroit: Gale, 1982), which explicates representative pieces from Perelman's canon and analyzes his style, all in a biographical context, was the forerunner of *S. J. Perelman: A Critical Study*. Terry Heller's "Sidney Joseph Perelman" in *Critical Survey of Short Fiction* (Los Angeles: Salem, 1981) provides a brief overview of Perelman's life and works, as do Michael T. Leech's "Sidney Joseph Perelman" in *Contemporary Dramatists* (ed. James Vinson, New York: St. Martin's, 1977) and Douglas Fowler's "S. J. Perelman" in *An Encyclopedia of American Humorists* (ed. by Steven H. Gale, New York: Garland, in preparation [1987]).

Of course, most Perelman scholarship has been confined to approximately 150 shorter articles of diverse quality that have appeared in journals. One of the best evaluations of Perelman's style is found in John Wain's insightful "A Jest is Season: Notes on S. J. Perelman, With a Digression on W. W. Jacobs" (*Twentieth Century* [June, 1960]: 530–44). Wain compares Perelman with the Edwardian humorist Jacobs to define "durable and non-durable humor" as a means of analyzing the twentieth-century writer's satire. Among the more interesting essays on various aspects of the humorist's canon are Alan Brien's "S. J. Perelman: The Man in the Ironic Mask" (*Quest/78* [November, 1978]: 71–74, 76); Philip French's "Perelman's Revenge or the Gift of Providence, Rhode Island" (*The Listener*, November 15, 1979, pp. 667–69), a transcribed radio round-table discussion between Woody Allen, Al Hirschfeld, John Hollander, Israel Shenker, and Caskie Stinnett. Joseph B. McCullough's "Mark Twain and Journalistic Humor Today" (*English Journal* [1971]: 591–95) is important as one of the first considerations of Perelman's work to appear in a scholarly journal. It identifies common links between Perelman and other twentieth-century humorists and newspaper humorists of the nineteenth century. "The Hollywood Metaphor: The Marx Brothers, S. J. Perelman, Nathanael West" by J. A. Ward (*Southern Review* [July, 1976]: 659–72) is an interesting examination of the material utilized by the Marxes, Perelman, and West through which Ward arrives at insights about the creative nature of these artists. In "S. J. Perelman: The Keenest Hatred of Chickens" (*Studies in American Humor* [Winter, 1985]) I discuss the author's treatment of money as a subject. A European perspective on American Humor is found in the German "Amerikanisher Humor—eine soziale Funktion" (*Merkur* [July, 1970]: 644–59) by Gert Raethel, who concludes that some of the interest in Perelman is related to the impact of McCarthyism.

Several revealing publications have appeared that comment specifically on Perelman's work in film. Joe Adamson's *Groucho, Harpo, Chico, and Sometimes Zeppo* (New York: Simon and Schuster, 1973) contains a great deal of material on the screenwriter's relationship with the Marx Brothers, as does Groucho Marx and Richard T. Anobile's *The Marx Bros.' Scrapbook* (New York: Darien House, 1973) and Hector Arce's *Groucho* (New York: Putnam's, 1979). Sanford Pinsker recounts Perelman's Hollywood experience in "Jumping on Hollywood's Bones, or How S. J. Perelman and Woody Allen Found It at the Movies" (*Midwest Quarterly* [1980]: 371–83). My "Around the World in Eighty Ways: S. J. Perelman as Screenwriter" (*Studies in American Humor* [Winter] 1985) surveys his filmscripts.

There have been literally hundreds of reviews of Perelman's books, plays, and films published in newspapers and magazines. By and large these have not been especially insightful, though there are some that are worth examining, if for no reason other than to determine what contemporary reactions to his work were. Among the more perceptive book reviewers were Ogden Nash, Dorothy Parker, Eudora Welty, and Tom Wolfe. Mourdant Hall and later Bosley Crowther of the *New York Times* and several writers for *Variety* reviewed a majority of Perelman's films positively. Critical reaction to the writer's plays was more mixed: Brooks Atkinson, the *New York Times* theater critic, expressed continued disappointment in the scripts, though Robert Brustein, writing for the *New Republic*, and Lewis Nichols of the *New York Times* found more positive elements in the plays to discuss.

Naturally, the above is only a small sampling of the scholarship that has been generated on Perelman's work. For a fuller listing and description of critical and scholarly reactions to Perelman's work, consult *S. J. Perelman: An Annotated Bibliography.*

Index

ABOUT THE AUTHOR

STEVEN H. GALE is Professor of English and Director of the Honors Program at Missouri Southern State College. He has published over 50 articles in scholarly journals, as well as two dozen essay reviews. He is the editor of *Harold Pinter: Critical Approaches* and the author of *Butter's Going Up: A Critical Analysis of Harold Pinter's Work, Harold Pinter: An Annotated Bibliography,* and *S. J. Perelman: An Annotated Bibliography.*

Recent Titles in
Contributions to the Study of Popular Culture

Common Culture and the Great Tradition: The Case for Renewal
Marshall W. Fishwick

Concise Histories of American Popular Culture
M. Thomas Inge, editor

Ban Johnson: Czar of Baseball
Eugene C. Murdock

Putting Dell on the Map: A History of the Dell Paperbacks
William H. Lyles

Behold the Mighty Wurlitzer: The History of the Theatre Pipe Organ
John W. Landon

Mighty Casey: All-American
Eugene C. Murdock

The Baker Street Reader: Cornerstone Writings about Sherlock Holmes
Philip A. Shreffler, editor

Dark Cinema: American *Film Noir* in Cultural Perspective
Jon Tuska

Seven Pillars of Popular Culture
Marshall W. Fishwick

The American West in Film: Critical Approaches to the Western
Jon Tuska

Sport in America: New Historical Perspectives
Donald Spivey, editor

Screwball Comedy: A Genre of Madcap Romance
Wes D. Gehring

Buckskins, Bullets, and Business: A History of Buffalo Bill's Wild West
Sarah J. Blackstone